D0152871

BLACKS
IN THE
AMERICAN
ARMED FORCES,
1776–1983

Recent Titles in
Bibliographies and Indexes in Afro-American and African Studies

Black-Jewish Relations in the United States: A Selected Bibliography
Compiled by Lenwood G. Davis

Black Immigration and Ethnicity in the United States: An Annotated Bibliography
Center for Afroamerican and African Studies, The University of Michigan

Education of the Black Adult in the United States: An Annotated Bibliography
Compiled by Leo McGee and Harvey G. Neufeldt

BLACKS IN THE AMERICAN ARMED FORCES, 1776–1983

A Bibliography

Compiled by
Lenwood G. Davis
and
George Hill

Forewords by
Benjamin O. Davis, Jr.,
and
Percy E. Johnston

Bibliographies and Indexes in Afro-American and African Studies, Number 3

Greenwood Press
Westport, Connecticut • London, England

Library of Congress Cataloging in Publication Data

Davis, Lenwood G.
   Blacks in the American armed forces, 1776–1983.

   (Bibliographies and indexes in Afro-American and
African studies, ISSN 0742-6924 ; no. 3)
   Includes index.
   1. United States—Armed Forces—Afro-Americans—
Bibliography. I. Hill, George. II. Title. III. Series.
Z1249.M5D38 1985   016.355 ′008996073   84-15697
[UB418.A47]
ISBN 0-313-24092-2 (lib. bdg.)

Copyright © 1985 by Lenwood G. Davis

All rights reserved. No portion of this book may be
reproduced, by any process or technique, without the
express written consent of the publisher.

Library of Congress Catalog Card Number: 84-15697
ISBN: 0-313-24092-2
ISSN: 0742-6924

First published in 1985

Greenwood Press
A division of Congressional Information Service, Inc.
88 Post Road West, Westport, Connecticut 06881

Printed in the United States of America

10 9 8 7 6 5 4 3 2 1

Contents

Foreword

Colonel "Lucky" Lester, one of America's outstanding Black airmen of World War II, tells the story of a young college student who had been beaten down by his professor that no Black pilots had participated in World War II. At the National Archives I learned in some detail about the important role played by Black Americans on both sides of our bloodiest war—the War Between the States, 1861-1865. I'd wager that you are unaware of the exploits of the "Buffalo Soldiers" and the Black cowboys who, after the Civil War, helped American pioneers migrate West and open up that vast unpopulated region to development and statehood.

The authors of *Blacks in the American Armed Forces, 1776-1983* provide a much-needed bibliography for all of us, white and Black, who have come to realize that the American history we were privileged to learn in high school and college skipped over in very large measure the key parts played by Black Americans. As stated in the introduction to this volume, no effort is made to chronicle the complete militrary contribution of Blacks to America's armed forces. Nor is this bibliography pointed necessarily to those who would engage in scholarly research; instead, it is a listing of writings about Black participation in America's wars and other significant periods of its military history. The introduction gives an overview of all of the writings, and following the bibliography are appendixes that provide, for the first time in one volume, valuable historical items of Black military history.

Throughout this bibliography runs the theme that (1) in every war Blacks aggressively volunteered to fight for America, (2) in most wars Blacks had to fight to get into the fighting forces, (3) in most wars Black participation as fighting men was not desired, (4) in all wars except Vietnam (and the United States Air Force in Korea), Black Americans fought in segregated units, (5) that only recently (since 1949 for the United States Air Force and during and since Vietnam for the rest of the United States armed forces) has the United States made a real effort to provide equal opportunity and treatment for Blacks, and (6) that even at present, with the United States Armed Forces sociologically far out in front of the United States' general population, there remains the vestige of individual racist attitudes that impedes progress toward full realization of American goals and ideals.

For these reasons, American history must be desegregated so that young Americans will learn in high school that Black American pilots fought outstandingly well in WWII, that Black Americans played important roles in every war America has fought, and that there were black cowboys alongside of the white cowboys who opened up the West.

If young Americans learn *all* of the facts of American history in the 1980s and 1990s, perhaps the parents of the twenty-first century will teach their children that Americans, be they Black or white, are Americans, and everyone should be treated the same. Only then will there be no need for *Blacks in the American Armed Forces, 1776-1983*. Today we need it badly to fill in some of the gaps in American history.

Benjamin O. Davis, Jr.
Brigadier General (Retired)
United States Air Force

Foreword

The father of modern Africana history, George Washington Williams, subtitled his seminal Black history (*History of the Negro Race in America from 1619-1880*) as follows: *Negroes As Slaves, As Soldiers, and As Citizens*. Now one century after the publication of Williams' pioneering work, Lenwood G. Davis and George Hill have compiled the first publication that has used the implications of that subtitle in a full epistemological sense. What seems to be common to Williams and to Davis and Hill is an insistence that historiography itself be interfaced with philosophy of history so that the matter of history can be researched critically.

The European and European-American tendency to be putatively objective can and has prevented scholars trained in those traditions from recognizing easily areas of potential research. Therefore, it is not surprising that Lenwood G. Davis and George Hill, Africanists and Afro-Americanists, would be the ones to produce *Blacks in the American Armed Forces, 1776-1983*.

That members of the Afro-American group as individuals and in concert have a history as rebels, revolutionaries, irregulars, regulars, volunteers, insurgents, guerrillas, militia, spies, counterspies, auxiliaries, and camp followers is not surprising to anyone who is aware of anthropological tendencies. But the specifics of military and paramilitary activity among Black or Negro (brown, tan, colored, sepia) folk for and against Anglo-America, the United States, or the Confederate States is not and has not been sufficiently documented in popular or scholarly literature outside of Negro or Black literature tradition or outside of official archives of the military establishment.

When George Washington Williams attempted to deal directly with the War Department in the 1880s to find out the condition of the celebrated Ninth, Tenth, Twenty-fourth, and Twenty-fifth Regiments, he was ignored. Williams did field work, however, using what anthropologists and sociologists would adopt as standard procedure, and anticipating the work method of W.E.B. DuBois by a full decade, Williams made direct observation (including interviews) of those infantry and cavalry regiments in Texas, Kansas, Indian Territory, and New Mexico.

Again, it is in the tradition of Williams and DuBois that Davis and Hill's present work can be seen with clarity. Like most of Black or Negro history, like most African diaspora history, Black military history has not been propagated to each generation in the normal course of education. The dream of Williams, of DuBois, of Carter G. Woodson, was not to merely expand "Negro History" week to "Black History" month. Nothing short of African history in its broadest context to Afro-American history to the present should be taught as Black history to Afro-Americans.

It is ironic that counterinsurgency was the source of liberty for "a slave of Robert Ruffin," who supplied information concerning a slave revolt in 1710 in Virginia and was, by an act of the Virginia General Assembly, given "manumission papers" for his espionage against his fellow Black slaves. But, this is not a generally well-known case even among historians. Had it been known, one can speculate that Afro-American social, educational, and resistance planning might have been different.

A history of Blacks in the military and the documents upon which such a history can be established involved a variety of subjects not ordinarily thought of as military. For example, when and where and under what circumstances were Blacks (Negroes) in possession of arms (particularly firearms)—or, when and under what circumstances were colored people in possession of wagons, tents, boats, or ships (nowadays aircraft)? Who and where were the brown people who were makers of weapons? Who and where were the Black people who were expert in the preparation of explosives and other ordnance? Who knew sanitation? Who knew engineering? Security? Telegraphy (after the demise of the drums)? Who knew quartermaster, supply, naval stores? And what about medicine, surgery, nursing, pharmacy? Need I mention music?

Lenwood G. Davis is the foremost compiler of source and bibliographic material in the western hemisphere. And in the case of his other source guides, for example, on sickle-cell anemia, on Paul Robeson, and on Black athletes, this guide on Blacks in the armed forces represents a tremendous sacrifice of time and effort from his own career as writer and researcher, not to mention his full-time teaching assignments. I do not think it can be overemphasized how important an all-encompassing reference work such as this can and will be to other writers and researchers. Davis, who is also a poet, has provided a work for poets, novelists, and playwrights as well.

Finally, let me say there are tons of gems to be mined out of the sources in *Blacks in the Armed Forces*, some from forgotten superstars of Black history like Captain Hugh Mulzac who wrote, in *A Star To Steer By* (New York: International, 1963),

Half-starved, sick and beaten as they were it was impossible for me then, as it is now, to be "fair" about the Germans. Sympathetic as I tried to be about the social and political forces which drove them to be what they were, I could not sympathize with them in person. Even in defeat they were arrogant, especially the officers. Most of those we carried were convinced they would be welcomed with open arms in America. . . .

describing his experience as senior captain among U.S. Merchant Marine officers when his ship USS *Booker T. Washington* transported "a raggedy bunch" of "this vaunted Wehrmacht" from Naples to Newport News. And as General Benjamin O. Davis, Sr., observed around the same time, "Nobody knows except the men in the front lines. . . ," or as Captain Mulzac might have amended it, "on deck." But what can be known depends on sources.

Percy E. Johnston
Executive Director
Afro American Philosophy
    Association, Inc.

Introduction

It should be pointed out that this collection is neither comprehensive nor definitive. It would be impossible to chronicle the complete contributions that Blacks have made to America's armed forces because they have been involved in the military for more than 450 years. Black Americans as nonslaves and slaves participated in military or quasi-military actions as early as 1528. Although Blacks have been involved in such actions, this book focuses on the American Revolution era through 1983 because these are the periods that can be documented. Hence, it is not the purpose of this work to chronicle the whole history of Blacks in the American military. It is the compilers' intent to present an overview of Black participation that relates to significant periods in United States military history.

Although much has been written about the Black soldier, to our knowledge there is no definitive compilation in one book on Blacks in the United States military. If one is to do serious research on Blacks in the United States military, one must start with the National Archives in Washington, D.C. The 128 volumes of the monumental *War of the Rebellion: A Compilation of Official Records of the Union and Confederate Armies,* however, contain the bulk of the material that is needed to study the Black soldier's role in the Civil War. In addition to the National Archives, there are also extensive collections of materials at the United States Army Military History Research Collection, Carlisle Barracks, Pennsylvania, and the Department of Defense, the Army and Navy. Black newspapers and periodicals are also indispensable sources of information and materials, as are former military men and women. Several Blacks have written about their lives in the military, and their stories offer personal insights on their struggle to be accepted as men and women on and off the battlefields.

Although many books and booklets have been written on the Black soldier, and most are listed in this collection, special attention needs to be given to the latest such work published by the United States Department of Defense. In 1982 this department released a 176-page booklet entitled *Black Americans in Defense of Our Nation.* This work gives an overview of the military heritage of Black Americans in defense of America from the Colonial Period (1528-1774) to the Post-Vietnam Era (1974-1981). There are also five other sections: "Black American Recipients of the Medal of Honor"; "Black Women in the Military Service of the United States"; "Black American Generals and Flag Officers by Military Service"; "The Military Academies and Black Americans"; and "Black Civilians in the Department of Defense." This work also has a number of photographs, illustrations, sketches, and broadsides. Each section has an introduction and conclusion. Unfortunately this work has no bibliographical references or footnotes.

This present volume is limited primarily to the printed materials on the Black soldier for two reasons. First, these sources are easily accessible to the general public and can be found in most good libraries. Second, this work is designed primarily for laymen and not scholars who deal mainly with primary or original documents and sources. Moreover as stated previously, the primary sources at the National Archives and elsewhere are too voluminous and out of the scope of this work to be listed in this book.

This work is divided into two parts. The first is a bibliography of books, articles, theses, and dissertations about Black soldiers in the various wars from the American Revolution to the Post-Vietnam era. It should be noted that in several instances the same book or article appears in different sections of this bibliography because they are general works and discuss various wars. Part Two consists of four appendixes and is followed by an extensive index that includes authors, coauthors, and editors.

Black American men and women have participated in every major war in which the United States has been involved. They saw themselves performing their obligation and responsibility as American citizens. Yet, in most instances, their services were not wanted except in national emergencies. Black soldiers received less pay and were insulted and sometimes physically abused on and off the military bases. The treatment of the Black soldier was a reflection of the treatment of the larger Black population. Blacks joined the military out of loyalty, duty, obligation, and economic necessity and proved to the world again and again that they were men and women who only wanted the same rights and privileges as other Americans.

We are indebted to our work-study student Debra Stevenson for helping with the proofreading and indexing. We would like also to thank Kitsy Smith for typing the final copy of the manuscript and for making several grammatical and technical corrections. Janie Harris assisted with the copying of citations and indexing. Several libraries also assisted us: the Schomburg Center for Research in Black Culture; the Moorland-Spingarn Research Center; Wake Forest University Library; New York Public Library; Winston-Salem University Library; and the Library of Congress.

Although many people assisted us in this endeavor, we take full responsibility for any errors or omissions and for all of its shortcomings.

We consulted all works that were available and attempted to give complete citation data. In a number of cases we saw only newspaper clippings of articles and not the complete newspapers. Many of the clippings did not give page numbers. Conversely, many of the papers are out of print and could not be located. We would like to point out that we did cite several major newspapers such as the *New York Times* and *Washington Post*. We also included most of the major Black newspapers such as the *New York Amsterdam News, Afro-American,* and *Pittsburgh Courier.* We believe that this volume is the most complete reference guide of works by and about the subject to date. It is our hope that this work will help others better understand and appreciate the contributions that Black men and women have made to American military history.

I.

Blacks in the American Revolution

1. "A British Officer in Boston in 1775," <u>Atlantic Monthly</u>, Vol. 39, 1877, pp. 389-401, 544-554.

2. Alexander, Arthur J. "How Maryland Tried to Raise Her Continental Quotas," <u>Maryland Historical Magazine</u>, Vol. 42, September, 1947, pp. 184-196.

3. Andrews, Charles M. "Slavery in Connecticut," <u>Magazine of American History</u>, Vol. 21, May, 1889, pp. 422-423.

4. Aptheker, Herbert. "Edward Griffin, Revolutionary Soldier," <u>Negro History Bulletin</u>, Vol. 13, November, 1949, pp. 38, 45.

5. _____. "Negroes Who Served in Our First Navy," <u>Opportunity</u>, Vol. 18, April, 1940, p. 117.

6. _____. <u>The American Revolution: 1763-1783</u>. New York: International Publishers, 1960. See Negroes in American Revolution, pp. 29, 65, 113, 119, 207-208, 251, 282.

7. Barnett, Paul. "The Black Continentals," <u>Negro History Bulletin</u>, Vol. 33, January, 1970, pp. 6-10.

8. Bettle, Edward. "Negro Slavery As Connected With Pennsylvania," <u>Historical Society of Pennsylvania, Memoirs</u>, Vol. I, 1826, pp. 367-416.

9. Billington, Ray Allen. "James Forten: Forgotten Abolitionist," <u>Negro History Bulletin</u>, Vol. 13, November, 1949, pp. 31-36.

10. Boatner, Mark M., III. "The Negro in the American Revolution," <u>American History Illustrated</u>, Vol. 4, August, 1969, pp. 36-44.

11. Boston City Council. A Memorial of Crispus Attucks, Samuel Maverick, James Caldwell, Samuel Gray and Patrick Carr. Miami, FL: Mnemosyne Publishing Co., Inc., 1969. Published originally in 1889.

12. Brown, Wallace. "Negroes and the American Revolution," History Today, Vol. 14, August, 1964, pp. 556-563.

13. Bull, Lisa A. "The Negro," Historical Journal of Western Massachusetts Supplement, 1976, pp. 67-74.

14. Bullock, James A. Black Patriots of the American Revolution: 1775-1783. Princeton: Carolingian Press, 1969.

15. "Bunker Hill," Historical Magazine, 2nd Ser. Vol. 3, 1868, pp. 321-340.

16. Coleman, Charles W. "The Southern Campaign, 1781," Magazine of American History, Vol. 7, 1881, pp. 201-216.

17. Collier, Thomas S. "The Revolutionary Privateers of Connecticut," New London Historical Society, Records and Papers, Vol. 1, pt. 4, 1892, pp. 3-45.

18. "Collier's and Mathew's Invasion of Virginia in 1779," Virginia Historical Register, Vol. 4, 1851, pp. 185-191.

19. Cooley, Timothy M. Sketches of the Life and Character of the Rev. Lemuel Haynes. New York: John S. Taylor, 1839, pp. 46, 83-86.

20. Cresto, Kathleen M. "The Negro: Symbol and Participant of the American Revolution," Negro History Bulletin, Vol. 39, November-December, 1976, pp. 628-631.

21. Crocker, James F. "The Parkers of Macclesfield, Isle of Wright, Va.," Virginia Magazine of History and Biography, Vol. 6, 1889, pp. 420-424.

22. Cropper, John. "Memoir of General John Cooper," By Burton H. Wise. Virginia Historical Society, Proceedings, Vol. 2, 1892, pp. 275-315.

23. Crow, Jeffrey J. The Black Experience in Revolutionary North Carolina. Raleigh, NC: Department of Cultural Resources, 1977.

24. David, Jay and Elaine Crane. The Black Soldier From the American Revolution to Vietnam. New York: William Morrow & Co., 1971.

25. Diman, J. Lewis. "The Capture of Prescott," Rhode Island Historical Tracts, Vol. 1, 1877, pp. 11-44.

26. Draper, Lyman C. King's Mountain (NC) and Its Heroes:
    History of the Battle of King's Mountain, October 7th,
    1780. Cincinnati: Peter G. Thomson, Publisher, 1881,
    pp. 42-43, 267-268, 583.

27. Drimmer, Melvin, Editor. Black History: A Reappraisal.
    Garden City, NY: Doubleday & Co., 1968, pp. 132-142.

28. Eckenrode, Hamilton J., Editor. List of Revolutionary
    Soldiers of Virginia. Richmond: Davis Bottom, 1912.

29. "Eighteenth Century Slaves as Advertised by Their
    Masters," Journal of Negro History, Vol. 1, April,
    1916, pp. 163-216.

30. Fisher, J. B. "Who Was Crispus Attucks?," American
    Historical Record, Vol. 1, 1872, pp. 531-533.

31. Fisher, Ruth Anna. "Manuscript Materials Bearing on
    the Negro in the British Museum," Journal of Negro
    History, Vol. 27, January, 1942, pp. 83-93.

32. Fiske, John. "Crispus Attucks," Negro History Bulletin,
    Vol. 33, March, 1970, pp. 58-68.

33. Fleming, Thomas. Give Me Liberty: Black Valor in the
    Revolutionary War. New York: Scholastic Book Services,
    1971.

34. Fogg, John S. H. "Inquest on Michael Johnson Alias
    Crispus Attucks," New England Historical and Genea-
    logical Register, Vol. 44, 1890, pp. 382-383.

35. Forten, James. A Series of Letters by a Man of Color.
    Philadelphia: n.p., 1813.

36. Frey, Sylvia R. "The British and the Black: A New
    Perspective," Historian, Vol. 38, February, 1976,
    pp. 225-238.

37. _____. "The British Soldier in the American
    Revolution." Unpublished Doctoral Dissertation, Tulane
    University, 1969.

38. Garrison, William Lloyd. The Loyalty and Devotion of
    Colored Americans in the Revolution and the War of
    1812. Boston: R. F. Wallcut, 1861.

39. Gasperetti, Elio. "An Italo-American Newspaper's
    Obituary of a Negro Revolutionary War Veteran," Negro
    History Bulletin, Vol. 18, December, 1954, p. 58.

40. Gibbs, C. R. "The First Black Army Officer (Col.
    Middleton, Revolutionary War)," Armed Forces Journal,
    Vol. 112, June, 1975, p. 24.

41. Gilmer, George R. Sketches of Some of the First
     (Austin Dabney, A Black Man) Settlers of Upper Georgia.
     Baltimore: Baltimore Genealogical Publishing Co., 1965.

42. Gobbel, Luther L. "The Militia in North Carolina in
     Colonial and Revolutionary Times," Trinity College
     Historical Society, Historical Papers, Vol. 13, 1919,
     pp. 35-61.

43. Gough, Robert J. "Black Men and the Early New Jersey
     Militia," New Jersey History, Vol. 88, Winter, 1970,
     pp. 227-238.

44. Green, Samuel A. "Slavery at Groton in Provincial
     Times," Massachusetts Historical Society, Proceedings,
     3rd Ser. Vol. 42, 1909, pp. 196-202.

45. Greene, Lorenzo J. "Some Observations on the Black
     Regiment of Rhode Island in the American Revolution,"
     Journal of Negro History, Vol. 37, April, 1952, pp.
     142-172.

46. _____. "The Negro in the Armed Forces of
     the United States, 1619-1783," Negro History Bulletin,
     Vol. 36, March, 1951, pp. 123-128.

47. Gwathmey, John H., Editor. Historical Register of
     Virginians in the Revolution. Soldiers, Sailors and
     Marines, 1775-1783. Richmond: Dietz Press, 1938.

48. Haarmann, Albert W. "The Siege of Pensacola: An Order
     of Battle," Florida Historical Quarterly, Vol. 44,
     January, 1966, pp. 193-199.

49. Hadaway, William S. "Negroes in the Revolutionary
     War," Westchester County Historical Society, Quarterly
     Bulletin, Vol. 6, 1930, pp. 8-12.

50. Harris, Janette H. "Crispus Attucks," Negro History
     Bulletin, Vol. 33, March, 1970, p. 69.

51. Hartgrove, W. B. "The Negro Soldier in the American
     Revolution," Journal of Negro History, Vol. I, April,
     1916, pp. 110-131.

52. Heitman, Francis B. Historical Register of Officers
     of the Continental Army During the War of the Revolu-
     tion, April, 1775 to December, 1783. Washington, DC:
     W. H. Lowdermilk & Co., 1893. See discussion of free
     Black soldiers from Massachusetts.

53. Holbrook, Stewart H. "The First American WAC: Deborah
     Sampson Gannett," Negro Digest, Vol. 3, November, 1944,
     pp. 39-43.

54. Jackson, Luther P. "Virginia Negro Soldiers and
     Seamen in the American Revolution," Journal of Negro
     History, Vol. 27, July, 1942, pp. 247-287.

55. _____. Virginia Negro Soldiers and Seaman
     in the Revolutionary War. Norfolk, VA: Guide Quality
     Press, 1944.

56. Jasper, John. "Biggest Hoax in the Revolutionary War,"
     Afro-American, Magazine Section, October 21, 1965, p. 1.

57. Johnson, Cecil. "Expansion in West Florida, 1770-1779,"
     Mississippi Valley Historical Review, Vol. 20, March,
     1934, pp. 481-496.

58. Johnson, Jesse J., Editor. Black Armed Forces Officers:
     1736-1971. Hampton, VA: Hampton Institute, 1971.

59. _____. A Pictoral History of Black
     Servicemen: Missing Pages in United States History.
     Hampton, VA: Hampton Institute, 1970.

60. Jordan, Winthrop. White Over Black: American Attitudes
     Toward the Negro, 1550-1812. Chapel Hill: University
     of North Carolina Press, 1968, pp. 302-306, 321-323.

61. Kaplan, Sidney. "A Negro Veteran in Shays' Rebellion,"
     Journal of Negro History, Vol. 33, April, 1948, pp.
     123-129.

62. _____. The Black Presence in the Era of the
     American Revolution, 1778-1800. New York: New York
     Graphic, 1973.

63. Langley, Harold D. "The Negro in the Navy and Merchant
     Service, 1798-1860," Journal of Negro History, Vol. 52,
     October, 1967, pp. 273-286.

64. "Lemuel Haynes: Revolutionary War Hero," Crisis,
     Vol. 82, December, 1072, p. 430.

65. Mann, JoAnn. "Black Americans in the War for Inde-
     pendence," Soldiers, Vol. 30, January, 1975, pp. 30-35.

66. Maslowski, Pete. "National Policy Toward the Use of
     Black Troops in the Revolution," South Carolina Histor-
     ical Magazine, Vol. 73, January, 1972, pp. 1-17.

67. McAllister, J. T. Virginia Militia in the Revolutionary
     War. Hot Springs, VA: McAllister Publishing Co., 1913.

68. Miller, William. "Effects of the American Revolution
     on Indentured Servitude," Pennsylvania History, Vol. 7,
     July, 1940, pp. 131-141.

69. Moore, George Henry. Historical Notes on the Employment of Negroes in the American Army of the Revolution. New York: C. T. Evans, 1862.

70. Morse, C. H. "Crispus Attucks," New England Historical and Genealogical Register, Vol. 13, 1859, p. 300.

71. Moss, Simon F. "The Persistence of Slavery and Involuntary Servitude in a Free State," Journal of Negro History, Vol. 35, July, 1950, pp. 289-314.

72. Mzack, Walter H. George Washington and the Negro. Washington, DC: Associated Publishers, 1932.

73. NAACP. Black Heroes of the American Revolution: 1775-1783. New York: NAACP, n.d.

74. Nell, William Cooper. The Colored Patriots of the American Revolution, With Sketches of Several Distinguished Colored Persons; To Which Is Added A Brief Survey of the Conditions and Prospects of Colored Americans. Boston: R. F. Wallcut, 1855.

75. _____. Services of Colored Americans, in the War of 1776 and 1812. Boston: Prentiss & Sawyer, 1851.

76. Nelson, Dennis D. The Integration of the Negro in the U. S. Navy, 1776-1947. New York: Farrar Straus, 1951.

77. Norton, Mary Beth. "The Fate of Some Loyalists of the American Revolution," Journal of Negro History, Vol. 58, October, 1973, pp. 402-426.

78. Observations on the Slaves and Indentured Servants, Inlisted in the Army, and the Navy of the United States. Philadelphia; n.p., 1777.

79. Payne, A. H. "The Negro in New York Prior to 1860," Howard Review, Vol. 1, 1923, pp. 23-35.

80. Pennington, Edgar L. "East Florida in the American Revolution, 1775-1778," Florida Historical Quarterly, Vol. 9, July, 1930, pp. 24-46.

81. Phillips, David E. "Slaves Who Fought in the Revolution," Journal of American History, Vol. 5, January-March, 1911, pp. 143-146.

82. Porter, Dorothy B. "The Black Role During the Era of the Revolution," Smithsonian, Vol. 4, August, 1973, pp. 52-57.

83. Pugh, Robert C.   "The Revolutionary Militia in the Southern Campaign, 1780-1781," William and Mary Quarterly, 3rd Ser. Vol. 14, April, 1957, pp. 154-175.

84. Quarles, Benjamin. "A Group Portrait: Black America
     at the Time of the American War," Ebony, Vol. 30,
     August, 1975, pp. 44-50.

85. _____. "Lord Dunmore as Liberator,"
     William and Mary Quarterly, Vol. 15, October, 1958,
     pp. 494-507.

86. _____. "The Colonial Militia and Negro
     Manpower," Mississippi Valley Historical Review, Vol.
     45, March, 1959, pp. 743-652.

87. _____. The Negro in the American Revolu-
     tion. Chapel Hill: University of North Carolina
     Press, 1961.

88. _____. "The Significance of the Revolu-
     tionary War for Black Americans," Black Heritage, Vol.
     21, November-December, 1981, pp. 25-35.

89. Rantoul, Robert S., Sr. "Negro Slavery in Massachu-
     setts," Historical Collections (Exxex Institute), Vol.
     14, 1887, pp. 81-100.

90. Reddick, Lawrence A.D. "The Negro Policy of the United
     States Army, 1775-1945," Journal of Negro History, Vol.
     34, January, 1949, pp. 9-29.

91. Reynolds, Helen W. "The Negro in Dutchess County in
     the Eighteenth Century," Dutchess County Historical
     Society, Yearbook, 1941, pp. 89-99.

92. Rider, Sidney Smith. An Historical Inquiry Concerning
     the Attempt to Raise a Regiment of Slaves by Rhode
     Island During the War of the Revolution. Providence,
     RI: S.S. Rider, 1880.

93. _____. "The Black Regiment of the
     Revolution," Rhode Island Historical Tracts (Providence),
     No. 10, 1880, p. 10.

94. _____. "The Rhode Island Black 'Regiment'
     of 1778," Rhode Island Historical Tracts, No. 10,
     1880, pp. 1-86.

95. Roberts, Wesley A. "The Black Experience and the
     American Revolution," Fides et Historia, Vol. 8, 1976,
     pp. 50-62.

96. Shaffer, E.T.H. "The Rejected Laurens-A Carolina
     Tragedy," South Carolina Historical Association,
     Proceedings for 1934 (Columbia), 1934, pp. 12-24.

97. "Slaves in the Revolutionary Army," Historical Maga-
     zine, 2nd Ser., Vol. 2, 1867, p. 44.

98.   Smith, Jonathan.   "How Massachusetts Raised Her Troops
      in the Revolution," Massachusetts Historical Society,
      Proceedings, 3rd Ser., Vol. 55, 1923, pp. 345-370.

99.   Smith, M.H.   "Connecticut Slaves in Revolutionary
      Times," Connecticut Magazine, Vol. 9, January, 1905,
      pp. 145-153.

100. Stickley, Julia Ward.   "The Records of Deborah Sampson
      Gannett, Woman Soldier of the Revolution," Prologue,
      Vol. 4, Winter, 1972, pp. 233-241.

101. Swett, Samuel.   Notes to His Sketch of Bunker-Hill
      Battle.   Boston: Munroe and Francis, 1825.

102. "The Boston Massacre and Crispus Attucks," Negro
      History Bulletin, Vol. 33, March, 1970, pp. 56-57.

103. "The Schooner Patriot," Virginia Historical Register,
      Vol. 1, 1848, pp. 76-80.

104. Thum, Marcella.   "Invisible Soldier in the Revolution-
      ary War," Black Collegian, November-December, 1975,
      pp. 16-18.

105. Thwaites, Reuben Gold.   "The British Regime in Wis-
      consin," State Historical Society of Wisconsin,
      Collections, Vol. 18, 1908, pp. 223-268.

106. Tyson, George F.,Jr.   "The Carolina Black Corps:
      Legacy of the Revolution (1783-1798)," Revista/Review
      Interamericana (Puerto Rico), Vol. 4, 1975, pp. 648-664.

107. Von, Eelking, Max.   "Military Operations in Rhode
      Island," Rhode Island Historical Tracts, No. 6, 1878,
      pp. 37-65.

108. Walker, James W. St. G.   "Blacks as American Loyalists:
      The Slaves' War for Independence," Historical Reflec-
      tions (Canada), Vol. 2, 1975, pp. 51-67.

109. Wax, Darold D.   "Black Heroes of the American Revolu-
      tion," Crisis, Vol. 83, August-September, 1976, pp.
      257-258.

110. _____.   "Black Heroes of the American Revolu-
      tion," Crisis, Vol. 83, December, 1976, pp. 360-362.

111. White, David O.   Connecticut's Black Soldiers 1755-
      1783.   Chester, CT: Pequot Press, 1973.

112. Wilkes, Laura Eliza.   Missing Pages in American
      History, Revealing the Services of the Negroes in the
      Early Wars in the United States of America, 1641-1815.
      New York: AMS Press, 1973. Published originally in
      1919.

113. Wilson, Joseph T. The Black Phalanx; A History of the
      Negro Soldiers of the United States in the Wars of
      1755-1812, 1861-1865. Hartford, CT: American Pub-
      lishing Co., 1887.

114. Winks, Robin W. The Blacks in Canada. New Haven, CT:
      Yale University Press, 1971. See pages 24-60.

II.

Blacks in the War of 1812

115. Arthur, Stanley C. The Story of the Battle of New
      Orleans. New Orleans: Louisiana Historical Society,
      1915.

116. Bowman, Larry G. "Virginia's Use of Blacks in the
      French and Indian War," Western Pennsylvania Historical
      Magazine, Vol. 53, January, 1970, pp. 57-104.

117. Cassell, Frank A. "Slaves of the Chesapeake Bay Area
      and the War of 1812," Journal of Negro History, Vol.
      57, April, 1972, pp. 144-156.

118. Christian, Marcus. Negro Soldiers in Battle of New
      Orleans. New Orleans, n.p.

119. Foner, Philip Sheldon. Morale Education in the Ameri-
      can Army: War for Independence, War of 1812, Civil
      War. New York: International Publishers, 1944.

120. Garrison, William Lloyd. The Loyalty and Devotion of
      Colored Americans in the Revolution and War of 1812.
      Boston: R.F. Wallcut, 1861.

121. Gilman, Charles. Story of the Jersey Blue. Redham,
      NJ: Arlington Laboratory for Clincal and Historical
      Research, 1962, p. 9.

122. Greene, Lorenze. "The Negro in the Armed Forces of
      the U.S., 1619-1783," Negro History Bulletin, Vol. 14,
      March, 1951, pp. 123-128.

123. _____. "The Negro in the War of 1812 and
      the Civil War," Negro History Bulletin, Vol. 14, March,
      1951, pp. 133-137.

124. Harrod, Frederick S. "Jim Crow in the Navy," U.S.
      Naval Institute Proceedings, Vol. 105, September, 1979,
      pp. 46-53.

125. Hyman, Mark. "Black Participation in the War of 1812,"
      Crisis, Vol. 85, December, 1978, pp. 355-358.

126. Johnson, Jesse J. A Pictorial History of Black Ser-
      vicemen: Missing Pages in United States History.
      Hampton, VA: Hampton Institute, 1970.

127. Langley, Harold D. "The Negro in the Navy and Merchant
      Service, 1789-1860," Journal of Negro History, Vol. 52,
      October, 1967, pp. 273-286.

128. Lyman, Olin L. Commodore Oliver Perry and the War on
      the Lakes. New York: New Amsterdam Book Co., 1905.

129. McConnell, Roland C. Negro Troops of Antebellum
      Louisiana. Baton Rouge, LA: Louisiana State Univer-
      sity, 1968.

130. Nell, William Cooper. Services of Colored Americans
      in the Wars of 1776 and 1812. Boston: Prentiss and
      Sawyer, 1851.

131. Owsley, Franke Lawrence, Jr. "The Role of the South
      in the British Grand Strategy in the War of 1812,"
      Tennessee Historical Quarterly, Vol. 31, Spring, 1972,
      pp. 22-38.

132. Reddick, Lawrence D. "The Negro Policy of the U.S.
      Army, 1775-1945," Journal of Negro History, Vol. 35,
      January, 1949, pp. 9-29.

133. "The Battle of New Orleans," Crisis, Vol. 9, March,
      1914, p. 258.

134. Wilson, Joseph Thomas. The Black Phalanx: A History
      of the Negro Soldiers of the United States in the Wars
      of 1775-1812, 1861-1865. Hartford, CT: American
      Publishing Co., 1887.

III.

Blacks in the Civil War

135. A History of the Negro Troops in the War of the Rebellion, 1861-1865, Preceeded by a Review of the Military Services of Negroes in Ancient and Modern Times. New York: Harper and Bros., 1888.

136. Abbott, Abial E. "The Negro in the War of the Rebellion," Military Essays and Recollections. Chicago: Dial Press, 1899.

137. Abbott, Richard H. "Massachusetts and the Recruitment of Southern Negroes, 1863-1865," Civil War History, Vol. 14, September, 1968, pp. 197-210.

138. Adams, Julius Walker. Letter to the Honorable Secretary of War, on the Examination of Field Officers for Colored Troops. New York: J.F. Lrow, Printer, 1863.

139. Addeman, Joshus McLancthon. Reminiscences of Two Years with the Colored Troops. Providence: N. Bangs Williams and Co., 1880.

140. Adjutant General's Office. The Negro in the Military Service of the United States, 1639-1886. Washington, DC, 1885-1888.

141. Akers, Capt. Frank H., Jr. "Blacks in the Civil War: They Fought for the Union and Equality," Army, Vol. 25, April, 1975, pp. 47-51.

142. _____. "They Fought For the Union and Equality: Blacks in the Civil War," Army, Vol. 25, March, 1975, pp. 47-51.

143. Aleckson, Sam. <u>Before the War, and After the Union:</u>
     <u>An Autobiography.</u> Boston: Gold Mine Publishing Co.,
     1929. An ex-slave from South Carolina who served in
     the Confederate Army during the Civil War writes about
     his life through 1914.

144. Anderson, Charles Carter. <u>Fighting by Southern</u>
     <u>Federals.</u> New York: Neale Publishing Co., 1912.

145. _____. <u>The South Reports the Civil</u>
     <u>War.</u> Princeton, NJ: Princeton University Press, 1970.

146. Anderson, Robert. <u>From Slavery to Affluence: Memoirs</u>
     <u>of Robert Anderson, Ex-Slave.</u> Hemingford, NB: Heming-
     ford Ledger, 1927. Anderson served in the Union Army
     during the Civil War.

147. Aptheker, Herbert. <u>Negro Casualties in the Civil War.</u>
     Washington, DC: The Association for the Study of
     Negro Life and History, Inc., n.d.

148. _____. "Negro Casualties in the Civil War,"
     <u>Journal of Negro History</u>, Vol. 32, January, 1947, pp.
     10-80.

149. _____. <u>The Negro in the Civil War.</u> New
     York: International Publishers, 1938.

150. _____. "The Negro in the Union Navy,"
     <u>Journal of Negro History</u>, Vol. 32, April, 1947, pp.
     169-200.

151. Austerman, Wayne R. "Baton Rouge and the Black Regu-
     lars," <u>Louisiana History</u>, Vol. 21, Summer, 1980, pp.
     277-286.

152. Ayers, James T. <u>The Diary of James T. Ayers, Civil</u>
     <u>War Recruiter.</u> Springfield: Printed by the State of
     Illinois, 1947.

153. Bahney, Robert Stanley. "Generals and Negroes:
     Education of Negroes by the Union Army, 1861-1865."
     Unpublished Doctoral Dissertation, University of
     Michigan, 1965.

154. Baird, Henry Carey. <u>General Washington and General</u>
     <u>Jackson, on Negro Soldiers.</u> Philadelphia: H.C. Baird,
     1863.

155. Bates, Samuel P. <u>History of Pennsylvania Volunteers,</u>
     <u>1861-1865.</u> Harrisburg, PA: B. Singerly Publisher,
     1869, Vol. 5, pp. 925, 966-969.

156. Belz, Herman. "Law, Politics, and the Race in the
     Struggle for Equal Pay During the Civil War," <u>Civil</u>
     <u>War History</u>, Vol. 22, September, 1976, pp. 197-213.

157. Benton, Josiah Henry. Voting in the Field: A Forgotten Chapter of the Civil War. Boston: Privately
Printed, 1951.

158. Berlin, Ira et al, Editors. Freedom: A Documentary
History of Emancipation, 1861-1867, Series II, The
Black Military Experience. London: Cambridge Univer-
sity Press, 1982.

159. Berry, Mary Frances. Military Necessity and Civil
Rights Policy: Black Citizenship and the Constitution,
1861-1868. Port Washington, NY: Kennikat Press, 1977.

160. _____. "Negro Troops in Blue and Gray:
The Louisiana Guard, 1861-1863," Louisiana History,
Vol. 8, Spring, 1967, pp. 165-190.

161. _____. "The Negro Soldier Movement and
the Adoption of the National Conscription, 1852-1865."
Unpublished Doctoral Dissertation, University of Michigan, 1966.

162. Biddle, Charles. The Alliance with the Negro. Washington, DC: L. Towers and Co., 1862.

163. Bigelow, John. On the Bloody Trail of Geronimo by Lt.
John Bigelow, Jr. with the Original Illustration of
Hooper, McDougall, Chapin, Hatfield and Frederic
Remington, Forward, Introduction and Notes by Arthur
Woodward. Los Angeles: Westernlore Press, 1968.

164. Bigelow, Martha M. "The Significance of Milliken's
Bend in the Civil War," Journal of Negro History,
Vol. 45, July, 1960, pp. 156-163.

165. Binder, Frederick M. "Pennsylvania Negro Regiments
in the Civil War," Journal of Negro History, Vol. 37,
October, 1952, pp. 383-417.

166. Bird, Francis W. Review of Governor Banks' Veto of
the Revised Code, on Account of Its Authorizing the
Enrollment of Colored Citizens in the Militia. Boston:
J.P. Jewett and Co., 1860.

167. Blassingame, John W. "Negro Chaplains in the Civil
War," Negro History Bulletin, Vol. 27, October, 1963,
pp. 23-24.

168. _____. "The Freedom Fighters," Negro
History Bulletin, Vol. 28, February, 1965, pp. 105-106.

169. _____. "The Organization and Use of
Negro Troops in the Union Army, 1863-1865." Unpublished Master's Thesis, Howard University, 1961.

170. _____. "The Recruitment of Colored Troops in Kentucky, Maryland and Missouri, 1863-1865," The Historian, 1967, pp. 533-545.

171. _____. "The Selection of Officers and Non-Commissioned Officers of Negro Troops in the Union Army, 1863-1865," Negro History Bulletin, Vol. 30, January, 1967, pp. 8-11.

172. _____. "The Union Army as an Educational Institution for Negroes, 1862-1865," Journal of Negro Education, Vol. 34, Spring, 1965, pp. 152-159.

173. Bliss, George J. Union League Club Report of the Committee on Volunteering Presented October 13, 1864. New York: n.p., 1864.

174. Boyd, Thomas James. "The Use of Negro Troops by Kansas During the Civil War." Unpublished Master's Thesis, Kansas State Teachers College, 1950.

175. Brague, S.B. Notes on Colored Troops and Military Colonies on Southern Soil, by an Officer of the 9th Army Corps. New York: n.p., 1863.

176. Brewer, James H. The Confederate Negro. Durham: Duke University Press, 1969.

177. Brewer, John Mason. Negro Legislators of Texas and Their Descendants: A History of the Negro in Texas Politics from Reconstruction to Disfranchisement. Dallas, TX: Mathis Publishing Company, 1935.

178. Brockett, L.P. The Camp, the Battle Field, and the Hospital, or Lights and Shadows of the Great Rebellion. St. Louis: National Publishing Co., 1866.

179. Brown, Frederick W. My Services in the U.S. Colored Cavalry. Cincinnati: Commandery of the Loyal Legion, 1908.

180. Brown, Ida C. Michigan Men in the Civil War. Ann Arbor, MI: University of Michigan, 1959.

181. Brown, William Wells. The Negro in the American Rebellion, His Heroism and His Fidelity. Boston: Lee and Sheppard, 1867.

182. Bruce, John Edward. A Defense of the Colored Soldiers Who Fought in the War of Rebellion. New York: n.p., n.d.

183. Bruner, Peter. A Slave's Adventures Toward Freedom: Not Fiction, But the True Story of a Struggle. Oxford, OH: The Author, 1925. Author served in the Union Army during the Civil War.

184. Bryant, William Cullen. "A Yankee Soldier Looks at the Negro," Civil War History, Vol. 7, June, 1961, pp. 133-148.

185. Burchard, Peter. One Gallant Rush; Robert Gould Shaw and His Brave Black Regiment. New York: St. Martin's Press, 1965.

186. Cahill, Carl. "Note on Two Va. Negro Civil War Soldiers: One Union, One Confederate," Negro History Bulletin, Vol. 29, November, 1965, pp. 39-40.

187. Califf, Joseph Mark. Record of the Services of the Seventh Regiment, U.S. Colored Troops, from September 1863, to November 1866. Providence, RI: E.L. Freeman and Co., 1878.

188. _____. History of the Seventh U.S. Colored Troops. Providence, RI: E.L. Freeman and Co., 1872.

189. Cashin, Hersel V. Under Fire, With the Tenth U.S. Cavalry, Being a Brief, Comprehensive View of the Negro's Participation in the Wars of the United States. Especially Showing the Valor and Heroism of the Negro Soldier of the Ninth and Tenth Cavalries, and the Twenty-Fourth and Twenty-Fifth Infantries...Famous Indian Campaigns and Their Results. New York: F.T. Neely, 1899.

190. Castel, Albert. "The Fort Pillow Massacre," Civil War History, Vol. 4, March, 1958, pp. 37-50.

191. _____. "Civil War Kansas and the Negro," Journal of Negro History, Vol. 51, April, 1966, pp. 125-138.

192. Chenery, William H. The 14th Regiment, Rhodes Island, Heavy Artillery (Colored) in the War to Preserve the Union, 1861-1865. Providence, RI: Snow and Farnham, 1898.

193. Civil War Official Records of the Union and Confederate Navies in the War of the Rebellion. Washington, DC: National Archives, 1927. 34 Vols.

194. Clark, Peter H. The Black Brigade of Cincinnati: Being A Report of Its Labors and A Muster-Roll of Its Members; Together With Various Orders, Speeches, Etc. Relating to It. Cincinnati: Joseph B. Boud, Publishers, 1864.

195. Cochrane, John. American Civil War. Memories of In-
      cidents Connected with the Origin and Culmination of
      the Rebellion that Threatened the Existence of the
      National Government:--Including Reminiscences of the
      Course of the Rebel Leaders in Congress and in the
      National Democratic Convention which Immediately Pre-
      ceeded the Outburst of Rebellion; Together with Move-
      ment in and Concerning the Army of the Potomac during
      the First Two Years of the War;--Including the Propo-
      sition made in a Speech at the Astor House, in New
      York in November, 1861, When, in Company with Simon
      Cameron...General John Cochrane...First Publicly
      Advocated the Arming of the Slaves in the War for the
      Union...From Writings on those Subjects (Printed for
      Private Use) by John Cochrane...Collected by Henry
      O'Rielly...(Designed as an Appendix to O'Rielly's
      "Brief History of the Organization of Colored Troops
      in the State of New York"--Deposited Among His Dona-
      tions to the New York Historical Society. New York:
      Rogers and Sherwood, 1879.

196. _____. Arming the Slaves in the War for the
      Union. New York: Rogers and Sherwood, 1875.

197. Colyer, Vincent. Report of the Services Rendered by
      the Freed People of the United States Army, in North
      Carolina, in the Spring of 1862, After the Battle of
      Newbern. New York: V. Colyer Publisher, 1864.

198. Conrad, Earl. Harriet Tubman. Negro Soldier and
      Abolitionist. New York: International Publishers,
      1942.

199. Cornish, Dudley T. "Kansas Negro Regiments in the
      Civil War," Kansas Historical Quarterly, Vol. 20,
      May, 1953, pp. 417-420.

200. _____. "Negro Troops in the Union Army,
      1861-1865." Unpublished Doctoral Dissertation,
      University of Colorado, 1950.

201. _____. The Sable Arm; Negro Troops in
      the Union Army, 1861-1865. New York: W.W. Norton,
      1966.

202. _____. "The Union Army as a Training
      School for Negroes," Journal of Negro History, Vol. 37,
      October, 1952, pp. 368-381.

203. Coston, William Hilary. A Freeman and Yet a Slave.
      Burlington, LA: Wohlwend Brothers Printers, 1888.

204. Coulter, Ellis Merton. The Civil War and Readjustment
      in Kentucky. Chapel Hill: University of North Caro-
      lina Press, 1926.

205. Cowden, Robert. A Brief Sketch of the Organization and Services of the Fifty-Ninth Regiment of United States Colored Infantry. Dayton, OH: United Brethren Publishing/Gause, 1883.

206. Cowdrey, Albert E. "Slave Into Soldier: The Enlistment by the North of Runaway Slaves," History Today, Vol. 20, October, pp. 704-715.

207. Crawford, Samuel J. Kansas in the Sixties. Chicago: n.p., 1911.

208. David, Jay and Elaine Crane. The Black Soldier--From the American Revolution to Vietnam. New York: William Morrow and Co., 1971.

209. Davis, William Watts Hart. History of the 104th Pennsylvania Regiment, From August 22nd, 1861 to September 30, 1864. Philadelphia: J.B. Rogers, 1866.

210. Dennet, George M. History of the Ninth U.S. Colored Troops. Philadelphia: King and Baird, 1866.

211. Dollard, R. United State Cavalry 2nd Colored Regiment, 1863-1866; Recollections of the Civil War and Going West to Grow up with the Country. Scotland, SD: P.A. Bliss, 1906.

212. Douglass, Frederick. Men of Color to Arms; A Call by Frederick Douglass. Rochester, NY: n.p., 1863.

213. Drinkard, Dorothy Lee. A Regiment History of the Twenty-Ninth Infantry, United States Colored Regiments, 1864-1865. Washington, DC: Howard University, 1963.

214. DuBois. W.E.B. "The Negro and the American War," Science and Society, Vol. 25, December, 1961, pp. 347-352.

215. Dyer, Brainerd. "The Treatment of Colored Union Troops by the Confederate, 1861-1865," Journal of Negro History, Vol. 20, July, 1935, pp. 273-286.

216. Dyer, Frederick. Compendium of the War of the Rebellion. Compiled and Arranged from Official Records of the Federal and Confederate Armies, Reports of the Adjutant Generals of the Several States, the Army Registers and Other Reliable Documents and Sources. Des Moines, IA: The Dyer Publishing Co., 1908.

217. Emilio, Louis F. A Brave Black Regiment: History of the Fifty-Fourth Massachusetts Volunteer Infantry, 1863-1865. Boston: Boston Book Co., 1891.

218. _____   The Assault on Fort Wagner, July 18, 1863. The Memorable Charge of the 54th Regiment of Massachusetts Volunteers, 1863-1865. Boston: Rand Avery Co., 1887.

219. Everett, Donald E.   "Ben Butler and the Louisiana Native Guards, 1861-1862," Journal of Southern History, Vol. 24, February, 1958, pp. 202-217.

220. _____. "Demands of the New Orleans Free Colored Population for Political Equality, 1862-1865," Louisiana Historical Quarterly, Vol. 38, April, 1955, pp. 43-64.

221. First Organization of Colored Troops in the State of New York. New York: n.p., 1864.

222. Fitts, James F.   "The Negro as a Soldier," Galaxy, Vol. 3, February 1, 1867, pp. 348-255.

223. Foner, Philip S.   "The First Negro Meeting in Maryland (Discusses Black Soldiers)," Maryland Historical Magazine, Vol. 66, Spring, 1971, pp. 60-67.

224. Forty-Fourth Regiment U.S. Colored Troops. Gettysburg, PA: J.E. Wible, 1866.

225. Foster, G. Allen.   "John Scobell-Union Spy in Civil War," Ebony, Vol. 33, October, 1978, pp. 73-76.

226. _____. "The Woman Who Saved the Union Navy," Ebony, Vol. 19, July, 1964, pp. 48-50, 52, 54-58.

227. Fox, Charles Bernard.   Record of the Service of the Fifty-Fifth Massachusetts Volunteer Infantry. Cambridge: The Regimental Association, 1868.

228. Fox, William F.   Regimental Losses in the American Civil War, 1861-1865. Albany, NY: William F. Fox, 1889.

229. Franklin, John Hope, Editor.   The Diary of James T. Ayers, Civil War Recruiter. Springfield, IL: n.p., 1947.

230. Freeman, Henry V.   "A Colored Brigade in the Campaign and Battle of Nashville," Military Essays and Recollections. Chicago: A. McClurg and Co., 1894.

231. French, Robert.   Colonel Robert G. Shaw. Boston: n.p., 1904.

232. Gerteis, Louis S.   From Contraband to Freedman: Federal Policy Toward Southern Blacks, 1861-1865. Westport, CT: Greenwood Press, 1973.

233. Goodman, M.H. "The Black Tar: The Black Enlisted Man
      in the Union Navy, 1861-1865." Unpublished Doctoral
      Dissertation, University of Nottingham, 1971.

234. Greene, Lorenze. "The Negro in the Armed Forces of
      the U.S., 1619-1783," Negro History Bulletin, Vol. 36,
      March, 1951, pp. 123-128.

235. Grimes, William W. Thirty-Three Years' Experience of
      an Itinerant Minister of A.M.E. Church. Lancaster,
      PA: E.S. Speaker, 1887. Author served in U.S. Navy
      during the Civil War.

236. Guthrie, James M. Camp-Fires of the Afro-American; or
      the Colored Man as a Patriot, Soldier, Sailor and Hero
      in the Cause of Free America. Philadelphia: Afro-
      American Publishing Co., 1899.

237. Hallowell, Norwood P. The Negro as a Soldier in the
      War of the Rebellion. Boston: Little and Brown, 1897.

238. Hansen, Chadwick. "The 54th Massachusetts Volunteer
      Black Infantry as a Subject for American Artists,"
      Massachusetts Review, Vol. 16, Autumn, 1975, pp. 745-
      749.

239. Harwickhall, Martin. "Negroes with Confederate Troops
      in West Texas and New Mexico," Pass Word, Vol. 13,
      Spring, 1968, pp. 11-12.

240. Harrington, Fred Harvey. "The Fort Jackson Mutiny,"
      Journal of Negro History, Vol. 27, October, 1942,
      pp. 420-431.

241. Harris, N. Dwight. The History of Negro Servitude in
      Illinois and of the Slavery Agitation in that State,
      1719-1864. Chicago: A.C. McClug and Company, 1904.

242. Hawkins, William George. Lunsford Lane; or Another
      Helper from North Carolina. Boston: Cosley and
      Nichols, 1863.

243. Heller, Charles E. "The 54th Massachusetts," Civil
      War Times Illustrated, Vol. II, April, 1972, pp. 32-41.

244. Hendricks, George Linton. "Union Army Occupation of
      the Southern Seaborad, 1861-1865." Unpublished
      Doctoral Dissertation, Columbia University, 1954.

245. Hesseltine, William B. Civil War Prisons. Columbus,
      OH: Ohio State University Press, 1930, pp. 87-89,
      112-113, 186-188, 216-230.

246. Hicken, Victor. "The Record of Illinois' Negro Soldier
      in the Civil War," Journal of the Illinois State
      Historical Society, Vol. 56, Spring, 1963, pp. 529-551.

247. Higginson, Thomas Wentworth. <u>Army Life in a Black Regiment</u>. Boston: Fields, Osgood and Co., 1870.

248. _____. "First Black Regiment: First South Carolina Colored Union Volunteers," <u>Outlook</u>, Vol. 59, July 2, 1898, pp. 521-531.

249. Hill, Isaac J. <u>A Sketch of the 29th Regiment of Connecticut Colored Troops</u>. Baltimore: Daugherty, Maguire and Co., 1867.

250. Hines, Marguerite McNeill. "Northern Negroes During the Civil War." Unpublished Master's Thesis, Howard University, 1940.

251. Hunt, Christine S. "Minden in the Civil War Years," <u>North Louisiana Historical Association</u>, Vol. 8, 1977, pp. 143-149.

252. Hunt, Sanford B. "The Negro as a Soldier," <u>Quarterly Journal of Psychological Medicine</u>, Vol. 1, 1867, pp. 161-186.

253. January, Alan Frank. "The First Nullification: The Negro Seamen Acts Controversy in South Carolina, 1822-1860." Unpublished Doctoral Dissertation, University of Iowa, 1976.

254. Johannsen, Robert W. "Spectors of Disunion: The Pacific Northwest and the Civil War," <u>Pacific Northwest Quarterly</u>, Vol. 44, July, 1953, pp. 106-114.

255. Johnson, Jessie J. <u>A Pictorial History of Black Servicemen: Missing Pages in United States History</u>. Hampton, VA: Hampton Institute, 1970.

256. Johnson, William Henry. <u>Autobiography of Dr. William Henry Johnson; Respectfully Dedicated to His Adopted Home, the Capital City of the Empire State</u>. Albany, NY: Argus Co., Printers, 1900. Author discusses his military service in the Union Army during the Civil War.

257. Jones, Howard J. "Letters in Protest of Race Prejudice in the Army During the American Civil War," <u>Journal of Negro History</u>, Vol. 61, January, 1976, pp. 97-98.

258. Kelly, William Darrah. <u>The Conscription</u>. Philadelphia: n.p., 1863.

259. Key, Vladimir O., Jr. <u>Southern Politics in State and Nation</u>. New York: Random House, 1949.

260. Krech, Shepard, III. "The Participation of Maryland Blacks in the Civil War: Perspectives from Oral History," <u>Ethnohistory</u>, Vol. 27, 1980, pp. 8-16.

261. Langley, Harold D. Social Reform in the United States Navy, 1798–1862. Urbana: University of Illinois Press, 1967.

262. Langston, John Mercer. From the Virginia Plantation to the National Capitol. Hartford, CN: American Publishing Co., 1894. Discussion of Black Soldiers in the Civil War.

263. Ledbetter, Billy D. "White Over Black in Texas: Racial Attitudes in the Ante-Bellum Period," Phylon, Vol. 34, 1973, pp. 406–418.

264. Lee, Irvin H. "Negro Heroes of the Civil War," Negro Digest, Vol. 24, February, 1966, pp. 20–25.

265. Lee, William Mack. History of the Life of Rev. William Mack Lee, Body Servant of General Robert E. Lee, Through the Civil War, Cook from 1861 to 1865; Still Living under the Protection of the Southern States. Norfolk, VA: Smith Printing Co., 1918.

266. Lester, Charles Edwards. The Light and Dark of the Rebellion. Philadelphia: George W. Childs, 1863.

267. Levstik, Frank R. "Robert A. Pinn: Courageous Black Soldier," Negro History Bulletin, Vol. 37, October/November, 1974, pp. 304–305.

268. Livermore, George. An Historical Research Respecting the Opinions of the Founders of the Republic on Negroes as Slaves, as Citizens, and as Soldiers. Boston: J. Wilson and Sons, 1862.

269. Livermore, Thomas L. Numbers and Losses in the Civil War in America: 1861–1865. Boston: Houghton, Mifflin and Co., 1900.

270. Long, Everette B. The Civil War Day by Day: An Almanac 1861–1865. New York: Doubleday, 1971, pp. 710–715.

271. Lord, Francis Alfred. "The Federal Volunteer Soldier in the American Civil War: 1861–1865." Unpublished Doctoral Dissertation, University of Michigan, 1949.

272. Love, William de Loss. Wisconsin in the War of the Rebellion. Chicago: Church and Goodman, 1866. See Black Units in Wisconsin during the Civil War.

273. Lovett, Bobby L. "The Negro's Civil War in Tennessee, 1861–1865," Journal of Negro History, Vol. 61, January, 1976, pp. 36–50.

274. Luke, Josephine. "From Slavery to Freedom in Louisiana, 1862-1865." Unpublished Master's Thesis, Tulane University, 1939.

275. MacGregor, Morris J. and Bernard C. Nalty, Editors. Blacks in the United States Armed Forces: Basic Documents. Wilmington, DE: Scholarly Resources, Inc., Vol. II, 1977, "Civil War and Emancipation."

276. Main, Edwin M. The Story of the Marches, Battles and Incidents of the Third United States Colored Cavalry, a Fighting Regiment in the War of the Rebellion, 1861-1865. With Official Orders and Reports Relating Thereto, Compiled from the Rebellion Records. by Ed. M. Main, Late Major, New Orleans, Louisiana. Louisville, KY: Globe Printing Co., 1908.

277. Mallory, William. Old Plantation Days. Hamilton, Ontario: n.p., n.d. (1902?). An Ex-slave discusses his services as a Union Army Officer during the Civil War.

278. Man, Albon P. "Labor Competition and the New York Draft Riots of 1863," Journal of Negro History, Vol. 36, October, 1951, pp. 375-405.

279. Marrs, Elijah Preston. Life and History of Rev. Elijah P. Marrs. Louisville, KY: Bradley and Gildert Co., 1885.

280. Matson, D. "The Colored Man in the Civil War," War Sketches and Incidents. Des Moines, IA: Kenyon Press, 1898.

281. McCarthy, Agnes. Worth Fighting For: A History of the Negro in the United States during the Civil War and Reconstruction. Garden City, NY: Doubleday, 1965.

282. McConnell, Roland C. Negro Troops of Antebellum Louisiana: A History of the Battalion of Free Men of Color. Baton Rouge, LA: Louisiana State University Press, 1968.

283. McPherson, James M. Marching Toward Freedom: The Negro in the Civil War, 1861-1865. New York: Alfred A. Knopf, 1968.

284. _____. The Negroes' Civil War. New York: Pantheon, 1965.

285. _____. The Negroes' Civil War: How American Negroes Felt and Acted during the War for the Union. New York: Vintage Books, 1967.

286. McRae, Norman. "Camp War, Detroit: Home of the First
      Michigan Colored Infantry Regiment," Bulletin of the
      Detroit Historical Society, Vol. 24, 1968, pp. 4-11.

287. Messner, William F. "The Federal Army and Blacks in
      the Gulf Department, 1862-1865." Unpublished Doctoral
      Dissertation, University of Wisconsin-Madison, 1972.

288. Meyer, Howard M. Colonel of the Black Regiment; the
      Life of Thomas Wentworth Higginson. New York: Norton,
      1967.

289. Michigan Adjutant General's Office. Record of Service
      of Michigan Volunteers in the Civil War, 1861-1865:
      First Colored Infantry. Kalamazoo, MI: Michigan
      Legislature, n.d.

290. Mickley, Jeremiah Marion. The Forty-Third Regiment
      United States Colored Troops. Gettysburg: J.E. Wible,
      1866.

291. Military Historical Society of Massachusetts. Civil
      and Mexican Wars, 1861, 1846. Boston: Military
      Historical Society of Massachusetts, 1913.

292. Minion, John A. Negro Soldiers in the Confederate
      Army. Rosedale, NY: n.p., 1969.

293. _____. "Negro Soldiers in the Confederate
      Army," Crisis, Vol. 77, June/July, 1970, pp. 230-232.

294. Montgomery, Horace. "A Union Officer's Recollections
      of the Negro as a Soldier," Pennsylvania History,
      Vol. 28, April, 1961, pp. 156-186.

295. Morgan, Thomas J. Reminiscences of Service with
      Colored Troops in the Army of the Cumberland, 1863-
      1865. Providence, RI: Soldiers and Sailors Histori-
      cal Society, 1885.

296. Morrison, Derrick. "Martin R. Delany and the Begin-
      nings of Black Nationalism," International Socialist
      Review, Vol. 33, April, 1972, pp. 10-13, 38-41.

297. Murry, Donald M. and Robert M. Rodney. "Colonel
      Julian E. Bryant: Chamption of the Negro Soldier,
      During the Civil War," Journal of the Illinois State
      Historical Society, Vol. 56, Summer, 1963, pp. 257-
      281.

298. Nankivell, John H. History of the Twenty-Fifth
      Regiment, United States Infantry, 1869-1926. Denver:
      Smith-Brooks Printing Co., 1926.

299. Nelson, Bernard H. "The Negro in the Confederacy,
      1861-1865." Unpublished Doctoral Dissertation,
      Howard University, 1935.

300.   Newton, Alexander Herritage. Out of the Briars: An
       Autobiography and Sketch of the Twenty-Ninth Regiment
       Connecticut Volunteers. Philadelphia: A.M.E. Book
       Concern, 1910. Author discusses his combat service in
       the Union Army during the Civil War.

301.   New York Association for Colored Volunteers. First
       Organization of Colored Troops in the State of New
       York. New York: Baker and Bodwin, 1864.

302.   Norton, Henry Allyn. "Colored Troops in the War of
       the Rebellion," Glimpse of the Nation's Struggle.
       St. Paul, MN: Review Publishing Co., 1903.

303.   Norton, Oliver Wilcox. Army Letters, 1861-1865.
       Chicago: O.L. Deming, 1903.

304.   Notes on Colored Troops and Military Colonies on
       Southern Soil. By An Officer of the 9th Army Corps.
       New York: n.p., 1863.

305.   Noyes, Edward. "The Negro in Wisconsin's Civil War
       Effort," Lincoln Herald, Vol. 69, 1967, pp. 70-82.

306.   Officer of the Ninth Corps. Notes on Colored Troops
       and Military Colonies on Southern Soil. New York:
       n.p., 1863.

307.   Official Records of the Union and Confederate Navies
       in the War of the Rebellion. 30 Vols. Washington,
       DC: Government Printing Office, 1894-1922.

308.   Page, Wilbur A. "Notes on George W. Williams: Soldier,
       Minister, Orator, Lecturer, Historian," Negro History
       Bulletin, Vol. 30, October, 1967, p. 12.

309.   Parker, Allen. Recollection of Slavery Times. Wor-
       cester, MA: Charles W. Burbank and Co., 1895. Author
       discusses his service in the U.S. Navy during the
       Civil War.

310.   Parton, James. General Butler in New Orleans.
       New York: Mason Brothers, 1864. Black Soldiers, pp.
       178, 264, 264-267, 489-490, 518, 580, 628.

311.   Perkins, Frances Beecher. "Two Years with a Colored
       Regiment, a Woman's Experience, 1864-1866," New Eng-
       land Magazine, Vol. 17, January, 1898, pp. 533-543.

312.   Pierce, E.L. The Negroes at Port Royal. Boston:
       R.F. Wallcut, 1862.

313.   Ponton, Mungo M. Life and Times of Henry M. Turner.
       Atlanta, GA: A.B. Caldwell Publishing Co., 1917,
       pp. 34-36.

314. Powell, E. Henry. The Colored Soldiers in the War of the Rebellion. n.p., 1893.

315. Preisser, Thomas M. "The Virginia Decision to Use Negro Soldiers in the Civil War, 1864-1865," Virginia Magazine of History and Biography, Vol. 83, January, 1975, pp. 98-113.

316. Quarles, Benjamin. "The Abduction of the 'Planter'," Civil War History, Vol. 4, 1958, pp. 5-10.

317. _____. The Negro in the Civil War. Boston: Little, Brown and Co., 1953.

318. Rampp, Lary C. "Negro Troop Activity in Indian Territory, 1863-1865," Chronicles of Oklahoma, Vol. 47, Spring, 1969, pp. 531-559.

319. Raney, William F. Wisconsin: A Story of Progress. New York: Appleton and Co., 1963. See Black units in Wisconsin during the Civil War, pp. 165-167.

320. Record of the Service of the Fifty-Fifth Regiment of Massachusetts Volunteer Infantry. Printed for Regimental Association. Cambridge: John Wilson and Son, 1868.

321. Record of the Service of the 7th Regiment, U.S. Colored Troops. Providence, RI: E.L. Freeman and Co., 1878.

322. Reddick, Lawrence D. "The Negro Policy of the U.S. Army, 1775-1945," Journal of Negro History, Vol. 34, January, 1949, pp. 9-29.

323. Redwood, R.C. "The Cook of the Confederate Army," Scribner's Monthly, Vol. 18, 1879, pp. 560-568.

324. Reid, John A. History of the 101st Regiment, Pennsylvania Veteran Volunteer Infantry, 1861-1865. Chicago: L.S. Dickey and Co., 1910.

325. Remond, Sarah Parker. The Negroes and Anglo-Africans as Freedmen and Soldiers. London: E. Faithfull, 1864.

326. Richard, James H. Personal Narratives, Services in the Colored Troops in Burnside's Corps. Providence: Soldiers and Sailors Historical Society of Rhode Island, 1894.

327. _____. Services with Colored Troops in Burnside's Corp. Providence: The Society, 1894.

328. Rider, Sarah Grace. "The Negro in Ohio with Especial Reference to the Influence of the Civil War." Unpublished Master's Thesis, Ohio State University, 1931.

329. Ripley, Charles Peter. "Black, Blue and Gray: Slaves
      and Freedmen in Civil War Louisiana." Unpublished
      Doctoral Dissertation, Florida State University, 1973.

330. Ritter, E. Jay. "Congressional Medal of Honor Winners
      (William H. Carney, 54th Massachusetts and Christian
      A Fleetwood, 4th U.S. Colored)," Negro History Bulletin,
      Vol. 26, January, 1963, pp. 135-136.

331. Robbins, Gerald. "Recruiting and Arming of Negroes in
      the South Carolina Sea Islands, 1862-1865," Negro
      History Bulletin, Vol. 28, April, 1965, pp. 150-151.

332. Robertson, James I., Jr. "Negro Soldiers in the Civil
      War," Civil War Times Illustrated, Vol. 7, October,
      1968, pp. 21-32.

333. Robinson, Mrs. W.S., Editor. Warrington Pen-Portraits.
      Boston: Lee and Shepard, 1877. See Black Soldiers in
      Massachusetts during the Civil War, pp. 298-299.

334. Robinson, William H. From Log Cabin to Pulpit; or
      Fifteen Years in Slavery. Eau Claire, WI: James H.
      Tifft Publishers, 1913. Author discusses his service
      in both the Confederate and Union Armies during the
      Civil War.

335. Roe, Alfred Seelye. The Thirty-Ninth Regiment
      Massachusetts Volunteers, 1862-1865. Worchester, MA:
      Regimental Veteran Association, 1914.

336. Rollins, Frank A. Life of Martin R. Delaney. Boston:
      Lee and Shepard, 1883.

337. Romeyer, Henry. With Colored Troops in the Army of
      the Cumberland. Washington, DC: Commandery of the
      District of Columbia, 1904.

338. Ruby, Barbara C. "General Patrick Cleburne's Proposal
      to Arm Southern Slaves," Arkansas Historical Quarterly,
      Vol. 30, Autumn, 1971, pp. 193-212.

339. Savitt, Todd L. "Captive Black Union Soldiers in
      Charleston-What To Do?," Civil War History, Vol. 28,
      March, 1982, pp. 28-44.

340. Schofield, John McAllister. Forty-Six Years in the
      Army. New York: The Century, 1897.

341. Seraile, William. "New York's Black Regiments During
      the Civil War." Unpublished Doctoral Dissertation,
      City University of New York, 1977.

342. _____. "The Struggle to Raise Black Regi-
      ment in New York State, 1861-1864," New York Historical
      Society Quarterly, Vol. 58, July, 1974, pp. 215-233.

343. Shannon, Fred A. "The Federal Government and the Negro
      Soldier, 1861-1864," Journal of Negro History, Vol. 11,
      October, 1926, pp. 563-583.

344. _____. Organization and Administration of the
      Union Army, 1861-1865. 2 Vols. Cleveland: Arthur
      H. Clark Co., 1928.

345. Sherman, George R. The Negro a Soldier. Providence:
      Soldiers and Sailors Historical Society of Rhode
      Island, 1913.

346. Silvestro, Clement Mario. "None But Patriots: The
      Union Leagues in Civil War and Reconstruction."
      Unpublished Doctoral Dissertation, University of
      Wisconsin-Madison, 1959.

347. Singletary, Otis A. Negro Militia and Reconstruction.
      Austin: University of Texas Press, 1957.

348. Smith, James Lindsay. Autobiography. Norwich, CT:
      Press of the Bulletin Co., 1881.

349. Smith, John D. "The Health of Vermont's Civil War
      Recruits," Vermont History, Vol. 43, Summer, 1975,
      pp. 185-192.

350. _____. "The Recruitment of Negro Soldiers in
      Kentucky, 1863-1865," Register of the Kentucky Histor-
      ical Society, Vol. 72, October, 1974, pp. 364-390.

351. Stanley, Robert. "Generals and Negroes: Education of
      Negroes by the Union Army, 1861-1865." Unpublished
      Doctoral Dissertation, University of Maryland, 1965.

352. Stein, A.H. History of the Thirty-Seventh Regiment,
      U.S. Colored Infantry from its Organization in the
      Winter of 1863 and 1864 to the Present Time. Phila-
      delphia: King and Baird, 1866.

353. Stein, Philip Van Doren. Soldiers Life in the Union
      and Confederate Armies. Bloomington: Indiana Univer-
      sity Press, 1961.

354. Sterling, Dorothy. Captain of the Planter: The Story
      of Robert Smalls. New York: Doubleday and Co., 1958.

355. Stone, Henry. "Hood's Invasion of Tennessee," Century
      Magazine, Vol. 12, August, 1887, pp. 597-616.

356. Strickland, Arvarh E. "The Illinois Background of
      Lincoln's Attitude Toward Slavery and the Negro,"
      Journal of the Illinois State Historical Society,
      Vol. 56, 1962, pp. 474-494.

357. Supervisory Committee for Recruiting Colored Regiments.
      Free Military School for Applicants for Command of
      Colored Troops, No. 1210 Chestnut St., Philadelphia:
      King and Baird, 1864.

358. Sutherland, G.E. Negro in the Later War. In Military
      Order of the Loyal Legion of the U.S. Milwaukee, WI:
      Wisconsin Commission War Papers, 1891.

359. Taggart, John H. Free Military School for Applicants
      for Command of Colored Troops. Philadelphia: King
      and Baird, 1864.

360. Taylor, Susie King. Reminiscences of My Life with the
      33rd United States Colored Troops. Boston: The
      Author, 1902.

361. "Teen-Age Civil War Nurse: Susie King Taylor," Ebony,
      Vol. 25, February, 1970, pp. 96-98, 100-102.

362. The Forty-Third Regiment U.S. Colored Troops. Gettys-
      burg: J.E. Wible, 1866.

363. The War of the Rebellion: A Compilation of Official
      Records of the Union and Confederate Armies. 128 Vols.
      Washington, DC: Government Printing Office, 1880-1910.

364. Thomas, Henry G. "The Colored Troops at Petersburg,"
      Century Magazine, Vol. 12, September, 1887, pp. 774-
      782.

365. Thompson, William F., Jr. "Pictorial Images of the
      Negro During the Civil War," Wisconsin Magazine of
      History, Vol. 48, Summer, 1965, pp. 282-294.

366. Toppin, Edgar A. "Humbly They Served, 'The Black
      Brigade' in the Defense of Cincinnati," Journal of
      Negro History, Vol. 48, April, 1963, pp. 75-97.

367. Trumbrull, Henry Clay. War Memoirs of a Chaplain.
      New York: Charles Scribner's Sons, 1898, pp. 188-195.

368. Ullman, Daniel. The Organization of Colored Troops
      and the Regeneration of the South. Washington: n.p.,
      1868.

369. United States War Department. The War of the Rebel-
      lion: A Compilation of the Official Records of the
      Union and Confederate Armies. Washington: United
      States Government Printing Office, 1892.

370. Uya, Okon Edet. From Slavery to Public Service:
      Robert Small, 1839-1915. New York: Oxford University
      Press, 1971. See "A Civil War Black Hero," pp. 11-31.

371. Valuska, David Lawrence. "The Negro in the Union Navy: 1861-1865." Unpublished Doctoral Dissertation, Lehigh University, 1973.

372. Villard, Oswald Garrison. "The Negro in the Regular Army (1863-1910)," Atlantic Monthly, Vol. 91, June, 1903, pp. 721-729.

373. Vlock, Laurel F. and Joel A. Levitch, Editors. Contraband of War; William Henry Singleton. New York: Funk and Wagnalls, 1970.

374. Voegeli, V. Jacque. Free But Not Equal: The Midwest and the Negro During the Civil War. Chicago: University of Chicago Press, 1967.

375. Wagandt, Charles Lewis. The Mighty Revolution: Negro Emancipation in Maryland. Baltimore: Johns Hopkins Press, 1964. See Chapters 9 and 13.

376. Webb, William. The History of William Webb, Composed by Himself. Detroit: Egbert Hoekstra, 1873. An ex-slave discusses his military experiences in the Union Army during the Civil War.

377. Weiss, Nathan. "General Benjamin Franklin Butler and the Negro: The Evolution of the Racial Views of a Practical Politician," Negro History Bulletin, Vol. 29, October, 1965, pp. 3-4, 14-16, 23.

378. Wesley, Charles H. and Patricia Romero. Negro Americans in the Civil War. Washington, DC: Russell, 1967.

379. _____. Ohio Negroes in the Civil War. Columbus: Ohio State University Press for the Ohio Historical Society, 1961.

380. _____. The Collapse of the Confederacy. Washington: Associated Publishers, Inc., 1936.

381. _____. "The Employment of Negroes as Soldiers in the Confederate Army," Journal of Negro History, Vol. 4, July, 1919, pp. 239-253.

382. Westwood, Howard C. "Captive Black Union Soldiers in Charles: What To Do?" Civil War History, Vol. 28, March, 1982, pp. 28-44.

383. Whyte, Elise Cornelia Stroud. History of the Twenty-Third and Thirty-Eighth Infantry United States Colored Regiments, 1863-1867. Washington, DC: Howard University, 1963.

384. Wilder, Burt Green. Fifty-Fifth Regiments of the Massachusetts Volunteer Infantry, Colored, June, 1863-September, 1865. 3rd ed. Chestnut Hill, MA: The Author, 1919.

385. Wiley, Bell Irvin. The Life of Billy Yank, the Common
      Soldier of the Union. Indianapolis: Bobbs-Merrill,
      1952.

386. _____. "The Negro in the Confederacy."
      Unpublished Doctoral Dissertation, Yale University,
      1938.

387. _____. Southern Negroes, 1861-1865. New
      Haven, CT: Yale University Press, 1938.

388. Williams, George Washington. A History of the Negro
      Troops in the War of the Rebellion, 1861-1865. New
      York: Bergman Publishers, 1968.

389. William, Harry. "Benjamin F. Wade and the Atrocity
      Propaganda of the Civil War," Ohio State Archaeological
      and Historical Quarterly, Vol. 48, January, 1939,
      pp. 40-43.

390. Wilson, James H. Under the Old Flag Recollection of
      Military Operations in the War for the Union, the
      Spanish War, the Boxer Rebellion, etc. 2 Vols. New
      York: D. Appleton and Co., 1912.

391. Wilson, Joseph Thomas. The Black Phalanx: A History
      of the Negro Soldiers of the United States in the
      Wars of 1775-1812, 1861-1865. Hartford, CT: American
      Publishing Co., 1892.

392. Wright, Elizui. To Men of Color. Boston: n.p., 1863.

393. Yelder, Jr. Booker Tee. "The Official Policy of the
      United States Regarding the Use of Negro Soldiers in
      the American Civil War, 1861 and 1862." Unpublished
      Master's Thesis, Howard University, 1962.

IV.

Blacks in the American West

394. Addeman, J.M. "Reminiscences of Two Years with the Color Troops." Personal Narratives of Events in the War of the Rebellion. Providence, RI: N. Bangs Williams and Co., 1880.

395. Alexander, Thomas G. and Leonard J. Arrington. "The Utah Military Frontier, 1872-1912: Forts Cameron, Thornburgh, and Duchesne," Utah Historical Quarterly, Vol. 32, Fall, 1964, pp. 330-354.

396. Anderson, Charles W. "The True Story of Fort Pillow," Confederate Veterans, Vol. 3, November, 1895, p. 326.

397. Andreas, Arthur T. History of the State of Kansas. Chicago: R.R. Donnelley and Sons, 1883.

398. Armes, Colonel George A. Ups and Downs of An Army Officer. Washington, DC, n.p., 1900.

399. Arnold, Paul T. "Negro Soldiers in the United States Army," Magazine of History, Vol. 11, March, 1910, pp. 119-125.

400. Athearn, Robert G. In Search of Canaan: Black Migration to Kansas, 1879-1880. Lawrence: Regents Press of Kansas, 1978.

401. Bagley, Asa W. "The Negro of Oklahoma." Unpublished Master's Thesis, University of Oklahoma, 1926.

402. Bailey, Sedell. "Buffalo Soldiers (Black Troops of the 9th and 10th Cavalries)," Armor, Vol. 83, January/February, 1974, pp. 9-12.

403. Baker, Edward I. Roster of Non-Commissioned Officers
      of the Tenth Cavalry. St. Paul, MI: n.p., 1897.

404. Barrow, William. "The Buffalo Soldiers: The Negro
      Cavalry in the West, 1866-1891," Black World, Vol. 16,
      July, 1967, pp. 34-37, 89.

405. Beasly, Delilah L. The Negro Trail Blazer of Cali-
      fornia. New York: Negro Universities Press, 1969.
      Published originally in 1919.

406. Bergman, G.M. "The Negro Who Rode with Fremont in
      1847 (Jacob Dodson)," Negro History Bulletin, Vol. 28,
      November, 1964, pp. 31-32.

407. Bonsal, Stephen. "The Negro Soldier in War and Peace,"
      North American Review, Vol. 185, June, 1907, pp. 321-
      327.

408. Bowman, Larry G. "Virginia's Use of Blacks in the
      French and Indian War," Western Pennsylvania Historical
      Magazine, Vol. 53, No. 1, January, 1970, pp. 57-104.

409. Brady, Cyrus T. Indian Fights and Fighters. New York:
      McClure Phillips and Co., 1904.

410. Brandes, Ray. Frontier Military Posts of Arizona.
      Globe: D.S. King, 1960, pp. 35-39.

411. Branley, Bill. "Black, White & Red: A Story of Black
      Cavalrymen in the West," Soldiers, Vol. 36, June, 1981,
      pp. 44-48.

412. "Brief History of Troops 'K' Tenth U.S. Cavalry,"
      Colored American Magazine, Vol. 7, December, 1904, pp.
      730-733.

413. Brown, Amanda Hardin. "A (Black) Pioneer in Colorado
      and Wyoming," The Colorado Magazine, Vol. 35, 1958,
      pp. 271-287.

414. Burt, Olive W. Negroes in the Early West. New York:
      Julian Messner, 1969.

415. Carlson, Paul H. "William R. Shafter, Black Troops
      and the Opening of the Llano Estacado, 1870-1875,"
      Panhandle-Plains Historical Review, Vol. 47, 1974,
      pp. 1-18.

416. Carpenter, W. Spencer. "The Negro Soldier's Contri-
      bution in the Wars of the United States," A.M.E. Review,
      Vol. 29, January, 1913, pp. 215-224.

417. Carriker, Robert C. Fort Supply, Indian Territory:
      Frontier Outpost on the Plains. Norman: University
      of Oklahoma, 1970.

418. Carroll, John M. The Black Military Experience in the
      American West. New York: Liveright Publishing Corp.,
      1971.

419. Carter, Kate B. The Negro Pioneers. Salt Lake City,
      UT: Utah Printing Company, 1965.

420. Cashin, Herschel V. et al. Under Fire With the Tenth
      Cavalry. Chicago: American Publishing House, 1899.

421. Castel, Albert. "Civil War Kansas and the Negro,"
      Journal of Negro History, Vol. 51, April, 1966, pp.
      125-138.

422. _____. "Fort Pillow: Victory or Massacre?,"
      American History Illustrated, Vol. 9, April, 1974, pp.
      4-10, 46-48.

423. Castle, Jean I. "The West: Crucible of the Negro,"
      Montana: The Magazine of Western History, Vol. 19,
      January, 1969, p. 19.

424. Chapman, Berlin B. "Freedmen and the Oklahoma Lands,"
      Southwestern Social Science Quarterly, Vol. 29, Sep-
      tember, 1948, pp. 150-159.

425. Cimprich, John and Robert C. Mainfort, Jr., Editors.
      "Fort Pillow Revisited: New Evidence About An Old
      Controversy," Civil War History, Vol. 28, December,
      1982, pp. 293-306.

426. Coffman, Edward M. "Army Life on the Frontier, 1865-
      1898," Military Affairs, Vol. 20, Winter, 1956, pp.
      193-201.

427. _____. "An Old Soldier's Story," Louis-
      ville Courier Journal, Vol. 2, December, 1956.

428. Colton,Ray Charles. The American Civil War in the
      Western Territories of New Mexico, Arizona, Colorado
      and Utah. Norman: University of Oklahoma Press, 1959.

429. Cook, John R. The Border and the Buffalo. Topeka, KA:
      Crance and Co., 1907. Black Soldiers, pp. 181, 238,
      240-241, 259-261, 265-267, 361-362.

430. Cornish, Dudley T. "Kansas Negro Regiments in the
      Civil War," Kansas Historical Quarterly, Vol. 20,
      May, 1953, pp. 417-420.

431. Cowden, Robert. A Brief Sketch of the Organization
      and Service of the 59th Regiment of the U.S. Colored
      Infantry. Dayton, OH: United Brethren Publishing Co.,
      1883.

432. Cox, Thomas C. Blacks in Topeka, Kansas: 1865-1915.
      Baton Rouge: Louisiana State University Press, 1982.

433. Crimmins, Colonel M.L. "Captain Nolan's Lost Troop on
      the Staked Plains," West Texan Historical Association
      Yearbook, Vol. 10, October, 1934.

434. _____. "Colonel Buell's Expedition
      into Mexico," New Mexico Historical Review, Vol. 10,
      April, 1935, pp. 133-142.

435. _____. "Shafter's Explorations in
      West Texas," West Texas Historical Association Year-
      book, Vol. 9, October, 1933.

436. Cromwell, Arthur, Jr., Editor. The Black Frontier.
      Lincoln: University of Nebraska Television, 1970.

437. Davidson, Homer K. Black Jack Davidson: A Cavalry
      Commander on the Western Frontier. The Life of
      General John W. Davidson. Glendale, CA: Arthur H.
      Clark Co., 1974.

438. Davis, Lenwood. Blacks in the American West: A
      Working Bibliography. Monticello, IL: Council of
      Planning Librarians, 1975.

439. _____. Blacks in the Pacific Northwest: A
      Bibliography. Monticello, IL: Council of Planning
      Librarians, 1975.

440. _____. Blacks in the State of Oregon: A
      Bibliography. Monticello, IL: Council of Planning
      Librarians, 1975.

441. _____. Blacks in the State of Utah: A
      Bibliography. Monticello, IL: Council of Planning
      Librarians, 1974.

442. _____. "Sources for History of Blacks in
      Oregon," Oregon Historical Quarterly, Vol. 63, Sep-
      tember, 1972, pp. 197-211.

443. _____. "Sources for History of Blacks in
      Washington State," Western Journal of Black Studies,
      Vol. 2, Spring, 1978, pp. 60-64.

444. Davison, Michael S. "The Negro As Fighting Man,"
      Crisis, Vol. 76, February, 1969, pp. 67-71.

445. Dinges, Bruce J. "Court Martial of Henry O. Flipper,"
      American West, Vol. 9, January, 1972, pp. 12-17, 59.

446. Dobak, William. "Black Regulars Speak," Panhandle-
      Plains Historical Review, Vol. 47, 1971, pp. 28-45.

447. Downey, Fairfax. The Buffalo Soldiers in the Indian
      Wars. New York: McGraw-Hill, 1969.

448. _____. Indian Fighting Army. New York:
      n.p., 1941.

449. Durham, Philip and Everett L. Jones. The Negro Cowboys.
      New York: Dodd Mead and Co., 1965.

450. Dwyer, Robert J. "The Negro in the United States
      Army," Sociology and Social Research, Vol. 38, No. 2,
      November/December, 1953, pp. 103-112.

451. "Events of Fifty-Six," Kansas Historical Collections,
      Vol. 7, 1910-1902, pp. 52-55.

452. Finley, Leighton. Notebook and Photograph Pertaining
      to Service as a Lieutenant with the 10th Cavalry, U.S.
      Army in Texas and Arizona During the Indian War.
      Tucson: University of Arizona Library, n.d.

453. Fisher, James A. "The Struggle for Negro Testimony in
      California, 1851-1863," Southern California Quarterly,
      Vol. 51, 1969, pp. 313-324.

454. Fleetwood, C.A. The Negro as a Soldier. Washington,
      DC: Howard University Print, 1895.

455. Fleming, Elvis Eugene. "Captain Nicholas Nolan: Lost
      on the Staked Plains," Texana, Vol. 4, Spring, 1966,
      pp. 1-13.

456. _____. Texas' Last Frontier: A
      History of Cochran County, Texas. Morton, TX: Cochran
      County Historical Society, 1965. Black Soldiers, pp.
      2-6.

457. Fletcher, Marvin E. "The Black Bicycle Corps,"
      Arizona and the West, Vol. 16, Autumn, 1974, pp. 219-
      232.

458. _____. "The Black in Blue: Negro Volun-
      teers in Reconstruction." Unpublished Master's Thesis,
      University of Wisconsin, 1964.

459. Flipper, Henry O. The Colored Cadet at West Point.
      New York: Homer and Lee, 1878.

460. _____. Negro Frontierman. El Paso, TX:
      Western College Press, 1963.

461. Foner, Jack D. The U.S. Soldier Between Two Wars:
      Army Life and Reforms, 1865-1898. New York: Human-
      ities Press, 1970.

462. Forbes, Jack D. "Black Pioneers: The Spanish-Speaking Afro-Americans of the Southwest," _Phylon_, Vol. 27, Fall, 1966, pp. 233-246.

463. Fowler, Arlen L. "The Negro Infantry in the West, 1869-1891." Unpublished Doctoral Dissertation, Washington State University, 1968.

464. _____. _The Black Infantry in the West, 1869-1891_. Westport, CT: Greenwood Publishing Corp., 1971.

465. Ganoe, William A. _The History of the United States Army_. New York: D. Appleton and Co., 1924.

466. Garfield, Marvin. "Defense of the Kansas Frontier, 1868-1869," _Kansas Historical Quarterly_, Vol. I, November, 1932, pp. 451-473.

467. Gilland, Mrs. George H. "The Texas Trail as Followed by a Pioneer in 1882," _Annals of Wyoming_, 1940, Vol. 12, pp. 253-263.

468. Glass, Edward L.N. _The History of the Tenth Cavalry: 1866-1921_. Tucson, AZ: Acme Printing Co., 1921.

469. Grimke, A.H. "Colonel Shaw and His Black Regiment," _New England Magazine_, Vol. 1, February, 1900, pp. 675-681.

470. Haley, J. Evetts. _Fort Concho and the Texas Frontier_. San Angelo, TX: Sangelo Standard-Times, 1952.

471. Hall, Martin. "Negro With Confederate Troops in West Texas and New Mexico," _Password_, Vol. 13, Spring, 1968, pp. 11-12.

472. Hanchett, William. "Yankee Law and the Negro in Nevada," _Western Humanities Review_, Vol. 10, 1956, pp. 241-249.

473. Harris, Theodore Delano. "Henry Ossian Flipper: The First Negro Graduate of West Point." Unpublished Doctoral Dissertation, University of Minnesota, 1971.

474. _____. _Negro Frontierman: The Western Memoirs of Henry O. Flipper_. El Paso: Texas Western College, 1963.

475. Harvey, James Rose. "Negroes in Colorado." Unpublished Master's Thesis, University of Denver, Colorado, 1941.

476. Hayman, Perry. "Ten Years of Exciting Experiences and Hard Service in the Tenth Cavalry," _Winners of the West_, March, 1925.

477.   Hayne, Paul Hamilton. "The Defense of Fort Wagner,"
        Southern Bivouac, February, 1886.

478.   Heard, J. Norman. The Black Frontiersmen: Adventures
        of Negroes Among American Indians 1528-1881. New York:
        John Day Co., 1969.

479.   Herr, John K. and Edward S. Wallace. The Story of the
        United States, 1775-1942. Boston: Little, Brown and
        Co., 1953. See section on Blacks in the American West.

480.   Hewman, William. Buffalo Soldier. New York: Dodd
        Mead and Co., 1969.

481.   Hill, Daniel G. "The Negro in the Early History of
        the West," The IIiff Review, (Denver, Colorado), Vol.
        3, Fall, 1946, pp. 132-142.

482.   _____. "Survey of Negroes in Oregon." Un-
        published Master's Thesis, University of Oregon, Eugene,
        1932.

483.   Hornsby, Alton, Jr. "The Freedmen's Bureau Schools in
        Texas, 1865-1870," Southwestern Historical Quarterly,
        Vol. 76, April, 1973, pp. 397-417.

484.   Hunter, John Warren. "A Trooper of the Ninth Cavalry,"
        Frontier Times, April, 1927.

485.   Hutcheson, Grote. "The Ninth Cavalry," By Valor and
        Arms, Vol. 1, Spring, 1975, pp. 48-55.

486.   _____. "The Ninth Regiment of Cavalry,"
        Journal of Military Service Institution of the United
        States, Vol. 8, 1892, pp. 215-224.

487.   _____. A Register of the Commissioned
        Officers Belonging to the Ninth U.S. Cavalry from Its
        Organization, July 28, 1866 to July 28, 1893. Fort
        Robinson: n.p., 1893.

488.   _____. History of the Ninth Cavalry. Los
        Angeles: n.p., 1894.

489.   Johnson, William H. History of the Colored Volunteer
        Infantry of Virgina, 1871-1899. Richmond, VA: n.p.,
        1923.

490.   Jordan, John L. "Was There a Massacre at Fort Pillow?,"
        Tennessee Historical Quarterly, Vol. 6, June, 1947, pp.
        122-132.

491.   Kansas Adjutant General. Official Military History of
        Kansas Regiments During the War for the Suppression
        of the Great Rebellion. Leavenworth, KA: n.p., 1870.

492. Katz, William Loren. The Black West. New York:
      Doubleday and Co., 1971.

493. Kirkland, John Robert. "Federal Troops in the South
      Atlantic States During Reconstruction 1865-1877."
      Unpublished Doctoral Dissertation, University of
      Illinois, 1970.

494. Kreidberg, Marvin and Merton G. Henry. History of
      Military Mobilization in the United States Army,
      1775-1945. Washington, DC: Department of the Army,
      1955.

495. Leckie, William H. The Buffalo Soldiers: A Narrative
      of the Negro Cavalry in the West. Norman: University
      of Oklahoma Press, 1967.

496. _____. The Military Conquest of the
      Southern Plains. Norman: University of Oklahoma
      Press, 1963.

497. Littlefield, Daniel F. and Lonnie E. Underhill.
      "Negro Marshalls in the Indian Territory," Journal
      of Negro History, Vol. 56, April, 1971, pp. 77-87.

498. Logan, Rayford W. The Betrayal of the Negro, From
      Rutherford B. Hayes to Woodrow Wilson. New York:
      Collin-Macmillan, Ltd., 1965.

499. Longacre, E.G. "Philadelphia Aristocrat With the
      Buffalo Soldiers," Journal of West, Vol. 18, April,
      1979, pp. 79-84.

500. Matlison, Ray H. "The Army Post on the Northern
      Plains, 1865-1885," Nebraska History, Vol. 35, 1954,
      pp. 17-43.

501. McConnell, Roland C. "Isaiah Dorman and the Custer
      Expedition," Journal of Negro History, Vol. 32, July,
      1948, pp. 344-352.

502. McCraken, Harold. Frederic Remington's Own West.
      New York: Dial Press, 1960. See Chapter 5.

503. Mills, Hazel W. and Nancy B. Pryor. The Negro in the
      State of Washington: 1788-1969. A Bibliography.
      Olympia, WA: Washington State Library, 1972.

504. Murray, Robert A. "The United States Army in the
      Aftermath of the Johnson County Invasion," Annals
      of Wyoming, Vol. 38, April, 1966, pp. 59-76.

505. Nankivell, John H., Editor. History of the Twenty-
      Fifth Regiment, United States Infantry, 1869-1926.
      Denver: Smith-Brooks Printing Co., 1927.

506. Nye, Wilbur S. Carbine and Lance: The Story of Old
      Fort Sill. Norman: University of Oklahoma, 1957.
      Revised Edition, 1969.

507. "Only All Negro Village in Kansas, Nicademus, is Fading
      Into History," Kansas City Times, May 28, 1959.

508. "Only Trace Left of Negro Colony," Argus Leader, (Sioux
      Falls), August 8, 1932.

509. Owens, Kenneth. "Pierce City Incident," Idaho Yester-
      days: The Quarterly Journal of the Idaho Historical
      Society, Vol. 3, Fall, 1959, p. 13.

510. Painter, Nell I. Exodusters: Black Migration to
      Kansas After Reconstruction. New York: Knopf, 1977.

511. Paynter, John H. Joining the Navy or Abroad With
      Uncle Sam. Hartford, CT: American Publishing Co.,
      1895.

512. Pelzer, Louis. "The Negro and Slavery in Early Iowa,"
      Iowa Journal of History and Politics, Vol. II, 1940,
      pp. 471-484.

513. Perry, Alexander Wallace. "The Ninth United States
      Cavalry in the Sioux Campaign of 1890," Journal of
      the United States Cavalry Association, Vol. 4, 1891,
      pp. 37-40.

514. Phillips, Thomas D. "The Negro Regulars: Negro
      Soldiers in the United States Army, 1866-1890."
      Unpublished Doctoral Dissertation, University of
      Wisconsin, 1970.

515. Porter, Kenneth W. "Negroes and Indians on the Texas
      Frontier," Southwestern Historical Quarterly, Vol. 53,
      October, 1949, pp. 151-163.

516. _____. The Negro on the American Frontier.
      New York: Arno Press, 1970.

517. _____. "The Seminole Negro Indian Scouts,
      1870-1881," Southwestern Historical Quarterly, Vol. 55,
      January, 1952, pp. 358-377.

518. Powell, Anthony. "Seminole Negro-Indian Scouts,"
      Vol. 20, November/December, 1980, pp. 30-37.

519. Prebble, John. The Buffalo Soldier. New York: Har-
      court, Brace, 1959.

520. Price, George F. Across the Continent with the Fifth
      Cavalry. New York: D. Van Nostrand Publishers, 1883.

521. Quarles, Benjamin. <u>The Negro in the Civil War</u>. Boston: Little, Brown and Co., 1953.

522. Reddick, Lawrence D. "The Negro Policy of the United States Army, 1775-1945," <u>Journal of Negro History</u>, Vol. 34, January, 1949, pp. 9-29.

523. Reeve, Frank D., Editor. "Frederick E. Phelps: A Soldier's Memoirs," <u>New Mexico Historical Review</u>, Vol. 25, 1950, pp. 187-221.

524. Remington, Frederic. "Artist Rides with 10th U.S. Cavalry, A Scout with the Buffalo Soldiers, Famous Negro Dragoons," <u>Butterfield Express; Historical Newspaper of the Southwest</u>, Vol. 4, August/September, 1966.

525. _____. "A Scout with the Buffalo Soldiers," <u>Century Magazine</u>, Vol. 37, April, 1889, pp. 899-912.

526. _____. "A Scout with the Buffalo Soldiers," <u>Pacific Historian</u>, Vol. 12, Spring, 1968, pp. 25-39.

527. Rice, Lawrence D. <u>The Negro in Texas: 1874-1900</u>. Baton Rouge: Louisiana State University Press, 1971.

528. Richard, James H. "Services with the Colored Troops in Burnside's Corps," <u>Personal Narrative of Events in the War of the Rebellion</u>. Providence, RI: Soldiers and Sailors Historical Society of Rhode Island, 1894.

529. Rickley, Don. "An Indian Wars Combat Record," <u>By Valor and Arms</u>, Vol. 2, 1975, pp. 4-11.

530. _____. <u>Forty Miles a Day on Beans and Hay</u>. Norman: University of Oklahoma Press, 1963.

531. Rodenbaugh, Theodore and William Haskin, Editors. <u>The Army of the United States. Historical Sketches of the 9th and 10th Regiments of Cavalry and the 24th and 25th Regiments of Infantry</u>. New York: Maynard, Merrill and Co., 1896.

532. <u>Roster of Non-commissioned Officers of the Tenth U.S. Cavalry, with Some Regimental Reminiscences, Appendices, etc., Connected with the Early History of the Regiment</u>. St. Paul: William Kennedy Printing Company, 1897.

533. Savage, W. Sherman. "The Role of Negro Soldier in Protecting the Indian Frontier from Intruders," <u>Journal of Negro History</u>, Vol. 36, January, 1951, pp. 25-34.

534. _____. "The Negro in the Westward Movement," <u>Journal of Negro History</u>, Vol. 25, October, 1940, pp. 531-539.

535.   Savage, W. Sherman. "The Negro of the Mining Frontier,"
       Journal of Negro History, Vol. 25, January, 1945, pp.
       30-46.

536.   Schoenberger, Dale T. "The Black Man in the American
       West," Negro History Bulletin, Vol. 32, March, 1969,
       pp. 7-11.

537.   Schubert, Frank N. "Black Soldiers on the White
       Frontier," Phylon, Vol. 32, Winter, 1971, pp. 410-415.

538.   _____. "The Suggs Affray," Western Histor-
       ical Quarterly, Vol. 4, January, 1973, pp. 57-68.

539.   Shaw, James, Jr. "Colonel of 7th United States Colored
       Troops." Our Last Campaign and Subsequent Service in
       Texas. Providence: The Society, 1905.

540.   Shaw, Van B. "Nicodemus Kansas: A Study in Isolation."
       Unpublished Doctoral Dissertation, University of Mis-
       souri, 1951.

541.   Sheridan, P.H. Personal Memoirs of P.H. Sheridan
       General United Army. New York: Charles L. Webster,
       1888, pp. 2-4.

542.   Singletary, Otis A. Negro Militia and Reconstruction.
       Austin: University of Texas Press, 1957.

543.   Smith, Gloria L. Black Americana in Arizona. Tucson,
       AZ: The Author, 1977. See Chapter 4.

544.   Smurr, J.W. and Ross Coole. Historical Essays on
       Montana and the Northwest. Helena, MT: The Western
       Press, 1957, pp. 149-203.

545.   Smythe, Donald. "John J. Pershing at Fort Assiniboine,"
       Montana, Vol. 18, 1968, pp. 19-23.

546.   "Soldier in Texas," Crisis, Vol. 1, May, 1911, pp. 14-15.

547.   Sommer, Richard J. "The Dutch Gap Affair: Military
       Atrocities and the Rights of Negro Soldiers," Civil
       War History, Vol. 21, March, 1975, pp. 51-64.

548.   Starr, Michelle. "Buffalo Soldier," Army, Vol. 31,
       January, 1981, pp. 41-43.

549.   Stotts, Gene. "The Negro Paul Revere (Henry Thompson)
       of Quantrill's Raid," Negro History Bulletin, Vol. 26
       February, 1963, pp. 169-170.

550.   Stover, Earl F. "Chaplain Henry V. Plummer, His
       Ministry and His Court Martial," Nebraska History,
       Vol. 56, Spring, 1975, pp. 20-50.

551.   "The Black Troopers," Leisure House, Vol. 19, 1876,
        pp. 353-417.

552.   Thomas, Henry Goddard. "The Colored Troops at Peters-
        burg," Century Magazine, Vol. 34, September, 1887, pp.
        771-782.

553.   Thompson, Erwin N. "The Negro Regiment of the United
        States Regular Army, 1866-1900." Unpublished Master's
        Thesis, University of California at Davis, 1966.

554.   _____. "The Negro Soldiers on the Frontier:
        A Fort Davis Case Study," Journal of the West, Vol. 7,
        April, 1968, pp. 217-235.

555.   Thompson, Lucille Smith and Alama Smith Jacobs. The
        Negro in Montana 1800-1945: A Selective Bibliography.
        Helena, MT: Montana State University, 1970.

556.   Thornbrough, Emma Lou. The Negro in Indiana. Indian-
        apolis: Indiana Historical Bureau, 1957.

557.   Thurman, Sue Bailey. Pioneers of Negro Origin in
        California. San Francisco: Acme Publishing Co., 1949.

558.   Troxel, Orlando C. "The Tenth Cavalry in Mexico,"
        Journal of the United States Cavalry Association, Vol.
        18, October, 1917, pp. 197-205.

559.   Tyler, Ronnie C. "Fugitive Slaves in Mexico," Journal
        of Negro History, Vol. 57, January, 1972, pp. 1-12.

560.   Ulrich, William John. "The Northern Military Mind in
        Regard to Reconstruction, 1865-1872: The Attitudes
        of Ten Leading Union Generals." Unpublished Doctoral
        Dissertation, Ohio State University, 1959.

561.   Unit Members. Historical and Pictorial Review, 9th
        Cavalry Regiment, Second Cavalry Division of the United
        States. Baton Rouge, LA: n.p., 1941.

562.   Utley, Robert M. Fort Davis National Historic Sites,
        Texas. National Park Service Historical Handbook
        Series No. 38. Washington, DC: U.S. Government
        Printing Office, 1965.

563.   _____. Frontier Regulars: The United States
        Army and the Indian 1866-1891. New York: Macmillian,
        1973. See Black Soldiers, p. 16.

564.   _____. "'Pecos Bill' on the Texas Frontier,"
        American West, Vol. 6, January, 1969, pp. 4-13, 61-62.

565.   Voegeli, V. Jacque. Free But Not Equal: The Midwest
        and the Negro During the Civil War. Chicago: Univer-
        sity of Chicago Press, 1970.

566. Warner, Ezra J. "A Black Man (Henry Ossian Flipper) in the Long Gray Line," American History Illustrated, Vol. 4, January, 1970, pp. 30-38.

567. Wellman, Paul I. The Indian Wars of the West. New York: Doubleday and Co., 1947, pp. 360-370.

568. Werner, Herman. On the Western Frontier with the United States Cavalry Fifty Years Ago. n.p., 1934.

569. Wharfield, Harold B. "Fight with the Yaquis at Bear Valley, 1918," Arizoniana, Vol. 4, Fall, 1963, pp. 1-18.

570. _____. 10th Cavalry and Border Fights. El Cajon, CA: Harold B. Wharfield, 1965.

571. _____. With Scouts and Cavalry at Fort Apache. Edited by John Alexander Carrol. Tucson: Arizona Pioneer Historical Society, 1965.

572. White, William Bruce. "The Military and the Melting Pot: The American Army and Minority Groups, 1865-1924." Unpublished Doctoral Dissertation, University of Wisconsin-Madison, 1968.

573. Whitman, Sidney Edgerton. The Troops: An Informal History of the Plains Cavalry, 1865-1890. New York: Hastings House, 1962.

574. Whitted, Burma Louise. "The History of the 8th United States Colored Troops." Unpublished Master's Thesis, Howard University, 1960.

575. Wolseley, Lord. "Negro As A Soldier," Forthnightly, Vol. 50, 1888, p. 689.

576. Woodward, Elon. The Negro in the United States Military Service: A Compilation of Official Records, State Papers, Historical Extracts, etc. Washington, DC: National Archives, 1888.

577. Yancy, James W. "The Negro of Tucson, Past and Present," Unpublished Master's Thesis, University of Arizona, 1933.

578. Young, Karl. "A Fight That Could Have Meant War," American West, Vol. 3, Spring, 1966, pp. 17-23, 90.

579. Zornow, William F. Kansas: A History of the Jayhawk State. Norman: University of Oklahoma Press, 1957.

V.

Blacks in the Spanish-American War

580. Alexander, Charles. <u>Battles and Victories of Allen Allensworth</u>. Boston: Sherman, French and Co., 1914. Author discusses the role of Blacks in the Spanish American War.

581. Alger, Russell A. <u>The Spanish-American War</u>. New York: Harper and Brothers, 1901. Writer discusses the role of Blacks in the Spanish American War.

582. Alstyne, Lawrence. <u>Diary of an Enlisted Man</u>. New Haven: Yale University Press, 1910. Author comments on role of Blacks in Spanish American War.

583. Astwood, H.C.C. "Blacks in Cuba," <u>Voice of Missions</u>, Vol. 6, October 1, 1898, p. 2.

584. Atkins, John B. <u>The War in Cuba: The Experiences of an Englishman with the United States Army</u>. London: Smith, Elder and Co., 1899.

585. Beale, Howard K. <u>Theodore Roosevelt and the Rise of America to World Power</u>. Baltimore: Johns Hopkins Press, 1956.

586. Bigelow, John, Jr. <u>Reminiscences of the Santiago Campaign</u>. New York: Harper and Brothers, 1898.

587. Blacksom, Augustus P., et al. <u>Affray at Brownsville, Texas, August 13 and 14, 1900, Investigation of the Conduct of U.S. Troops</u>. Washington, DC: U.S. Government Printing Office, 1906.

588. Blount, James H. <u>The American Occupation of the Philippines 1898-1912</u>. New York: G.P. Putnam's Sons, 1912.

589. Bond, Horace Mann. "The Negro in the Armed Forces of the United States Prior to World War I," Journal of Negro Education, Vol. 12, Summer, 1943, pp. 263–287.

590. Bonsal, Stephen. "The Negro Soldier in War and Peace," North American Review, Vol. 156, June, 1907, pp. 321–328.

591. Braxton, George H. "Company 'L' in the Spanish-American War," Colored American Magazine, Vol. 1, May, 1900, pp. 19–25.

592. Bullard, Robert L. "The Negro Volunteer: Some Characteristics," Journal of the Military Service Institution of the United States, Vol. 29, July, 1901, pp. 27–39.

593. Burt, Andrew S. "The Negro as a Soldier," Crisis, Vol. 1, February, 1911, pp. 23–25.

594. Campbell, Nicholas H. "The Negro in the Navy," Colored American, Vol. 6, June, 1903, pp. 406–413.

595. Chenery, William H. The Fourteenth Regiment Rhode Island Heavy Artillery (Colored) in the War to Preserve the Union. Providence, RI: Snow and Farnham, 1898.

596. Chew, Abraham A. A Biography of Colonel Charles Young. Washington, DC: R.L. Pendleton, 1923.

597. Clark, Michael James. "A History of the Twenty-Fourth United States Infantry Regiment in Utah: 1896–1900." Unpublished Doctoral Dissertation, University of Utah, 1979.

598. Clendened, Clarence C. Blood on the Border. New York: Macmillan, 1969. Writer discusses role of Blacks in Spanish-American War.

599. Coston, William Hilary. The Betrayal of the American Negroes as Citizens, as Soldiers and Sailors, by the Republican Party in Deference to the People of the Philippine Island. n.p., n.d.

600. _____. The Spanish-American War Volunteer. Middletown, PA: W.H. Coston, 1899.

601. Cousins, Phyllis M. A History of the 33rd United States Colored Troops. Washington, DC: Howard University, 1961.

602. Crane, Charles J. The Experiences of a Colonel of the Infantry. New York: The Knickerbocker Press, 1923.

603. Curtis, Mary. The Black Soldier, or the Colored Boys of the United States Army. Washington: Murray Brothers, 1915.

604. David, Jay and Elaine Crane. The Black Soldier - From
      the American Revolution to Vietnam. New York: William
      Morrow and Co., 1971.

605. Davis, Richard Harding. The Cuban and Porto Rican
      Campaigns. New York: Charles Scribner's Sons, 1898.

606. Downey, Fairfax D. Indian-Fighting Army. New York:
      Charles Scribner's Sons, 1941.

607. Durnham, John S. "Confession of a Man Who Did,"
      Southern Workman, Vol. 27, May, 1899, pp. 168-172.

608. Early, Gerald H. "The Negro Soldier in the Spanish-
      American War." Unpublished Master's Thesis, Shippen-
      burg State College, 1970.

609. Edwards, Frank B. The '98 Campaign of the 6th Massa-
      chusetts V.S.V. Boston: Little Brown and Co., 1899.

610. Faust, Karl I. Campaigning in the Philippines. San
      Francisco: The Hicks-Judd Company, 1899.

611. Fleetwood, Christian A. The Negro as A Soldier:
      Written by Christian A. Fleetwood, Late Sergeant-
      Major 4th U.S. Colored Troops, From the Negro Congress
      at the Cotton States and International Exposition,
      Atlanta, Ga., November 11, to November 23, 1895. Wash-
      ington, D.C.: Howard University Print, 1895.

612. Fletcher, Marvin E. "Negro Soldier and the U.S. Army,
      1891-1917." Unpublished Doctoral Dissertation, Uni-
      versity of Wisconsin, 1968.

613. _____. The Black Soldier and Officer in
      the United States Army, 1891-1917. Columbus, MO:
      University of Missouri Press, 1974.

614. _____. "The Black Volunteers in the
      Spanish-American War," Military Affairs, Vol. 38, 1974,
      pp. 48-53.

615. Foley, Albert S. God's Men of Color. New York: Far-
      rar, Strauss and Co., 1955.

616. Foote, Mary H. "Coeur D'Alene," Century Magazine, Vol.
      48, May, 1894, pp. 102-115.

617. Foraker, Joseph B. Notes of a Busy Life. 2 Vols.
      Cincinnati: Stewart and Kidd Company, 1916.

618. Freidel, Frank. The Splendid Little War. Boston:
      Little Brown and Company, 1958.

619. Funston, Frederick. Memories of Two Wars. New York:
      Scribners, 1914.

620. Gatewood, Willard B., Jr.   "Alabama's Negro Soldier Experiment," Journal of Negro History, Vol. 57, October, 1972, pp. 333-351.

621. _____. "Black Americans and the Quest for Empire, 1890-1903," Journal of Southern History, Vol. 38, November, 1972, pp. 545-566.

622. _____. "John Hanks Alexander of Arkansas: Second Black Graduate of West Point," Arkansas Historical Quarterly, Vol. 41, No. 2, Summer, 1982, pp. 103-128.

623. _____. "Indiana Negroes and the Spanish-American War," Indiana Magazine of History, Vol. 69, 1973, pp. 115-139.

624. _____. "Kansas Negroes and the Spanish-American War," Kansas Historical Quarterly, Vol. 37, Autumn, 1971, pp. 300-313.

625. _____. "Negro Troops in Florida, 1898," Florida Historical Quarterly, Vol. 49, July, 1970, pp. 1-15.

626. _____. "North Carolina's Negro Regiment in the Spanish-American War," North Carolina Historical Review, Vol. 48, October, 1971, pp. 370-387.

627. _____. "Ohio's Negro Battalion in the Spanish-American War," Northwestern Ohio Quarterly, Vol. 45, Spring, 1973, pp. 55-66.

628. _____. "Smoked Yankees" and the Struggle for Empire: Letters from Negro Soldiers 1898-1902. Urbana: University of Illinois Press, 1971.

629. Gardner, Bettye Jane. "A History of the Third United States Colored Cavalry." Unpublished Master's Thesis, Howard University, 1964.

630. Gianakos, Perry E. "The Spanish-American War and the Double Paradox of the Negro American," Phylon, Vol. 26, Spring, 1965, pp. 34-49.

631. Glass, Edward. History of the Tenth Cavalry. Tucson: Acme Printing Co., 1921.

632. Goode, W.T. The 8th Illinois. Chicago: The Blakely Printing Company, 1899.

633. Green, Robert E. "Colonel Charles Young, Soldier and Diplomat." Unpublished Master's Thesis, Howard University, 1972.

634.   Guthrie, James M. Camp Fires of the Afro-American.
       Philadelphia: Afro-American Publishing Co., 1899.

635.   Hall, Charles W. "The Eighth Illinois, U.S.V.,"
       Colored American Magazine, Vol. 1, June, 1900, pp. 94-
       103.

636.   Hamilton, James Cleveland. "The Negro as a Modern
       Soldier," Anglo-American Monthly, Vol. 2, August, 1899,
       pp. 113-124.

637.   Head, William H. "The Negro as an American Soldier,"
       World Today, Vol. 12, March, 1907, pp. 322-324.

638.   Hemment, John C. Cannon and Camera: Sea and Land
       Battles of the Spanish-American War in Cuba; Camp Life
       and the Return of the Soldiers. New York: D. Appleton
       and Company, 1898.

639.   Heini, Nancy. "Colonel Charles Young: Pointman,"
       Army, Vol. 27, March, 1977, pp. 30-33.

640.   Higginson, Thomas Wentworth. "Colored Troops Under
       Fire," Century, Vol. 32, 1897, pp. 193-195.

641.   _____. "Negro Regiment, First,"
       Outlook (NY), Vol. 59, July 2, 1898, pp. 521-531.

642.   Johnson, Charles, Jr. "Black Soldiers in the National
       Guard, 1877-1949." Unpublished Doctoral Dissertation,
       Howard University, 1976.

643.   Johnson, Edward Austin. History of Negro Soldiers in
       the Spanish-American War. Raleigh: Capital Printing
       Co., 1899.

644.   Johnson, Jesse J. A Pictorial History of Black Ser-
       vicemen Missing Pages in United States History.
       Hampton, VA: Hampton Institute, 1970.

645.   Johnson, William H. History of the Colored Volunteer
       Infantry of Virginia, 1871-1899. Richmond, VA: n.p.,
       1923.

646.   Kelly, Josephine. Dark Shepherd. Paterson, NJ: St.
       Anthony Guild Press, 1967.

647.   Kennedy, Philip W. "The Concept of Racial Superiority
       and United States Imperialism, 1890-1910." Unpublished
       Doctoral Dissertation, St. Louis University, 1962.

648.   Lane, Ann J. The Brownsville Affair: National Crisis
       and Black Reaction. Port Royal Washington, NY: Ken-
       nikat Press, 1977.

649.   Lemus, Rienzi B. "The Enlisted Man in Action, or the
        Colored American Soldier in the Philippines," Colored
        American Magazine, Vol. 5, May, 1902, pp. 46-54.

650.   Leroy, James A. The American in the Philippines. 2
        Vols. Boston: Houghton Mifflin Company, 1914.

651.   Lynch, John Roy. Reminiscences of an Active Life:
        The Autobiography of John Ray Lynch. Chicago: Uni-
        versity of Chicago Press, 1970. Author discusses his
        duties as a U.S. Army Officer during and after the
        Spanish-American War.

652.   Lynk, Miles Vandahurst. The Black Troops; or The
        Daring Heroism of the Negro Soldiers in the Spanish-
        American War. Jackson, TN: M.V. Lynk Publishing
        House, 1899. Reprinted by AMS Press, 1971.

653.   MacGregor, Morris J. and Bernard C. Nalty, Editors.
        Blacks in the United States Armed Forces: Basic
        Documents. Wilmington, DE: Scholarly Resources, Inc.,
        1977. Vol. III, "Freedom and Jim Crow, 1865-1917."

654.   Medley, Jensen. Illustrated Review, Ninth U.S. Cal-
        vary. Fort D.A. Russell, Wyoming, 1910.

655.   Miley, John D. In Cuba with Shafter. New York:
        Charles Scribner's Sons, 1899.

656.   Miller, Randall M. and Jon W. Zophy. "Unwelcome
        Allies: Billy Yank and the Black Soldier," Phylon,
        Vol. 39, September, 1978, pp. 234-240.

657.   Montague, Ludwell L. Haiti and the United States:
        1714-1938. Durham, NC: Duke University Press, 1940.

658.   Morgan, Thomas Jefferson. The Negro in America and
        the Ideal American Republic. Philadelphia: America
        Baptist Publication Society, 1898.

659.   Moss, James A. Memories of the Campaign of Santiago.
        San Francisco: The Mysell-Rollins Co., 1899.

660.   Muller, William R. The Twenty-Fourth Infantry, Past
        and Present. n.p., 1923.

661.   Nankivell, John H. History of the Twenty-Fifth Regi-
        ment of the United States Infantry, 1869-1926. Denver:
        Smith-Brooks Printing Co., 1927.

662.   "Negro As Soldier and Officer," Nation, Vol. 73,
        August 1, 1901, p. 85.

663.   "Negro Soldiers," Colored American Magazine, Vol. 6,
        November, 1902, p. 48.

664. "Negroes as Soldiers: Force of San Antonio," _Independent_, Vol. 70, April 13, 1911, pp. 805-806.

665. "Negroes In Our Army," _Richmond (Virginia) Dispatch_, August 5, 1904.

666. Newton, A.H. _Out of the Briars: Personal Experiences and Reflections of the Negro 29th Regiment of Connecticut Volunteers_. Philadelphia: A.M.E. Book Co., 1910.

667. "No Praise For Negro," _Washington Post_, December 27, 1898.

668. O'Connor, Richard. "'Black Jack' of the 10th (Cavalry)," _American Heritage_, Vol. 18, February, 1967, pp. 14-25, 102-107.

669. _____. Black Jack Pershing_. Garden City, NY: Doubleday, 1961.

670. Palmer, Frederick. "White Man and Brown Man in the Philippines," _Scribner's Magazine_, Vol. 27, January, 1900, pp. 76-86.

671. Parker, John H. _History of the Gatling Gun Detachment, Fifth Army Corps, at Santiago_. Kansas City, MO: Hudson-Kimberly Publishing Co., 1898.

672. Parker, W. Thornton. "The Evolution of the Colored Soldier," _North American Review_, Vol. 168, February, 1899, pp. 223-228.

673. Payne, William C. _The Cruise of the USS Dixie or On Board with the Maryland Boys in the Spanish-American_. Washington, DC: E.C. Jones, 1899.

674. Perkins, Frances Beecher. "Two Years with a Colored Regiment, A Woman's Experience," _New England Magazine_, Vol. 17, January, 1898, pp. 533-543.

675. Phillips, James R. "Little-Known Negro Rough Riders," _Negro History Bulletin_, Vol. 27, December, 1963, p. 59.

676. "Race Discrimination in the Philippines," The _Independent_, Vol. 54, February 13, 1902, pp. 416-417.

677. "Record of the 24th Infantry," _Manila Times_, June 29, 1902.

678. Reddick, Lawrence D. "The Negro Policy of the U.S. Army, 1775-1945," _Journal of Negro History_, Vol. 35, January, 1945, pp. 9-29.

679. Remington, Frederic. "Vagabonding with the Tenth Horse," _Cosmopolitan_, Vol. 22, February, 1897, pp. 347-354.

680. Rippy, J. Fred. "Some Precedents of the Pershing
      Expedition into Mexico," Southwestern Historical
      Quarterly, Vol. 60, July, 1956, pp. 23-35.

681   Rodenbough, Theodore F. and William L. Hasken, Editors.
      The Army of the United States. New York: Maynard,
      Merrill and Co., 1896.

682. Roosevelt, Theodore. "The Rough Riders," Scribner's
      Magazine, Vol. 25, April, 1899, pp. 420-450.

683. _____. The Rough Riders. New York:
      Macmillan, 1961.

684. Rulh, Arthur. "The Gallery at San Antonio," Collier's
      Weekly, Vol. 47, April 29, 1911, p. 13.

685. Sargent, Herbert H.   The Campaign of Santiago de Cuba.
      3 Vols. Chicago: A.C. McChurch and Co., 1907.

686. Scipio, L. Albert. The Last of the Black Regulars: A
      History of the 24th Infantry Regiment (1869-1951).
      Silver Spring, MD: Roman Publications, 1983.

687. Sexton, William T. Soldiers in the Sun: An Adventure
      in Imperialism. Harrisburg, PA: The Military Service
      Publishing Company, 1939.

688. Sherman, George R. The Negro as a Soldier. By George
      R. Sherman Captain Seventh United States Colored In-
      fantry and Brevet-Lieut.-Colonel United States Volun-
      teers. Providence: The Society, 1913.

689. Stanton, Harry, et al. History of the Eighth Illinois
      Volunteers Infantry Regiment. Chicago: E.F. Harmon
      Co., 1899.

690. Steele, Matthew F. "The 'Color Line' in the Army,"
      North American Review, Vol. 183, December, 1906, pp.
      1285-1288.

691. Stevens, Walter James. Chip on My Shoulder: Auto-
      biography of Walter J. Stevens. Boston: Meador Pub-
      lishing Co., 1946. Author discusses his combat service
      with the U.S. Army during the Spanish-American War.

692. Steward, Theophilus G. Active Service; or Gospel Work
      Among U.S. Soldiers. New York: U.S. Army Association,
      n.d.

693. _____. Colored Regulars in the United
      States Army. Philadelphia: A.M.E. Book Concern, 1904.

694. Steward, Theophilus G.   From 1864 to 1914, Fifty Years
      in the Gosepl Ministry; Twenty-Seven Years in the Pas-
      torate; Sixteen Years' Active Service as Chaplain in
      the U.S. Army; Seven Years Professor in Wilberforce
      University; Two Trips to Europe; A Trip to Mexico.
      Philadelphia: A.M.E. Book Concern, 1921.

695. _____. How the Black St. Domingo
      Legion Saved the Patriot Army in the Siege of Savannah.
      Washington, DC: The Academy, 1899.

696. _____. "Two Years in Luzon," Colored
      American Magazine, Vol. 4, November, 1901, pp. 4-10.

697. Taylor, (Mrs.) Susie King. Reminiscences of My Life
      in Camp with the 33rd U.S. Colored Troops. Boston:
      The Author, 1902.

698. Teamoh, R.T. Sketch of the Life and Death of Col.
      Robert Gould, Shaw. Boston: The Author, 1904.

699. _____. The Spanish-American War: The Events of
      the War Described by Eye Witnesses. Chicago and New
      York: H.S. Stone and Co., 1899.

700. Terrell, Mary Church. "Taft and the Negro Soldiers,"
      Independent, Vol. 65, July 23, 1908, pp. 189-190.

701. "The Manufacture of Prejudice," Crisis, Vol. 1, March,
      1911, pp. 25-27.

702. "The Negro as a Soldier and Officer," Nation (NY), Vol.
      73, August 1, 1901, pp. 85-86.

703. "The Negro as a Soldier," Public Opinion, Vol. 27,
      August 17, 1899, p. 198.

704. "The Negro in the Spanish-American War," Negro History
      Bulletin, Vol. 15, October, 1951, pp. 3-4, 22.

705. "The Negro Soldier," The Voice, Vol. 3, 1906. Whole
      issue devoted to Negro soldiers.

706. Thweatt, Hiram M., Compiler. What the Newspapers Say
      of the Negro Soldier in the Spanish-American War.
      Thomasville, GA: n.d.

707. Tompkins, Frank. Chasing Villa. Harrisburg, PA: The
      Military Service Publishing Co., 1934.

708. Van Alstyne, Lawrence. Diary of an Enlisted Man.
      New Haven, CT: Tuttle, Morehouse and Taylor Co., 1910.

709. Villard, Oswald G. "The Negro in the Regular Army,"
      Atlantic Monthly, Vol. 91, June, 1903, pp. 721-729.

710. Villard, Oswald G. "Negroes as Soldiers," Nation (NY),
      Vol. 73, 1901, p. 85.

711. "Virginia's Colored Volunteers," Southern Workman,
      Vol. 27, July, 1898, p. 132.

712. Washington, Booker T. Heroes in Black Skins. New
      York: n.p., 1903.

713. _____. The Colored Soldier in the
      Spanish-American War. Chicago: Chicago Library Com-
      mission, 1899.

714. _____. The Story of the Negro. New
      York: Doubleday, Page and Co., 1909. Chapter XV
      discusses Black Soldiers Fight for Freedom.

715. Wesley, Charles H. The Quest for Equality: From
      Civil War to Civil Rights. New York: Publisher's Co.,
      1968, pp. 80-90.

716. Wharfield, Harold B. "The Affair at Carrizal: Per-
      shing's Punitive Expedition," Montana, Vol. 18, October,
      1968, pp. 24-39.

717. Wilson, James H. Under the Old Flag: Recollections
      of Military Operations in the War for the Union, the
      Boxer Rebellion, etc. 2 Vols. New York: D. Appleton
      and Company, 1912.

718. Wynne, Lewis N. "Brownsville: The Reaction of the
      Negro Press," Phylon, Vol. 33, Summer, 1972, pp. 153-
      160.

719. Young, Charles. Military Morale of Nations and Races.
      Kansas City: Franklin Hudson Publishing Co., 1912.

720. Young, James R. and J. Hampton Moore, Editors. Remin-
      iscences and Thrilling Stories of the War by Return
      Heroes. Philadelphia, PA: National Publishing Co.,
      1899.

VI.

Blacks in World War I

721. "A Futile Attempt at Sedition," Outlook, Vol. 115, April 18, 1917, p. 684.

722. "A Negro's Faith in American Justice," Southern Workman, Vol. 47, December, 1918, pp. 591-592.

723. "A Negro's March with Muffled Drums," Survey, Vol. 38, August 4, 1917, pp. 405-406.

724. "A New Color Line," The Public, Vol. 22, February 8, 1919, p. 129.

725. "A Philosophy in Time of War," Crisis, Vol. 16, August, 1918, p. 164.

726. A Pictorial History of the Negro in the Great World War, 1917-1918. New York: Touissant Pictorial Co., 1919.

727. Adams, Thomas Richard. "Houston Riot of 1917." Unpublished Master's Thesis, Texas A & M University, 1972.

728. Aldrich, Mildred. The Peak of the Load. Boston: Small, Maynard and Co., 1918.

729. Allen, Henry T. The Rhineland Occupation. Indianapolis: Bobbs-Merrill, 1927.

730. "American Negro as a Fighting Man," Review of Reviews, Vol. 58, August, 1918, pp. 210-211.

731. "American Negro in France," Current History, Vol. 2, March, 1921, pp. 479-480.

732. Anderson, Jervis. A. Philip Randolph: A Biographical
      Portrait. New York: Harcourt Brace Jovanovich, 1973.

733. Anderson, William L. "Soldiers, World War I," Crisis,
      Vol. 20, May, 1920, p. 49.

734. Atwell, E.T. "The Experience of the War in Organizing
      Recreation for Colored Soldiers and Its Application to
      Peace Time," National Conference of Social Work, Pro-
      ceedings, Vol. 47, 1920, pp. 331-333.

735. Baker, Newton D. "The Negro and the National Guard,"
      Crisis, Vol. 20, July, 1920, p. 137.

736. Baker, Ray S. "Gathering Clouds Along the Color Line,"
      World's Work, Vol. 32, June, 1916, pp. 232-236.

737. _____. "The Negro Goes North," World's Work,
      Vol. 34, July, 1917, pp. 314-319.

738. Baldridge, C. Leroy. I Was There. New York: G.P.
      Putnam's Sons, 1919.

739. Barbeau, Arthur Edward. "The Black American Soldier
      in World War I." Unpublished Doctoral Dissertation,
      University of Pittsburgh, 1970.

740. _____ and Florette Henri. The Unknown
      Soldiers: Black American Troops in World War I. Phil-
      adelphia: Temple University Press, 1974.

741. Barksdale, Norvel P. "France and the Negro," Lincoln
      University Record, October, 1924, pp. 8-16.

742. Barton, R.C. Race Consciousness and the American Negro.
      Copenhagen: Norrebros Central Printing, 1934.

743. Bass, Urbane F. "Soldiers, World War," Crisis, Vol.
      15, May, 1917, pp. 226-228.

744. Berry, Mary Frances and John W. Blassingame. Long
      Memory: The Black Experience in America. New York:
      Oxford University Press, 1982. See "The First World
      War," pp. 314-317.

745. "Black Soldiers," Crisis, Vol. 15, November, 1917, pp.
      33-35.

746. "Blacks in World War I: A Little Known Chapter in
      American History," New York Amsterdam News, June 3,
      1978, p. A-8.

747. Blanton, Joshua E. "Men in the Making," Southern Work-
      man, Vol. 42, January, 1919, pp. 17-24.

748. Bliss, James G. History of the 805th Pioneer Infantry.
St. Paul: Privately Published, 1919.

749. Blount, Samuel R. Reminiscences of Samuel E. Blount,
Corporal and Company Clerk, Company B, 367th Infantry,
92nd Division, U.S. National Army. n.p., 1934.

750. Bond, Horace Mann. "The Negro in the Armed Forces of
the United States Prior to World War I," Journal of
Negro Education, Vol. 12, Summer, 1943, pp. 268-287.

751. _____. "What the Army 'Intelligence' Test
Measured," Opportunity, Vol. 2, July, 1924, pp. 197-
202.

752. Bonsal, Stephen. The Negro Soldier in War and Peace.
New York: n.p., 1917.

753. Bougue, Allan, Thomas D. Phillips, and James E. Wright.
The West of the American People. Itasca, IL: F.E.
Peacock Publishers, Inc., 1970.

754. Bradden, William S. "Articles on Negro Soldiers by the
8th Regiment's Chaplain," Chicago Broad Ax, May/June,
1919.

755. _____. Under Fire with the 370th Infantry,
A.E.F. Chicago: The Author, n.d.

756. Braithwaite, William S., Compiler. Victory. Boston:
Small, Maynard and Company, 1918.

757. Broadus, Lewis. "Soldiers," Crisis, Vol. 14, June,
1917, pp. 60, 73, 85.

758. Brock, George D., Compiler. Within the Heart of the
Colored Soldier. n.p., n.d.

759. Broonzy, William Lee Conley. Big Bill Blues: William
Boonzy's Story. London: Cassell and Co., 1955. There
is a section in this book about the author's military
experiences in Europe during World War I.

760. Brown, Hugh. "Negro in the Great War," Southern Workman, Vol. 46, August, 1917, pp. 427-430.

761. Bruce, John Edward. A Tribute for the Negro Soldier.
New York: Bruce and Franklin, 1918.

762. Buchanan, Walter S. The Negro's War Aims. Birmingham,
AL: n.p., 1918.

763. Bullard, Robert L. American Soldiers Also Fought.
New York: Longmans, Green, 1936.

764. Bullard, Robert L. Personalities and Reminiscences of
      the War. New York: Doubleday, Page, 1925.

765. Bullock, M.W. "What Does the Negro Want?," Outlook,
      Vol. 73, September, 1919, p. 110.

766. "Bush Germans Better Watch that 'Chocolate Front',"
      Literary Digest, Vol. 57, June 15, 1918, pp. 43-47.

767. Butler, Alban. Happy Days. New York: Coward and
      McCann, 1929.

768. Cade, John B. Twenty-Two Months with Uncle Sam.
      Atlanta, GA: n.p., 1929.

769. Chase, Hal S. "Struggle For Equality: Fort Des Moines
      Training Camp For Colored Officers, 1917," Phylon, Vol.
      39, December, 1978, pp. 297-310.

770. Chew, Abraham. A Biography of Col. Charles Young.
      Washington: R.L. Pendleton, 1923.

771. Circle for Negro War Relief. Report of the Circle
      for Negro War Relief. n.p., n.d.

772. Clark, Chief Justice Walter. "Negro Soldier (in North
      Carolina)," The North Carolina Booklet, Vol. 18, No. 1,
      July, 1918, pp. 57-62.

773. Clement, Rufus E. "Problems of Demobilization and
      Rehabilitation of the Negro Soldier after World War
      I and II," Journal of Negro Education, Vol. 12, Summer,
      1943, pp. 533-542.

774. Cobb, Irvin S. The Glory of the Coming. New York:
      George H. Doran, 1918.

775. Cochell, William H.W. My Travel in France in World's
      War. Memphis, TN: n.p., n.d.

776. Coffman, Edward M. The War to End All Wars. New York:
      Oxford University Press, 1968.

777. "Col. Bill Hayward and His Black Watch," Literary
      Digest, Vol. 60, March 8, 1919, p. 58.

778. "Close Ranks," Crisis, Vol. 16, July, 1918, p. 111.

779. Colson, William N. "An Analysis of Negro Patriotism,"
      Messenger, Vol. 2, August, 1919, pp. 23-25.

780. _____. "Propaganda and the American Negro
      Soldier," Messenger, Vol. 2, July, 1919, pp. 24-25.

781. _____. "The Social Experience of the Negro
      Soldier Abroad," Messenger, Vol. 2, October, 1919, pp.
      26-27.

782. Colson, William N. and A.B. Nutt. "The Failure of the
      Ninety-Second Division," Messenger, Vol. 2, September,
      1919, pp. 22-25.

783. Complete History of the Colored Soldiers in World Wars;
      Authentic Story of the Greatest War of Civilized Times
      and What the Colored Man Did to Uphold Democracy and
      Liberty. New York: Bennett and Churchill, 1919.

784. Cooley, Rosa B. "Is There an Explanation?," Outlook,
      Vol. 123, September, 1919, p. 39.

785. Coppin, Levi. Unwritten History. Philadelphia: A.M.E.
      Book Concern, 1919.

786. "Croix de Guerre and Rare Praise for American Negro
      Troops," Literary Digest, Vol. 60, January 18, 1919,
      pp. 55-60.

787. Crowder, Enoch. Second Report of the Provost Marshal
      General. Washington: n.p., 1919.

788. Crowell, Benedict and R.F. Wilson. The Road to France.
      New Haven, CT: Yale University Press, 1921. 2 Vols.

789. Curtis, Mary. The Black Soldiers; or the Colored Boys
      of the United States Army. Washington: Murray Bro-
      thers, 1918.

790. David, Jay and Elaine Crane. The Black Soldier--From
      the American Revolution to Vietnam. New York: William
      Morrow and Company, 1971.

791. Davis, Benjamin O. "Soldiers," Crisis, Vol. 39, July,
      1932, p. 225.

792. Davis, Paul C. "The Negro in the Armed Forces," Vir-
      ginia Quarterly Review, Vol. 24, 1948, pp. 499-520.

793. Dawes, Charles G. A Journal of the Great War. 2 vols.
      Boston: Houghton-Mifflin, 1921.

794. DeCastlebled, Maurice. History of the AEF. New York:
      Bookcraft, 1937.

795. Deckard, Percy E. List of Officers Who Served With
      the 371st Infantry and Headquarters 186th Infantry
      Brigade During the World War. Allegany, NY: The
      Allegany Citizen, 1929.

796. "Defenders of Liberty and Human Rights," Crisis, Vol.
      16, July, 1913, pp. 122-214.

797. Deland, Margaret. Small Things. New York: D. Apple-
      ton and Company, 1919.

798.   Delsante, Walter W. Negro Democracy and the War.
        Detroit: Wolverine Printing Co., 1919.

799.   "Democracy and the Colored Soldier," Playground, Vol.
        13, September, 1919, pp. 259-266.

800.   Delsante,Walter William. The Negro Democracy and the
        War. Detroit: Wolverine Printing Co., 1919.

801.   Dickman, Joseph T. The Great Crusade. New York:
        D. Appleton and Company, 1927.

802.   "Discovery of France by Jos. Williams Colored Doughboy,"
        Literary Digest, Vol. 61, April 12, 1919, pp. 80-84.

803.   Drinker, Frederick. Our War for Human Rights. Wash-
        ington: Austin-Jenkins, 1917.

804.   DuBois, W.E.B. "The Black Man in the Revolution of
        1914-1918," Crisis, Vol. 17, March, 1919, pp. 218-223.

805.   _____. "An Essay Toward a History of the
        Black Man in the Great War," Crisis, Vol. 18, June,
        1919, pp. 63-87.

806.   _____. "The Negro Soldier in Service Abroad
        During the First World War," Journal of Negro Educa-
        tion, Vol. 12, Summer, 1943, pp. 324-334.

807.   _____. "Documents of the War," Crisis, Vol.
        18, May, 1919, pp. 16-21.

808.   _____. "Black Labor Moves North," Nation, Vol.
        116, May, 9, 1923, pp. 539-541.

809.   _____. "The Problem of Problems," The Inter-
        collegiate Socialist, December/January, 1917-1918,
        pp. 5-9.

810.   Dunton, W. Herbert. "The Fair in the Cow Country,"
        Scribner's Magazine, Vol. 55, April, 1914, pp. 454-
        465.

811.   Dwyer, Norval. "The Camp Upton Story, 1917-1921,"
        Long Island Forum, Vol. 33, 1970, pp. 6-10; (2):31-34;
        (3):54-57.

812.   Edward, William J. Twenty-Five Years in the Black
        Belt. Boston: Cornhill, 1918.

813.   Eleazer, Robert B. America's Tenth Man. Atlanta:
        Commission on Interracial Cooperation, 1931.

814.   _____, Compiler. Singers in the Dawn.
        Atlanta: Conference on Education and Race Relations,
        1934.

815.   Embee, E.R. "With the Negro Troops," Survey, Vol. 40,
        August 10, 1918, pp. 537-538.

816.   Emmett, Chris. Give Way to the Right. San Antonio,
        TX: The Naylor Co., 1934.

817.   Ferguson, David L. "With This Black Man's Army,"
        Independent, Vol. 92, March 15, 1919, pp. 368, 385.

818.   Ferguson, George O. "The Intelligence of Negroes at
        Camp Lee, Virginia," School and Society, Vol. 9, June
        14, 1919, pp. 721-726.

819.   _____. "The Mental Status of the American
        Negro," Scientific Monthly, Vol. 12, June, 1921, pp.
        533-543.

820.   Finch, Minnie.   The NAACP: Its Fights for Justice.
        Metuchen, NJ: Scarecrow Press, 1981. See Chapter VI,
        "Segregation in the Armed Forces--World War I," pp. 37-
        44.

821.   Fleming, William F. "American Negro Combat Soldiers
        in World War I." Unpublished Doctoral Dissertation,
        Western Reserve University, 1975.

822.   Ford, James W. The Negro and the Imperialist War of
        1914-1918. n.p., 1929.

823.   Foster, Obahiah M. The Modern Warfare and My Exper-
        iences in France. Washington: The Goines Printing
        Co., 1919.

824.   Franklin, John Hope. From Slavery to Freedom: A
        History of Negro Americans. New York: Alfred A. Knopf,
        1980. See "World War I," pp. 323-342.

825.   Frazier, Thomas A. "Soldier's in 'World War I',"
        Crisis, Vol. 17, February, 1919, p. 197.

826.   Gannett, Lewis S. "Those Black Troops on the Rhine-
        and the White," Nation, Vol. 112, May 25, 1921, pp.
        733-734.

827.   Garvin, Charles H. "The Trail of the Buffaloes,"
        Crisis, Vol. 35, November, 1928, pp. 367-385.

828.   _____. "An Unsung Hero," Crisis, Vol. 35,
        February, 1928, p. 47.

829.   "German Plots Among Negroes," Literary Digest, Vol. 54,
        April 21, 1917, p. 1153.

830.   Giddings, Franklin H. "The Black Man's Rights,"
        Independent, Vol. 99, August 2, 1919, p. 153.

831. Gibbons, Floyd. And They Thought We Wouldn't Fight.
      New York: George H. Doran Co., 1918.

832. Gleason, Arthur. Our Part in the Great War. New York:
      Fredrick A. Stokes, 1917.

833. Gould, William B. "Soldiers," Crisis, Vol. 26, August,
      1923, p. 176.

834. Graf, William S. "Henry Johnson of the 369th Colored
      U.S. Infantry Regiment Was A Fighting Man (First Amer-
      ican to Win the French Croix de Guerre)," Soldiers,
      Vol. 30, April, 1975, pp. 10-11.

835. Grant, Frances B. "Negro Patriotism and Negro Music,"
      Outlook, Vol. 121, February 26, 1919, pp. 343-347.

836. Grant, Lucius L. The Destiny of the American Negro.
      Nashville, TN: S.S. Publishing Board, 1920.

837. Green, (Elisha) Ely. Ely: Too Black, Too White.
      Amherst, MA: University of Massachusetts Press, 1970.
      Author discusses his military experiences in Europe in
      the U.S. Army during World War I.

838. Griffin, William W. "Mobilization of Black Militiamen
      in World War I: Ohio's Ninth Battalion," The Historian,
      Vol. 40, August, 1978, pp. 686-703.

839. Grimke, Francis James. A Word of Greeting to Colored
      Soldiers Delivered at the Opening of the Rest Rooms
      for Colored Soldiers. Washington, DC: July 13, 1918.

840. Hagood, Johnson. The Services of Supply. Boston:
      Houghton-Mifflin, 1920.

841. Hanford, Cornelius Holgate. Seattle and Environs:
      1852-1924. (Contains a list of Negroes who served in
      World War I). Chicago: Pioneer Historical Publishing
      Co., 1924.

842. Harbord, James G. The American Army in France. Boston:
      Little Brown and Co., 1936.

843. _____. Leaves From a War Diary. New York:
      Dodd, Mead, 1925.

844. Harrison, William H. Colored Boys' and Girls' In-
      spiring United States History. n.p., 1921.

845. Hart, Irving S. "Keeping Up Morale at Camp Alexander,
      Virginia," Southern Workman, Vol. 47, May, 1919, pp.
      225-230.

846. Harvey, Bartle M. Me and Bayes Eyes and Slim. n.p.,
      Charles F. Davis, 1932.

847.   Hayes, D.H.   The Colored Man's Part in the War.
        Atlanta, GA: Robinson Hamilton Co., 1919.

848.   Haynes, George E.   "The Negro and National Reconstruc-
        tion," The Public, Vol. 22, February 8, 1919, pp. 131-
        133.

849.   _____.   "Race Riots in Relation to Democra-
        cy," Survey, Vol. 42, August 8, 1919, pp. 697-699.

850.   _____.   "What Negroes Think of the Race
        Riots," The Public, Vol. 22, August 9, 1919, pp. 848-
        849.

851.   Haynes, Robert V.   A Night of Violence: The Houston
        Riot of 1917.   Baton Rouge: Louisiana State University
        Press, 1976.

852.   _____.   "The Houston Mutiny and Riot of 1917,"
        Southwestern Historical Quarterly, Vol. 76, April, 1973,
        pp. 418-439.

853.   Henri, Florette.   Black Migration: Movement North,
        1900-1920.   Garden City, NY: Doubleday, 1975.   There
        is one Chapter in this work entitled "In the Great
        War for Democracy" that deals with the Black Soldier
        in World War I.

854.   Heroes of 1918:   Stories From the Lips of Black Fight-
        ers.   Chicago: O. Walker, 1919.

855.   Herring, Kate M.   "How the Southern Negro Is Supporting
        the Government," Outlook, Vol. 120, November 20, 1918,
        pp. 452-453.

856.   _____.   "The Negro and War Savings in North
        Carolina," Southern Workman, Vol. 48, July, 1919, pp.
        364-367.

857.   Heywood, Chester Dodd.   Negro Combat Troops in the
        World War, the Story of the 37th Infantry.   Worchester,
        MA: Commonwealth Press, 1928.

858.   Hilts, Helen M.   "Hampton Training and War Service,"
        Southern Workman, Vol. 47, July, 1918, pp. 335-344.

859.   History of the 19th Regiment, Field Artillery Replace-
        ment Depot.   Columbia: Camp Jackson, S.C.   By its
        Officers and Men, 1918.

860.   "Honor to Whom Honor Is Due," Outlook, Vol. 121, Feb-
        ruary 26, 1919, p. 329.

861.   House, Grace B.   Soldiers of Freedom.   n.p., n.d.

862.   Houston, Charles H. "Saving the World For Democracy," Pittsburgh Courier, July 20/October 12, 1940.

863.   "How French and American Black Troops Performed Deeds of Valor on Many Battlefields," Current History, Vol. 5, December, 1919, pp. 536-541.

864.   "How Shall the Black Man's Burden Be Lifted," Current Opinion, Vol. 61, August 19, 1919, pp. 111-112.

865.   "How the War Brings Unprophesied Opportunities to the Negro Race," Current Opinion, Vol. 61, December, 1916, pp. 404-405.

866.   Hunton, Addie W. and Kathryn M. Johnson. Two Colored Women With the American Expeditionary Forces. Brooklyn: Brooklyn Eagle Press, 1920.

867.   "Intelligence of Negroes as Compared with Whites," Current Opinion, Vol. 61, November, 1921, pp. 640-641.

868.   Jamieson, J.A., et al. Complete History of the Colored Soldier in the World War. New York: Bennett and Churchhill, 1919.

869.   Johnson, Charles B. The World War and Democracy, as Regards the Negro. (The Truth), n.p., n.d.

870.   Johnson, Charles S. "Mental Measurements of Negro Groups," Opportunity, Vol. 1, February, 1923, pp. 23-25.

871.   Johnson, Henry H. The Black Man's Part in the War. London: Simpkin, Marshall, Hamilton, Ken and Co., 1917.

872.   Johnson, James Weldon. "Negro in War-Time; Reply to B. Smith," Public, (Chicago) Vol. 21, September 21, 1919, pp. 1218-1219.

873.   _____. "What the Negro Is Doing for Himself," Liberator, Vol. I, June, 1919, pp. 29-31.

874.   Johnson, Jessie J. A Pictorial History of Black Servicemen: Missing Pages in United States History. Hampton, VA: Hampton Institute, 1970.

875.   Johnson, Walker H. With Old Eph in the Army: By a Soldier From France. Baltimore: R.E. Houch and Co., 1919.

876.   Johnston, Harry Hamilton. The Black Man's Part in the War. London: Simpkin and Marshall, 1917.

877.   Jordan, W.H. With "Old Eph" in the Army. Baltimore: H.E. Houck, 1919.

878.   Judy, William L. A Soldier's Diary. Chicago: Judy
        Publishing Co., 1930.

879.   Keene, Royal D. The Light Still Shines. New York:
        Carlton Press, 1961. Author discusses his military
        experiences in the U.S. Army during World War I.

880.   Kerlin, Robert T. The Negro's Reaction to the World
        War. Norfolk, VA: n.d.

881.   Khorat, Pierre. "Colored Soldiers," Living Age, Vol.
        314, September 2, 1922, pp. 575-578.

882.   Koger, A. Briscoe. The Maryland Negro in Our Wars.
        Baltimore, MD: Clarke Press, 1942.

883.   Lane, Anne J. The Brownsville Affair: National Crisis
        and Black Reaction. Port Washington, NY: Kennikat
        Press, 1971.

884.   "Last Year's Lynching Record," Outlook, Vol. 115, Jan-
        uary 17, 1917.

885.   Laurence, H.B. "Why the Negro Fights," Southern Work-
        man, Vol. 47, August, 1918, p. 400.

886.   Lauzurne, Stephane. "The Black Troops," Outlook, Vol.
        127, March 16, 1921, pp. 432-434.

887.   Lee, George W. A Brave Black Division. Memphis, TN:
        n.p., 1923.

888.   _____. "After Eleven Years," Opportunity,
        Vol. 7, November, 1929, pp. 337-340.

889.   Liggett, Hunter. Commanding An American Army. Boston:
        Houghton-Mifflin Co., 1925.

890.   _____. AEF. New York: Dodd, Mead and
        Company, 1928.

891.   Link, Arthur S. Woodrow Wilson and the Progressive
        Era: 1910-1917. New York: Harper and Row, 1943.

892.   Little, Arthur W. From Harlem to the Rhine: The
        Story of New York's Colored Volunteers. New York:
        Covice Friede, 1936.

893.   Litwack, Leon F. Been in the Storm So Long: The
        Aftermath of Slavery. New York: Alfred A. Knopf, 1979.
        See Chapter 2, pp. 64-103.

894.   Logan, Rayford W. The Betrayal of the Negro, From
        Rutherford B. Hayes to Woodrow Wilson. New York:
        Collin-Macmillan, Ltd., 1965.

895. Long, Francis T. The Negores of Clarke County, Georgia During the Great War. Athens, GA: n.p., 1919.

896. Long, Howard H. "The Negro Soldier in the Army of the United States," Journal of Negro Education, Vol. 127, Summer, 1943, pp. 307-315.

897. Love, A.G. and C.B. Davenport. "A Comparison of White and Colored Troops in Respect to Incidence of Disease," Proceedings of National Academy of Sciences, Vol. 5, March, 1919, pp. 58-67.

898. Lovewell, Reinette. "Backing the Negro Troops," Southern Workman, Vol. 47, November, 1917, pp. 524-526.

899. Lucas, Wilmer F. "The 36th Infantry, New York National Guard," Crisis, Vol. 37, April, 1930, pp. 120-122.

900. Lynde, Lt. Charles C. "Mobilizing 'Rastus'," Outlook, Vol. 118, March 13, 1918, pp. 415-417.

901. Lynk, Miles Vandahurst. The Negro Pictorial Review of the Great World War: A Visual Narrative of the Negro's Glorious Part in the World's Greatest War. Memphis, TN: Twentieth Century Art Co., 1919.

902. MacIntyre, William Irwin. Colored Soldiers. Macon, GA: J.W. Burke Co., 1923.

903. Madelbaum, David. Soldier Groups and Negro Soldiers. Berkeley, CA: University of California Press, 1952.

904. "Making Soldiers in Dixie," Colliers Weekly, April 27, 1918.

905. March, Peyton. A Nation at War. Garden City, NJ: Doubleday Doran, 1932.

906. Marcossan, Isaac. S.O.S.: America's Miracle in France. New York: John Lane Co., 1919.

907. Marshall, Napoleon Bonaporte. "Soldiers, World War I," Crisis, Vol. 17, February, 1919, p. 178.

908. _____. The Providential Armistice, A Volunteer's Story. Washington: n.p., 1930.

909. Marshall, S.L.A. The American Heritage History of World War I. New York: American Heritage, 1964.

910. Mason, Monroe and Arthur Furr. The American Negro With the Red Hand of France. Boston: Cornhill, 1920.

911. Matthews, Carl S. "After Booker T. Washington: The Search for a New Negro Leadership, 1915-1925." Unpublished Doctoral Dissertation, University of Virginia, 1971.

912.   McCarthy, C.F.   A Year at Camp Gordon.   Wilkes-Barre,
       PA: T.F. McCarthy, 1920.

913.   McCormack, Rorbert R.   The Army of 1918.   New York:
       Harcourt-Brace, 1920.

914.   McCougall, William.   Is America Safe for Democracy?
       New York: Charles Scribner's Sons, 1921.

915.   McIntyre, Irwin W.   Colored Soldiers.   Macon, GA:
       Burke, 1923.

916.   McKaine, Osceola E.   "The Buffaloes," Outlook, Vol.
       119, May 22, 1918, pp. 144-147.

917.   _____.   "With the Buffaloes in France,"
       Independent, Vol. 97, January 11, 1919, p. 50.

918.   McKay, Claude.   A Long Way From Home.   New York:
       Furman, 1937.

919.   McMaster, John B.   The United States in the World War.
       New York: D. Appleton and Co., 1918.

920.   McNutt, William S.   "Making Soldiers in Dixie," Col-
       lier's Weekly,   Vol. 61, April 27, 1918, p. 7.

921.   McRae, Norman.   "Camp Ward, Detroit: Home of the First
       Michigan Colored Infantry Regiment," Detroit Historical
       Society Bulletin, Vol. 24, 1968, pp. 4-11.

922.   Miller, E.E.   "The War and Race Feeling," Outlook,
       Vol. 123, September 10, 1919, pp. 52-56.

923.   Miller, Kelly.   Appeal to Conscience.   New York:
       Macmillan, 1918.

924.   _____.   Kelly Miller's History of the World
       War For Human Rights; Being an Intensely Human and
       Brilliant Account of the World War and Why and For
       What Purpose American and the Allies are Fighting and
       the Important Part Taken By the Negro.   Including the
       Horrors and Wonders of Modern Warfare, the New and
       Strange Devices.   Washington: Austin Jenkins Co., 1919.

925.   _____.   New Pictorial History of the World War
       for Human Right.   Washington, DC: Austin Jenkins Co.,
       1919.

926.   _____.   The Disgrace of Democracy.   Washington:
       The Author, 1917.

927.   _____.   The Everlasting Stain.   Washington:
       Associated Publishers, 1924.

928. Miller, Kelly. World War For Human Rights. Washington: A. Jenkins and C. Keller, 1919.

929. Miller, Warren H. The Boys of 1917. Boston: L.C. Page, 1939.

930. Miner, Uzziah, et al. Modern Artillerymen. Camp Dix, NJ: n.p., 1919.

931. Moore, Lewis B. Patriotism Through Education. New York: n.p., 1919.

932. _____. How the Colored Race Can Help in the Problems Issuing from the War. New York: National Security League, 1919.

933. Moorland, Jesse. "The Y.M.C.A. with Colored Troops," Southern Workman, Vol. 48, April, 1919, pp. 171-175.

934. Morel, E.O. The Horror of the Rhine. n.p., (England?), 1920.

935. Moss, James A. "The Negro as a Soldier," Southern Workman, Vol. 47, June, 1918, p. 313.

936. Moss, Pauline Cooper. "At Home and At War, 1917-1919 (With Lt. George P. Cooper)," Negro History Bulletin, Vol. 45, April/May/June, 1982, pp. 43-45.

937. Moton, Robert Russa. "American Negro and the World War I," World's Work, Vol. 36, May, 1918, pp. 74-77.

938. _____. "Negro Troops in France," Southern Workman, Vol. 54, July, 1925, pp. 304a-d.

939. _____. "Fifty Thousand and Fifty Million," Outlook, Vol. 120, November 20, 1918, pp. 451-452.

940. _____. Finding A Way Out: An Autobiography. Garden City, NY: Doubleday, Page, 1920.

941. _____. "The Lynching Record for 1918," Outlook, Vol. 121, January 22, 1919, p. 159.

942. _____ and K.M. Herring. "Patriotism of the Negro Citizen," Outlook (NY), Vol. 120, November 20, 1918.

943. Mueller, William G. "The Negro in the Navy," Social Forces, Vol. 27, October, 1945.

944. _____. The Twenty-Fourth Infantry Past and Present: A Brief History of the Regiment Compiled From Official Records Under the Direction of the Regimental Commander. Fort Benning, Columbus, GA: n.p., 1923.

945.   Murray, Paul Thom. "Blacks and the Draft: An Analysis
       of Institutional Racism, 1917-1971." Unpublished
       Doctoral Dissertation, Florida State University, 1972.

946.   _____. "Blacks and the Draft: A History
       of Institutional Racism," Journal of Black Studies,
       Vol. 2, September, 1971, pp. 57-76.

947.   Muston, W.H. Over There. Yoakum, TX: Baners Printing
       Co., 1923.

948.   National Association for the Advancement of Colored
       People. Burning at the Stake in the United States.
       New York: The Association, 1919.

949.   Nave, George F. The Negro's Attitude Toward His
       Government. Muskegee, OK: The Author, 1917.

950.   Nearing, George. Black America. New York: Vanguard
       Press, 1929.

951.   "Negro Conscription," New Republic, Vol. 12, October
       20, 1917, pp. 317-318.

952.   "Negro Educators and Our War Effort," Survey, Vol. 40,
       May 4, 1918, pp. 132-133.

953.   "Negro Patriotism," Southern Workman, Vol. 48, October
       20, 1919, pp. 510-511.

954.   "Negro Veterans of the World War," Crisis, Vol. 23,
       April, 1922, p. 270.

955.   Niles, John J. Singing Soldiers. New York: Charles
       Scribner's Sons, 1927.

956.   "Not One of the Famous 39th Was Taken Alive," Literary
       Digest, Vol. 60, March 15, 1919, pp. 94-96.

957.   O'Connor, Richard. "Black Jack of the 10th," American
       Heritage, Vol. 18, February, 1967, pp. 14-17.

958.   "Other Hampton Men at the Front," Southern Workman,
       Vol. 48, January, 1919, pp. 43-46.

959.   "Our Own Race War," North American Review, Vol. 210,
       October, 1919, pp. 436-438.

960.   "Our Own Subject Race Rebels," Literary Digest, Vol.
       57, August 2, 1919, p. 25.

961.   "Our Special Grievances" and "The Rewards," Crisis,
       Vol. 16, September, 1918, pp. 217, 238.

962.   Page, Arthur W. Our 110 Days Fighting. Garden City,
       NY: Doubleday, Page, 1920.

963. Palmer, Frederick. _American in France_. New York:
      Dodd, Mead and Company, 1918.

964. Park, Phocian Samuel. "The Twenty-Fourth Infantry
      Regiment and the Houston Riot of 1917." Unpublished
      Master's Thesis, University of Houston, 1917.

965. Park, Robert E. "Negro Race Consciousness as Reflected
      in Race Literature," _American Review_, Vol. 1, September/
      October, 1923, pp. 505-517.

966. Patton, Gerald Wilson. "War and Race: The Black Offi-
      cer in the American Military: 1915-1925." Doctoral
      Dissertation, University of Iowa, 1978. See next entry.

967. _____. _War and Race: The Black Offi-
      cer in the American Military, 1915-1941_. Westport, CT:
      Greenwood Press, 1981. This is a revision of his
      dissertation.

968. Pearson, Paul F. _Army War College Carlisle Barracks
      Pa. The Development of National Policy Regarding
      Black Combat Soldiers in U.S. Army 1912-1925_. Wash-
      ington, DC: U.S. Government Printing Office, March 3,
      1972.

969. Peixotto, Ernest C. _The American Front_. New York:
      Charles Scribner's Sons, 1919.

970. Percy, William A. _Lanterns on the Levee_. New York:
      A.A. Knopf, 1940.

971. Pershing, John J. _Final Report, Commander in Chief
      American Expeditionary Forces_. Washington: n.p., 1919.

972. _____. _My Experiences in the World War_.
      New York: Frederick A. Stokes Co., 1931.

973. Pickens, William. "Tit For Tat, How Colored Soldiers
      Defeated the Real Enemy at Grandvillars," _Crisis_,
      Vol. 19, March, 1920, pp. 260-262.

974. _____. _The Negro in the Light of the
      Great War_. Baltimore: The Daily Herald Printing Co.,
      n.d.

975. Pierce, Lucy F. "Training Colored Soldiers," _Review
      of Reviews_, Vol. 56, December, 1917, p. 640.

976. Poling, Daniel A. _Huts in Hell_. Boston: Christian
      Endeavor World, 1918.

977. _____. "Physically Competent and Morally
      Fit," _Outlook_, Vol. 119, July 10, 1918, pp. 415-417.

978. Pottle, Frederick A. _Stretchers_. New Haven, CT:
      Yale University Press, 1929.

979. Powell, A. Clayton. Patriotism and the Negro. New
      York: Beehive Press, n.d.

980. Proctor, H.H. Between Black and White. New York:
      Pilgrim Press, 1925.

981. Raschke, Phillip. "Harlem's Hellfighters (The All-
      Black 369th of WWI)," Soldiers, Vol. 32, August, 1977,
      pp. 49-52.

982. Rass, Joyce B. J.E.Spingarn and the Rise of the
      NAACP, 1911-1939, New York: Sheed and Ward, 1972.

983. "Recreation for Colored Soldiers," Southern Workman,
      Vol. 47, December, 1918, pp. 572-574.

984. Refutation of the Charges Made in the Campaign Against
      the French Colored Troops in the Rhenish Occupied
      Territories. n.p., n.d.

985. Reid, Ira de A. "Critical Summary: The Negro on the
      Home Front in World Wars I and II," Journal of Negro
      Education, Vol. 12, Summer, 1943, pp. 511-520.

986. "Returning Soldiers," Crisis, Vol. 18, May, 1919, pp.
      13-14.

987. Reynolds, Elijah. Colored Soldiers and the Regular
      Army. Washington, D.C.: n.p., 1934.

988. Rhodes, Harrison. "The Negro and the War," Metropoli-
      tan Monthly, Vol. 48, October, 1918, pp. 32-33, 40-44.

989. Richards, John. "Some Experiences with Colored Sold-
      iers," Atlantic Monthly, Vol. 41, August, 1919, pp.
      184-190.

990. Riegelman, Harold. War Notes of a Casual. New York:
      The Author, 1931.

991. Riggs, Arthur S. With Three Armies. Indianapolis, IN:
      Bobbs-Merrill Co., 1918.

992. Ross, B. Joyce. J.E. Spingarn and the Rise of the
      NAACP, 1911-1939. New York: Sheed and Ward, 1972.

993. Ross, Warner D. My Colored Battalion. Chicago: The
      Author, 1920.

994. Ross, William D. and Duke L. Slaughter. With the
      351st in France. Baltimore: Afro-American Co., 1919.

995. Rush, Mallahiew W. "Soldiers-World War," Crisis, Vol.
      17, February, 1917, p. 177.

996.   Sadler, James E. The Negro from Jamestown to the
        Rhine. n.p., 1919.

997.   Saunder, Vincent. "The War," Crisis, Vol. 18, May,
        1919, p. 33.

998.   Scherer, James A.B. The Nation at War. New York:
        George H. Doran Co., 1918.

999.   Schirmer, Daniel. Republic or Empire. Cambridge, MA:
        Harvard University Press, 1917.

1000.   Schoenfeld, Seymour J. The Negro in the Armed Forces.
        Washington: Association Publishers, 1945.

1001.   Schuyler, George Samuel. Black and Conservative:
        The Autobiography of George S. Schuyler. New Rochelle,
        NY: Arlington House, 1966. Author discusses his
        service in the U.S. Army during World War I.

1002.   Scott, Emmett. Scott's Official History of the Ameri-
        can Negro in World War. Chicago: Homewood Press, 1919.

1003.   _____. "The Participation of Negroes in World
        War I: An Introductory Statement," Journal of Negro
        Education, Vol. 12, Summer, 1943, pp. 288-297.

1004.   Scully, Charles A. The Course of the Silver Greyhound.
        New York: Putnam, 1936.

1005.   Sears, Cyrus. Paper of Cyrus Sears, Late Lieut. Col.
        of the 49th U.S. Colored Infantry Cols. of African
        Descent--Originally 11th La. Vol. Infantry--A.D. of
        Harpster, Ohio. Columbus: F.J. Heer Printing Co.,
        1919.

1006.   Seligmann, Herbert. The Negro Faces America. New
        York: Harper, 1922.

1007.   Sexton, Vincent L. "The Negro American and World War
        I." Unpublished Doctoral Dissertation, University of
        Georgia, 1972.

1008.   Shanks, David S. As They Passed Through the Port.
        Washington: Cory Publishing Co., 1927.

1009.   Shaw, Charles A. "The Colored Americans in France,"
        Crisis, Vol. 17, February, 1919, pp. 167-168.

1010.   Shufeldt, R.W. America's Greatest Problem: The Negro.
        Philadelphia: Davis, 1915.

1011.   Singleton, George Arnett. The Autobiography of George
        A. Singleton. Boston: Forum Publishing Co., 1964.
        Author discusses his military service in the U.S. Army
        during World War I.

1012. Skillman, Willis R. The AEF. Phildelphia: Jacobs,
       1920.

1013. Slosson, Preston. The Great Crusade and After. New
       York: MacMillan, 1930.

1014. Smith, Bolton. "The Negro in War-Time," The Public,
       Vol. 21, August 13, 1918, pp. 1110-1113.

1015. Smith, Charles V. American All. Boston: Lorthrop,
       Lee and Shepherd Co., 1925.

1016. Snively, Harry H. The Battle of the Non-Combatants.
       New York: The Business Borse Publishers, 1933.

1017. Snyder, E.E., Editor. Colored Soldiers in France.
       n.p., n.d.

1018. Spencer, Seldon P. The Racial Question. Washington,
       n.p., 1920.

1019. Spingarn, Arthur E. "The Health and Morals of Negro
       Troops," Crisis, Vol. 16, August, 1918, pp. 166-168.

1020. _____. "The War and Venereal Disease
       Among Negroes," Social Hygiene, Vol. 4, July, 1918,
       pp. 333-346.

1021. "Soldiers, World War I," Crisis, Vol. 17, February,
       1919, pp. 192-193.

1022. "Soldiers, World War I," Crisis, Vol. 17, April, 1919,
       p. 295.

1023. "Soldiers, World War I," Crisis, Vol. 18, December,
       1919, p. 81.

1024. Stallings, Lawrence. The Doughboys. New York:
       Haprer and Row, 1963.

1025. Stephenson, Mary L. "The Red Cross and Negro Troops,"
       Southern Workman, Vol. 47, December, 1918, pp. 593-
       594.

1026. Stoddard, Lothrup. The Rising Tide of Color Against
       White World Supremacy. New York: Scribner's Sons,
       1920.

1027. Stringfellow, John. Hell! No! Boston: Meador Pub-
       lishing Co., 1936.

1028. Sullivan, Vincent F. With the Yanks in France. New
       York: V.F. Sullivan Co., 1922.

1029. Sweeney, W. Allison. History of the American Negro in
       the Great World War. Chicago: Cuneo-Henneberry, 1919.

1030. Tate, Merze. "The War Aims of World War I and II and
       Their Relation to the Darker Peoples of the World,"
       Journal of Negro Education, Vol. 12, Summer, 1943,
       pp. 521-532.

1031. "The American Negro as a Fighting Man," Review of
       Reviews, Vol. 58, August, 1918, pp. 210-211.

1032. "The American Negro in France," Current History Maga-
       zine, Vol. 13, March, 1921, pp. 479-480.

1033. "The Army Clears the Record," Newsweek, Vol. 80,
       October 16, 1972, p. 36.

1034. "The Black Troops on the Rhine," Nation, Vol. 112,
       March 9, 1921, pp. 365-366.

1035. "The Colored Americans in France," Crisis, Vol. 17,
       February, 1919, pp. 167-168.

1036. "The Discovery of France by Jos. Williams, Colored
       Dough-Boy," Literary Digest, Vol. 61, April 12, 1919,
       pp. 80-84.

1037. "The Failure of the Ninety-Second Division," Messenger,
       Vol. 2, September, 1919.

1038. "The Health of Colored Troops," Literary Digest, Vol.
       61, June 14, 1919, p. 23.

1039. "The Houston Mutiny," Outlook, Vol. 77, September 5,
       1917, pp. 10-11.

1040. "The Looking Glass: Lost Echoes," Crisis, Vol. 17,
       January, 1919, p. 133.

1041. "The Looking Glass: Over There," Crisis, Vol. 16,
       August, 1918, p. 179.

1042. "The Negro at Bay," Nation, Vol. 107, June 14, 1919,
       p. 931.

1043. "The Negro in the War: How French and American Black
       Troops Performed Deeds of Valor on Many Battlefields,"
       Current History, Vol. 11, December, 1919, pp. 536-541.

1044. "The Negro Officer," National Service With the Inter-
       national Military Digest, Vol. 5, March, 1919, p. 134.

1045. "The Negro Volunteer: Some Characteristics," Military
       Service Institution of the United States, Vol. 29,
       July, 1919.

1046. "The Ninety-Second Division in Action," Southern Work-
       man, Vol. 48, January, 1919, pp. 41-43.

1047. "The Problem of the Negro Soldier," Outlook, Vol. 117,
       October 24, 1917, pp. 279-280.

1048. "The Turning of the Tide," Crisis, Vol. 15, December,
       1917, p. 77.

1049. "The Twenty-Fourth Infantry Prisoners," Crisis, Vol.
       22, November, 1921, pp. 21-22.

1050. "These Colored Fighters Never Lost Their Sense of
       Humor," Literary Digest, Vol. 61, May 10, 1919, pp.
       63-64.

1051. Thirkield, Wilbur. "No Longer 'Nigger' But American
       Negro," Christian Advocate, Vol. 93, October 31, 1918,
       p. 1386.

1052. Thomas, Shipley. The History of the AEF. New York:
       n.p., 1920.

1053. Thornbrough, Emma Lou. "The Brownsville Episode and
       the Negro Vote," Mississippi Valley Historical Review,
       Vol. 44, December, 1957, pp. 469-493.

1054. Tinsley, James A. "The Brownsville Affray." Unpub-
       lished Master's Thesis, University of North Carolina,
       1948.

1055. "Training Negroes For Officers," Literary Digest, Vol.
       55, July 21, 1917, pp. 50-51.

1056. "Twenty-Fourth Infantry," Crisis, Vol. 39, January,
       1932, p. 464.

1057. Union League Club. The Presentation of Colors to the
       367th Regiment of Infantry. New York: S.L. Parson
       Co., 1918.

1058. United States, Adjutant General's Office. Summary of
       Casualties in the AEF. Washington, 1919.

1059. United States, American Expeditionary Forces, Engineer
       Corps. Historical Report of the Chief Engineer.
       Washington, 1918.

1060. United States Army, Adjutant General. Report of the
       Adjutant General of the Army, 1918. Washington, 1918.

1061. United States Army, General Staff, Historical Branch.
       Brief Histories of Divisions, U.S. Army, 1917-1918.
       Washington, 1921.

1062. United States Army, General Staff, Historical Branch.
       Organization of the Services of Supply. Washington,
       1921.

1063.   United States Army, Surgeon General. Report of Negro
        Soldier Regular Army, Diseases, etc. Washington, 1923.

1064.   United States Army, War College. Colored Soldiers in
        the U.S. Army. Washington, 1942.

1065.   United States, Committee on Foreign Affairs, House.
        Hearings on H.R. 9694 Authorizing the Erection of a
        Monument to the 93rd Division. Washington, 1926.

1066.   United States, Committee on the Library, House. Negro
        Soldiers' and Sailors' Memorial, Hearings on. Wash-
        ington, 1919.

1067.   United States, Congress. Congressional Record. Wash-
        ington, 65th and 66th Congresses, 1917-1920.

1068.   United States, Congress, House. Selective Service Act,
        Hearings on. Washington, 1918.

1069.   United States, Congress, Senate. Alleged Executions
        Without Trial in France. Washington, 1923.

1070.   United States, Department of Labor, Division of Negro
        Economics. The Negro at Work During the World War and
        Reconstruction. Washington, 1921.

1071.   United States, Department of State. Colored Soldiers
        in the French Army. Washington, 1919.

1972.   _____. Colored Troops in
        the French Army; a Report from the Department of State
        Relating to the Colored Troops in the French Army and
        the Number of French Colonial Troops in the Occupied
        Territory. Washington, 1921.

1073.   United States, War Department. Annual Reports, 1918.
        Washington, 1919.

1074.   _____. Battle Participation
        of Organizations of the American Expeditionary Forces
        in France, Belgium and Italy. Washington, 1920.

1075.   _____. The Medical Department
        of the United States Army in the World War. Washing-
        ton, 1925. Vol. XV Statistics.

1076.   _____. The Official Record
        of the United States' Part in the Great War. Wash-
        ington, 1923.

1077.   _____, Militia Bureau. Mili-
        tary Protection, U.S. Guard. Washington, 1919.

1078.   _____. Report of the Acting
        Chief of the Militia Bureau, 1918. Washington, 1918.

1079. Van Every, Dole. The AEF in Battle. New York:
       Appleton, 1923.

1080. Vardaman, James K. The Great American Race Problem
       and Its Relation to the Present War. n.p., 1917.

1081. Varlin, Eugene. The Negro and the U.S. Army. New
       York: Pioneer Publishers, n.d.

1082. War Camp Community Service. The War Camp Community
       Service and the Negro Soldier. n.p., 1920.

1083. Weaver, John D. The Brownsville Raid: The Story of
       America's Black Dreyfus Affair. New York: Norton,
       1970.

1084. Webster, Edgar H. Chums and Brothers. Boston:
       Richard G. Padger, 1920.

1085. Weil, F.E.G. "The Negro in the Armed Forces," Social
       Forces, Vol. 26, October, 1947, pp. 95-98.

1086. Westover, Wendell. Suicide Battalions. New York:
       Putnam, 1929.

1087. "What the Negro Did for the War," World Outlook, Vol.
       5, October,1919, p. 36.

1088. "What the Negro is Doing to Help Win the War," Literary
       Digest, Vol. 58, July 27, 1918, pp. 39-40.

1089. "Where to Encamp the Negro Troops," Literary Digest,
       Vol. 55, September 29, 1917, pp. 14-15.

1090. White, William L. "Negro Officers: 1917 and Now,"
       Survey Graphic, Vol. 19, April, 1942, pp. 192-194.

1091. Whitehouse, Arch. Heroes and Legends of World War I.
       New York: Modern Literary Editions, 1964.

1092. Wilgus, William J. Transporting the AEF in Western
       Europe. New York: Columbia University Press, 1931.

1093. Williams, Charles H. Sidelights on Negro Soldiers.
       Boston: B.J. Brimmer Co., 1923.

1094. Williams, John H. A Negro Looks at War. New York:
       New Workers Library, 1940.

1095. Williams, John R. A Trench Letter. n.p., 1918.

1096. Williams, Walter Bruce. "Soldiers," Crisis, Vol. 35,
       December, 1928, p. 412.

1097. Williams, W.T.B. "The World War and the Negro,"
       Southern Workman, Vol. 47, January, 1918, pp. 9-16.

1098. Wilson, Charles Henry. "The American Negro's Part in the World's War." Unpublished Master's Thesis, University of Southern California, Los Angeles, 1929.

1099. Winterich, John T., Editor. Squads Write. New York: n.p., 1931.

1100. "With the Negro Troops," Southern Workman, Vol. 48, January, 1919, pp. 31–32.

1101. Woodson, Carter G. The Negro in Our History. Washington: Associated Publishers, 1928. See section on Black soldiers.

1102. Woolcott, Alexander. The Command Is Forward. New York: New Century Co., 1919.

1103. Work, Monroe N. "The Negro and Democracy," Southern Workman, Vol. 42, May, 1918, pp. 219–222.

1104. _____, Editor. Negro Year Book, An Annual Encyclopedia of the Negro. Tuskegee Institute, AL: Negro Year Book Co. See 1916–1917 Edition, pp. 62–64; 1918–1919 Edition, pp. 125–129, 215–228; 1921–1922 Edition, pp. 189–193; 1925–1926 Edition, pp. 250–253.

1105. York, William H. "Soldiers," Crisis, Vol. 7, January, 1914, p. 212.

1106. Young, Charles. "Soldiers," Crisis, Vol. 11, January, 1916, p. 130.

VII.

Blacks in World War II

1107. "A General (Joseph T. McNarney) on Negroes," <u>Newsweek</u>, Vol. 28, September, 1942, p. 25.

1108. "A London Diary," <u>New Statesman and Nation</u>, Vol. 21, August 22, 1942, p. 121.

1109. "A Negro Enlisted Man, Jim Crow in the Army Camps," <u>Crisis</u>, Vol. 47, December, 1940, p. 385.

1110. "A Negro in the Army," <u>New Republic</u>, Vol. 110, June 26, 1944, p. 851.

1111. "A Negro Pursuit Squadron," <u>Opportunity</u>, Vol. 19, April, 1941, pp. 98-99.

1112. "A New War Song Inspired By Corporal Joe Louis," <u>New York Sunday Mirror</u>, July 5, 1942, pp. 2, 15.

1113. "A White Folk's War," <u>Common Ground</u>, Vol. 2, Spring, 1942, pp. 28-31.

1114. "Accomplishments of Bilalian U.S. Pilots in World War II Recounted," <u>Bilalian News</u>, August 22, 1980, p.7.

1115. "Air Corps," <u>Crisis</u>, Vol. 49, February, 1942, p. 51.

1116. "Air Forces Used Women Mechanics," <u>East Tennessee News</u>, December 17, 1942.

1117. "Air Pilots, But Segregated," <u>Crisis</u>, Vol. 48, February, 1941, p. 39.

1118. Alder, Morris H. "The Management of the Maladjusted Soldier at the Basic Training Center," <u>Journal of Clinical Psychopathology</u>, Vol. 7, April, 1946, pp. 713-729.

1119.   Alan, M. Osur. Blacks in the Army, Air Force During
        World War II: The Problem of Race Relation. Washing-
        ton, DC: Office of Air Force History, 1977.

1120.   Aldridge, Madeline L. "Let's Look at the Record,"
        Opportunity, Vol. 23, Winter, 1945, pp. 4,13, 30-43.

1121.   Alexander, Raymond Pace. The Negro Soldier in the
        United States Army-With Certain Recommendations.
        Philadelphia: The Author, 1950.

1122.   "Along the N.A.A.C.P. Battle Front," Crisis, Vol. 51,
        July, 1944, p. 226.

1123.   "Along the N.A.A.C.P. Battle Front," Crisis, Vol. 50,
        December, 1943, p. 371.

1124.   American Battle Monuments Commission. 92nd Division
        Summary of Operations in the World War. Washington,
        DC: United States Government Printing Office, 1944.

1125.   _____. 93rd Division
        Summary of Operations in the World War. Washington,
        DC: United States Government Printing Office, 1944.

1126.   "American Nazism," Opportunity, Vol. 19, February,
        1941, p. 35.

1127.   "American Negro as a Fighting Man," Review of Reviews,
        Vol. 58, August, 1918, pp. 210-211.

1128.   Amidon, Beulah. "Negroes and Defense," Survey Graphic,
        Vol. 30, June, 1941, pp. 320-326.

1129.   "An Immoral Cultural Lag: Our War Treatment of
        Negroes," Frontier of Democracy, February, 1942, pp.
        134-135.

1130.   Anderson, Trezzvant W. Come Out Fighting: The Epic
        of the 761st Tank Battalion, 1942-1945. Salzburg,
        Austria: Salsburger Druckerci, 1945, pp. 15-21.

1131.   Aptheker, Herbert. "Literacy, The Negro and World War
        II," Journal of Negro Education, Vol. 15, Fall, 1946,
        pp. 595-602.

1132.   "Armed Forces," Our World, Vol. 5, June, 1950, pp.
        11-35.

1133.   "Armed Service Jim Crow Policy Ends," Crisis, Vol. 56,
        May, 1940, p. 137.

1134.   "Army Air Corps," Crisis, Vol. 47, November, 1940,
        p. 358.

1135.   "Army Air Corps Smoke Screen," Crisis, Vol. 48, April,
        1941, p. 103.

1136.   "Army Court Convicts 4 Negro Wacs of Disobeying Super-
        ior," Washington Post, March 21, 1945, p. 4.

1137.   "Army Can Have Jim Crow in Selective Services Act,"
        Crisis, Vol. 48, January, 1941, p. 22.

1138.   "Army Labor Battalions," Crisis, Vol. 45, April, 1944,
        p. 104.

1139.   Army Service Forces. Leadership and the Negro Soldier.
        Washington, DC: United States Government Printing
        Office, 1933. Vol. 5.

1140.   Army Services Manual M5, Leadership and the Negro
        Soldier. Heardquarters, Army Service Forces, October,
        1944.

1141.   "Aviation Ground Service Training For Negroes at Tus-
        kegee," Opportunity, Vol. 19, October, 1941, p. 313.

1142.   Baker, Warren. "North of the Border (Negro Troops
        Help Build the Alcan Military Highway)," Negro Digest,
        Vol. 1, March, 1943, pp. 39-41.

1143.   Becker, John. "Mixed Division," Commonweal, June 19,
        1942, p. 206.

1144.   Beecher, John. "S.S. Booker T. Washington," New Re-
        public, Vol. 111, October 2, 1944, pp. 421-423.

1145.   _____. "This is the Picture," Common Ground,
        No. 4, 1943, pp. 11-16.

1146.   Beighlter, Robert S. The Negro in the Armed Forces.
        Unpublished Thesis, Army Pentagon Library, 1948.

1147.   Bekessy, Jean. Walk in Darkness. Translated by
        Richard Hanser. New York: G.P. Pubnam's Sons, 1948.

1148.   Bell, W.Y.,Jr. "The Negro Warrior's Homefront,"
        Phylon, Vol. 5, Third Quarter, 1944, pp. 271-278.

1149.   Benet, William Rose. "The Phoenix Nest," Saturday
        Review of Literature, Vol. 27, March 18, 1944, p. 28.

1150.   Bergman, William C. The Politics of Civil Rights in
        the Truman Administration. Columbus, OH: Ohio State
        University Press, 1970.

1151.   Berry, Mary Frances and John W. Blassingame. Long
        Memory: The Black Experience in America. New York:
        Oxford University Press, 1982. See "Service in the
        Second World War," pp. 320-328.

1152.   "Black and White in America and Britain," New States-
        man and Nation, Vol. 161, August 4, 1945, p. 74.

1153. "Black and White Rape," Crisis, Vol. 51, July, 1944, p. 217.

1154. "Black Division," Time, Vol. 51, December 29, 1941, p. 49.

1155. Black, Lowell D. "The Negro Volunteer Militia Units of the Ohio National Guard, 1870–1954: The Struggle for Military Recognition and Equality in the State of Ohio." Unpublished Doctoral Dissertation, Ohio State University, 1976.

1156. Blook, Kathryn. "Women Warriors," Pulse, Vol. 1, December, 1943, pp. 20–21.

1157. Bolte, Charles G. and Louis Harris. Negro Veterans. New York: New York Public Affairs Committee, 1947.

1158. Bond, Horace M. "Should the Negro Care Who Wins the War?," The Annals, Vol. 223, September, 1942, pp. 81–84.

1159. Bowen, Paul. "The Historical Background of the Negro as A Soldier," Virginia Teachers Bulletin, Vol. 17, November, 1940, pp. 29–31.

1160. Bowker, Benjamin C. Out of Uniform. New York: Norton, 1946.

1161. Bradford, Roark. "Black Bullets For Hitler," Negro Digest, Vol. 1, February, 1943, pp. 25–28.

1162. Brearley, H.C. "The Negro's New Belligerency," Phylon, Vol. 5, 4th Quarter, 1944, pp. 339–371.

1163. Brown, Earl. "American Negroes and the War," Harper's Magazine, Vol. 184, April, 1942, pp. 545–552.

1164. _____. "Colored Soldiers, U.S.A.," Survey Graphic, Vol. 31, November, 1942, pp. 475–477, 563.

1165. _____ and George R. Leighton. The Negro and the War. New York: Public Affairs Committee, 1942.

1166. Brown, Nugent. "Tuskegee, World's Only Army Flying School For Negroes," Service, Vol. 7, September, 1942, pp. 9–10.

1167. Brown, Sterling A. "Out of Their Mouths," Survey Graphic, Vol. 31, November, 1942, p. 485.

1168. Brown, Wesley A. "First Negro Graduate of Annapolis Tells His Story," Saturday Evening Post, Vol. 221, June 25, 1949, pp. 26–27, 111.

1169.   "Brown Women Making History As American Pilots," Black
         Dispatch, January 23, 1943, p. 1.

1170.   Brunson, Sergeant Warren J.   "What a Negro Soldier
         Thinks About," Social Service Review, Vol. 18, Decem-
         ber, 1944.

1171.   Buchan, A. Russell.   Black Americans in World War II.
         Santa Barbara, CA: CLIO Press, 1977.

1172.   Buck, Al.   "Louis Helps Boost Morale of Soldiers,"
         New York Post, March 17, 1942, p. 9.

1173.   Bunche, Ralph J.   "The Negro in the Political Life of
         the United States," Journal of Negro Education, Vol.
         10, July, 1941, pp. 567-584.

1174.   Bureau of Naval Personnel.   Guide to Command of Negro
         Naval Personnel. Washington, DC: Navy Department,
         1944.

1175.   Burnham, Louis E.   "These Are Our Heroes," Negro Digest,
         Vol. 2, February, 1944, pp. 47-49.

1176.   Burns, Ben.   "United They Fight," Negro Digest, Vol. 2,
         February, 1944, pp. 47-49.

1177.   _____.   "Democracy Afloat," Crisis, Vol. 52,
         April, 1945, pp. 107-108.

1178.   Butler, Mary Frances.   "For What Are the Negroes
         Fighting?," Scholastic, May 15, 1944, pp. 3, 8.

1179.   Byers, Jean.   A Study of the Negro in Military Service.
         Washington, DC: United States Department of Defense,
         1950.

1180.   Caliver, Ambrose, Editor.   Post War Education of
         Negroes: Educational Implications of Negro Veterans
         and War Workers. Washington, DC: Federal Security
         Agency, U.S. Office of Education, 1945.

1181.   Caproel, Joan.   "Big Welcome In Britain For Negro
         WACS," P.M., February 14, 1945.

1182.   Carter, Elmer A.   "A Negro Pursuit Squadron," Oppor-
         tunity, Vol. 19, April, 1941, pp. 98-99.

1183.   _____.   "Brigadier General Benjamin O. Davis,"
         Opportunity, Vol. 18, November, 1940, p. 323.

1184.   _____.   "Defense Industry," Opportunity,
         Vol. 19, October, 1941, pp. 290-291.

1185.   _____.   "Negro Medical Officers," Opportunity,
         Vol. 19, June, 1941, p. 163.

1186.   Carter, Elmer A. "The Army Makes a Discovery," _Opportunity_, Vol. 19, June, 1941, p. 162.

1187.   _____. "The Negro in the U.S. Army," _Opportunity_, Vol. 18, July, 1940, p. 195.

1188.   _____. "The Negro Pilot," _Opportunity_, Vol. 18, September, 1940, p. 258.

1189.   _____. "The 369th Departs," _Opportunity_, Vol. 19, February, 1941, p. 35.

1190.   _____. "Trouble in the South," _Opportunity_, September, 1941, p. 258.

1191.   _____. "The Negroes and War," _Opportunity_, Vol. 18, May, 1940, pp. 130-131.

1192.   Carter, Joseph. _The History of the 14th Armored Division_. Atlanta: Love, n.d.

1193.   Carter, Vincent D. _The Bern Book: A Record of a Voyage of the Mind_. New York: John Day, 1973. Author discusses his military experiences in Europe in the U.S. Army during World War II.

1194.   Caudill, William A. _Negro G.I.s Come Back_. Chicago: The Clearing House, American Council on Race Relations, 1945.

1195.   Cayton, Horace R. "Negro Morale," _Opportunity_, Vol. 19, December, 1941, pp. 371-375.

1196.   _____. "Fighting For White Folk?," _Nation_, Vol. 155, September 26, 1942, pp. 267-270.

1197.   _____. "The Negro's Challenge," _Nation_, Vol. 156, July 3, 1943, pp. 10-11.

1198.   Cheers, Michael. "Black World War II Tank Unit Gets Presidential Award," _Jet_, Vol. 55, February 23, 1978, pp. 76-77.

1199.   Chivers, Walter R. "Trend of Race Relations in the South During War Times," _Journal of Negro Education_, Vol. 13, January, 1944, pp. 104-111.

1200.   Christian, Marcus B. "James Lewis," _Negro History Bulletin_, Vol. 5, March, 1942, p. 139.

1201.   Clark, Kenneth B. "Morale of the Negro on the Home Front: World Wars I and II," _Journal of Negro Education_, Vol. 13, July, 1943, pp. 417-428.

1202.   Clarke, John. _Black Soldier_. Garden City, NY: Doubleday, 1968.

1203.   Clement, Rufus. "Problems of Demobilization and Re-
        habilitation of the Negro Soldier After World Wars I
        and II," Journal of Negro Education, Vol. 12, July,
        1943, pp. 553-542.

1204.   "Coast Guard Officers," Crisis, Vol. 51, July, 1944,
        p. 234.

1205.   Cocklin, Robert F. "Report on the Negro Soldier,"
        Infantry Journal, Vol. 54, December, 1946, pp. 15-17.

1206.   Collier, John and Saul K. Padover. "An Institute for
        Ethnic Democracy," Common Ground, Vol. 4, August, 1943,
        pp. 3-7.

1207.   "Color, Unfinished Business of Democracy," Survey
        Graphic, Vol. 31, November, 1942, entire issue.

1208.   "Colored Officer Candidates Included in the WAAC,"
        Opportunity, Vol. 20, August, 1942, p. 249.

1209.   "Colored Troops in Britain," New Statesman and Nation,
        Vol. 24, August 22, 1942, p. 121.

1210.   "Colored WAAC Units With D.C. Officers Arrive in
        Arizona," Washington Star, December 1, 1942.

1211.   Commager, Henry S. "Negroes and the War," Scholastic,
        Vol. 42, March 8, 1942, p. 9.

1212.   "Congressman (Adam) Powell Asks F.D.R. to Commission
        Sgt. Joe Louis," Chicago Defender, March 17, 1945, p.18.

1213.   Cook, Lawrence Hugh. "The Brownsville Affray of 1906."
        Unpublished Master's Thesis, University of Colorado,
        1942.

1214.   Council For Democracy. The Negro and Defense: A Test
        of Democracy. New York: Council For Democracy, 1941.

1215.   _____ . The Negro in America: How We
        Treat Him and How We Should. New York: Council For
        Democracy, 1945.

1216.   Cripps, Thomas and D. Culbert. "Negro Soldier (During
        World War II) Film Propaganda in Black and White,"
        American Quarterly, Vol. 31, Winter, 1979, pp. 616-640.

1217.   Crumes, Coles, Sr. My Life Is An Open Book. New York:
        Carlton Press, 1965. Author discusses his military
        experiences in Africa and Italy during World War II.

1218.   Curran, Joseph. "How to Fight Racial Discrimination,"
        New Republic, Vol. 109, July 2, 1943, p. 49.

1219. Curtis, Constance H. "All Seamen Are The Same," _Crisis_, Vol. 50, January, 1943, pp. 26-28.

1220. Dabney, Virginius. "Nearer and Nearer the Precipice," _Atlantic Monthly_, Vol. 171, January, 1943, pp. 94-100.

1221. _____. "Press and Morale," _Saturday Review of Literature_, July 4, 1942, pp. 5-6, 24-25.

1222. Dalfiume, Richard M. "Desegregation of the United States Armed Forces, 1939-1953." Doctoral Dissertation, University of Missouri, 1966. See next entry.

1223. _____. _Desegregation of the United States Armed Forced Forces: Fighting on Two Fronts, 1939-1953_. Columbia, MO: University of Missouri Press, 1969. This is a revision of his dissertation.

1224. _____. "Military Segregation and the 1940 Presidential Election," _Phylon_, Vol. 30, Spring, 1969, pp. 42-55.

1225. Daniels, Jonathan. "New Patterns For Old," _Survey Graphic_, Vol. 31, November, 1942, pp. 485-487, 561.

1226. Davenport, Roy K. "Implications of Military Selection and Classification in Relation to Universal Military Training," _Journal of Negro Education_, Vol. 15, Fall, 1946, p. 590.

1227. _____. "The Negro in the Army: A Subject of Research," _Journal of Social Issues_, Vol. 3, Fall, 1947, pp. 32-39.

1228. David, Jay and Elaine Crane. _The Black Soldier-From the American Revolution to Vietnam_. New York: William Morrow and Co., 1971.

1229. Davis, Arthur P. "Will a Long War Aid the Negro," _Negro Digest_, Vol. 2, November, 1943, pp. 43-47.

1230. Davis, John A. "The Negro Outlook Today," _Survey Graphic_, Vol. 31, November, 1942, pp. 500-503, 562-563.

1231. Davis, John P., Editor. _The American Negro Reference Book_. Englewood Cliffs, NY: Prentice-Hall, 1966. See Section on "Negro Soldier."

1232. Davis, John W. "The Negro in the United States Navy, Marine Corps and Coast Guard," _Journal of Negro Education_, Vol. 12, July, 1943, pp. 345-349.

1233. Davis, Paul C. "The Negro in the Armed Service," _Virginia Quarterly Review_, Vol. 24, October, 1948, pp. 499-520.

1234.   Davis, Ralph N.   "The Negro Newspaper and the War,"
        Sociology and Social Research, Vol. 27, May, 1943,
        pp. 373-380.

1235.   Davis, Sammy, Jr.   Yes I Can.   New York: Farrar,
        Straus, 1965.   Author discusses his Army life, pp.
        51-74.

1236.   DeBow, Charles H.   "I Got Wings," American Magazine,
        Vol. 234, August, 1942, pp. 28-29†.

1237.   "Defeat at Detroit," Nation, Vol. 157, July 3, 1943,
        p. 4.

1238.   "Democracy for Fighters," Survey Midmonthly, Vol. 80,
        October, 1944, p. 291.

1239.   "Detroit Negro Worker Upgraded for Defense Production,"
        Opportunity, Vol. 20, March, 1942, p. 88.

1240.   Director of Selective Service.   Selective Service in
        Wartime,   2nd Report, 1941-1952.   Washington, DC:
        United States Government Printing Office, 1943.

1241.   _____ .   As the Tide of the War
        Turns,   3rd Report, 1943-1944.   Washington, DC: United
        States Government Printing Office, 1945.

1242.   _____ .   Selective Service and
        Victory,   4th Report, 1944-1945.   Washington, DC:
        United States Government Printing Office, 1948.

1243.   "Discrimination Softens Under Pressure," Christian
        Century, Vol. 61, March 8, 1944, p. 292.

1244.   Dollard, Charles and Donald Young.   "The Negro in the
        Armed Forces," Survey Graphic, Vol. 36, January, 1947,
        pp. 66-69, 111-116.

1245.   "Dorie Miller: First U.S. Hero of World War II,"
        Ebony, Vol. 25, December, 1969, pp. 132-138.

1246.   Douglas, Helen.   The Negro Soldier: A Partial Record
        of Negro Devotion and Heroism in the Cause of Freedom
        Gathered from the Files of the War and Navy Department.
        Washington, DC: United States Government Printing
        Office, 1946.

1247.   Driberg, Tom.   "Dixie Goes to Britain," Negro Digest,
        Vol. 2, December, 1943, pp. 15-16.

1248.   DuBois, W.E.B.   "An Essay Toward a History of the
        Black Man in the Great War," Crisis, Vol. 49, June,
        1942, pp. 63-87.

1249. DuBois, W.E.B. "The Black Man in the Revolution of
       1941-1942," Crisis, Vol. 49, March, 1942, pp. 218-223.

1250. _____. "The Negro Soldier in Service Abroad
       During the First World War," Journal of Negro Educa-
       tion, Vol. 12, July, 1943, pp. 342-334.

1251. DuBose, Carolyn. "'Chappie' James," Ebony, Vol. 25,
       October, 1970, pp. 152-154, 156.

1252. Durham Statement, Atlanta Statement, Richmond State-
       ment. Atlanta, GA: Commission on Interracial Cooper-
       ation, Inc., 1943.

1253. Eastland, James O. "Are Negroes Good Soldiers?,"
       Negro Digest, Vol. 4, December, 1945, pp. 28-30.

1254. Ebon, Martin. "The Negro Looks Abroad," Free World,
       May, 1945, pp. 64-65.

1255. Editorial. "Honor Given to World War II Heroes,"
       Chicago Defender, May 3, 1979, p. 9.

1256. Editorial. "How 'Practical' Is a Racially Segregated
       Army?," Politics, Vol. 1, July, 1944, pp. 184-185.

1257. Editorial. "Joe Louis Typifies Negro Patriotism,"
       (Louisville) Courier-Journal, January 20, 1942, p. 6.

1258. Editorial. "Negro Soldier (in World War II) Betrayed,"
       Crisis, Vol. 52, April, 1945, p. 97.

1259. Effrat, Louis. "Joe Louis Returns After Long Tour:
       Champion, in 14-Month Trip of 30,000 Miles, Entertained
       2,000,000 Service Men," New York Times, October 11,
       1944, p. 25.

1260. Embree, Edwin R. "Balance Sheet in Race Relations,"
       Atlantic Monthly, Vol. 175, May, 1945, pp. 87-91.

1261. _____. "For Whose Freedom," Asia, April,
       1942, pp. 221-224.

1262. _____. "Negroes and the Commonweal," Survey
       Graphic, Vol. 31, November, 1942, pp. 491-492, 494.

1263. Evans, James C. "Adult Education for Negroes in the
       Armed Forces," Journal of Negro Education, Vol. 14,
       Summer, 1945, pp. 437-442.

1264. _____ and David A. Lane, Jr. "Integration in
       the Armed Service," Annals, Vol. 304, March, 1956, pp.
       78-85.

1265. _____. The Negro in the Army, Policy and
       Practice. Washington, DC: United States Department
       of the Army, 1948.

1266.   Evers, Charles. Evers. Cleveland: World Publishing
        Co., 1971. Author discusses his military experiences
        in the Pacific with the U.S. Army during World War II.

1267.   "Experiment Proved?," Time, Vol. 42, September 20,
        1943, pp. 66-68.

1268.   "Exploits of Tuskegee Airmen in World War II," Atlanta
        World, August 7, 1980, p. 1.

1269.   "Fighting the Jim Crow Army," Crisis, Vol. 55, May,
        1948, p. 136.

1270.   "Fighters Over the World," Infantry Journal, March,
        1943, pp. 38-43.

1271.   Finch, Minnie. The NAACP: Its Fight For Justice.
        Metuchen, NJ: Scarecrow Press, 1981. See Chapter
        XIII, "World War II," pp. 101-114.

1272.   Finkle, Lee. "The Conservative Aims of Militant
        Rhetoric: Black Protest During World War II," Journal
        of American History, Vol. 60, December, 1973, pp. 692-
        713.

1273.   "First Bomber Pilots," Crisis, Vol. 51, January, 1944,
        p. 7.

1274.   "First Lieutenant Top Rank?," Crisis, Vol. 50, March,
        1943, p. 72.

1275.   "First Negro Officer Commissioned in U.S. Air Corps,"
        Opportunity, Vol. 20, April, 1942, p. 120.

1276.   "First WACS Overseas," Headlines, Vol. 1, March, 1945,
        p. 33.

1277.   "First Waves Win Praise," Headlines, Vol. 1, February,
        1945, p. 18.

1278.   Foner, Jack D. Blacks and the Military in American
        History: A New Perspective. New York: Praeger
        Publisher, 1974.

1279.   "For Manhood in National Defense," Crisis, Vol. 47,
        December, 1940, p. 375.

1280.   Ford, James W. The War and the Negro People. New
        York: Workers Library Publishers, 1942.

1281.   Ford, Nick Aaron. "What Negroes Are Fighting For,"
        Vital Speeches, Vol. 9, February 1, 1943, pp. 240-242.

1282.   Forman, Clark. "Race Tension in the South," New
        Republic, Vol. 107, September 21, 1942, pp. 340-342.

1283. "41st Engineers, the First Regiment of Negro Engineers in the New Army," _Time_, Vol. 38, July 21, 1941, pp. 32-33.

1284. Francis, Charles E. _Tuskegee Airman: The Story of the Negro in the ASAAF_. Boston: Bruce Humphries, 1955.

1285. _____. "Tuskegee Airman: The Story of the Negro in the U.S. Air Force," _Air Force Times_, Vol. 16, June 30, 1956, p. 25.

1286. Franklin, John Hope. _From Slavery to Freedom: A History of Negro Americans_. New York: Alfred A. Knopf, 1980. See "Negroes in the Service," pp. 428-444.

1287. Franklin, Zilpha C. "On the Local Front," _National Municipal Review_, December, 1942, pp. 620-621.

1288. Frazier, Edward Franklin. "Ethnic and Minority Groups in Wartime, With Special Reference to the Negro," _American Journal of Sociology_, Vol. 48, November, 1942, pp. 369-377.

1289. Fritz, Ernest W., Compiler. _393rd Infantry (99th Division) in Review: A Pictorial Account of 393rd Infantry Regiment in Combat, 1944-1945_. Salt Lake City: Robert E. Freed, 1946.

1290. "From Fighters to Laborers," _Crisis_, Vol. 51, May, 1944, p. 136.

1291. Furr, Arthur. _Democracy's Negroes: A Book of Facts Concerning the Activities of Negroes in World War II_. Boston: House of Edinboro, 1947.

1292. Gallagher, Buell B. "How Does Negro Youth Feel About the War?," _Frontiers of Democracy_, Vol. 9, November 15, 1942, pp. 42-44.

1293. Garvin, Charles. "The Negro in the Special Services of the United States Army: Medical Corps, Dental Corps, and Nurses Corps," _Journal of Negro Education_, Vol. 12, July, 1943, pp. 335-344.

1294. "Germany Meets the Negro Soldier," _Ebony_, Vol. 1, October, 1946, pp. 5-11.

1295. Ginzburg, Eli. _The Negro Potential_. New York: Columbia University Press, 1956. See "The Negro Soldier," pp. 61-91.

1296. Gleed, Col. Edward C. "The Story of America's Black Air Force," _Tony Brown's Journal_, January/March, 1983, pp. 4-7.

1297. "Good News," Crisis, Vol. 51, March, 1944, p. 72.

1298. Goodman, George W. "The Englishman Meets the Negro,"
       Common Ground, Vol. 5, Autumn, 1944, pp. 3-11.

1299. Gorham, Thelma Thurston. "Negro Army Wifes," Crisis,
       Vol. 50, January, 1943, pp. 21-23.

1300. "Government Blesses Separation," Crisis, Vol. 50,
       April, 1943, p. 105.

1301. Graham, Frank. "Joe Louis and the Army," New York Sun,
       October 15, 1941, p. 14.

1302. Granger, Lester B. "The Negro Views Peace," Far
       Eastern Survey, August 29, 1945, pp. 237-239.

1303. _____. "Negro Citizens in a Democracy at
       War," National Conference of Social Work, 1942, pp.
       119-128.

1304. _____. "Techniques in Race Relations,"
       Survey Midmonthly, December, 1943, pp. 322-326.

1305. _____. "Barriers to Negro War Employment,"
       Annals, Vol. 223, September, 1942, pp. 72-80.

1306. _____. "Victory Through Unity," Oppor-
       tunity, Vol. 21, October, 1943, pp. 147-151.

1307. _____. "Women Are Vital To Victory,"
       Opportunity, Vol. 21, April, 1943, p. 36.

1308. Graves, John Temple. "The Southern Negro and the War
       Crisis," Virginia Quarterly Review, October, 1942,
       pp. 500-517.

1309. Greenfield, Kent Roberts, et al. The Organization of
       Ground Combat Troops, United States Army in World War
       II. Washington, DC. United States Government Print-
       ing Office, 1947.

1310. Gregg, John A. Of Men and of Arms. Nashville, TN:
       A.M.E. Sunday School Union Press, 1945.

1311. Gregory, George, Jr. "Wartime Guidance For Tomorrow's
       Citizens," Opportunity, Vol. 21, April, 1943, pp. 70-
       71, 90.

1312. Grove, Gene. "The Army and the Negro," New York Times
       Magazine, July 24, 1966, pp. 4-5, 49-51.

1313. Guzman, Jessie P., Editor. Negro Year Book: A Review
       of Events Affecting Negro Life, 1914-1946. Tuskegee:
       Department of Records and Research of Tuskegee Insti-
       tute, 1947. See "Negro Soldiers in World War II."

1314. Hackey, Thomas. "Walter White and the American Negro
       Soldier in World War II: A Diplomatic Dilemma for
       Britain," Phylon, Vol. 39, September, 1978, pp. 241-
       249.

1315. Hall, E.T.,Jr. "Prejudice and Negro-White Relations
       in the Army," American Journal of Sociology, Vol. 52,
       March, 1947, pp. 401-409.

1316. Halsey, Margaret. "Memo to Junior Hostesses," Common
       Ground, No. 2, 1944, pp. 103-105.

1317. Hamlin, P.G. "Camptocormia: The Hysterical Bent Back
       Soldiers," Military Surgeon, Vol. 92, March, 1943, pp.
       295-300.

1318. Hampton Conference on Participation of the Negro in
       National Defense. VA: Hampton Institute, 1940.

1319. Hampton, Elizabeth C. "Negro Women and the WAAC,"
       Opportunity, Vol. 21, April, 1943, pp. 54-55, 93.

1320. Hanley, J. "Minority Report," Fortnightly, June, 1943,
       pp. 419-422.

1321. Hansen, Morris H., Compiler. Statistical Abstracts
       of the United States 1944-1945. Washington, DC:
       United States Government Printing Office, 1946, pp.
       174-177.

1322. Hard, William. "White and Black Can Work Together,"
       Reader's Digest, Vol. 44, March, 1944, pp. 17-22.

1323. Hargrove, Hondon. "Lt. John Fox's Bravery in World
       War II," Michigan Chronicle, February 28, 1981, p. A-1.

1324. Harris, Gabe. "Tenth Man Travels in Wartime," Service,
       Vol. 7, September, 1942, pp. 12-13.

1325. Harris, Paul Nelson. Base Company 16. New York:
       Vantage Books, 1963. Author discusses his military
       experiences in the U.S. Navy during World War II.

1326. Hastie, William Henry. The Negro in the Army Today.
       Philadelphia: American Academy of Political and
       Social Science, 1942.

1327. _____. On Clipped Wings: The Story
       of Jim Crow in the Army Air Corps. New York: National
       Association for the Advancement of Colored People, 1943.

1328. _____. "Negro in the Army Today,"
       Annals, Vol. 223, September, 1942, pp. 55-59.

1329. _____. "Negro Officers in Two World
       Wars," Journal of Negro Education, Vol. 123, July,
       1943, pp. 316-323.

1330.   Hausrath, Alfred H. "Utilization of Negro Manpower in
         the Army," Journal of the Operations Research Society
         of America, Vol. 2, February, 1954, pp. 17-30.

1331.   "Help for the Negro," Newsweek, Vol. 17, April 28,
         1941, p. 47.

1332.   Heningburg, Alphonse. "The Negro Veteran Comes Home,"
         Opportunity, Vol. 23, Winter, 1945, p. 3.

1333.   Henri, Florette. Bitter Victory: A History of Black
         Soldiers in World War II. Garden City, NY: Doubleday,
         1970.

1334.   Henry, John. "From a Negro Division," Common Sense,
         Vol. 21, January, 1943, pp. 457-459.

1335.   Hepburn, David. "Were Negro Soldiers Cowards?," Our
         World, March, 1947, p. 4.

1336.   Hershey, General Lewis B. "They're in the Army,"
         Negro Digest, Vol. 1, December, 1942, pp. 70-72.

1337.   Heymen, Dorothy. "Manifestations of Psychoneurosis in
         Negroes," Mental Hygiene, April, 1945, pp. 231-235.

1338.   Hicks, James L. "Negro WACS Barred From Overseas
         Stations By Top General's Orders," Call and Post,
         July 20, 1946, p. 1.

1339.   High, Stanley. "How the Negro Fights for Freedom,"
         Reader's Digest, Vol. 41, July, 1942, pp. 113-118.

1340.   Hinkson, D. "The Role of the Negro Physician in the
         Military Services from World War I through World War
         II," National Medical Association, January, 1972,
         pp. 75-76.

1341.   Hoegh, Leo A. and Howard J. Doyle. Timberwolf Tracks:
         The History of the 104th Infantry Division, 1942-1945.
         Washington: The Infantry Journal Press, 1946.

1342.   Holbrook, Stewart H. "The First American WAC," Negro
         Digest, Vol. 3, November, 1944, pp. 39-43.

1343.   "Honors for Negroes," Time, Vol. 43, May 29, 1944, p.62.

1344.   Hornsby, Henry Haywood. The Trey of Sevens. Dallas,
         TX: Mathis, Van Nortand Co., 1946.

1345.   Houser, George M. Erasing the Color. New York:
         Fellowship Publications, 1945.

1346.   Houston, Charles H. "Critical Summary: The Negro in
         the United States Armed Forces in World Wars I and II,"
         Journal of Negro Education, Vol. 12, July, 1943, pp.
         364-366.

1347.   Houston, Charles H.   "The Negro Soldier," Nation, Vol.
        159, October 21, 1944, pp. 496-497.

1348.   "How About Navy Pilots?," Crisis, Vol. 49, October,
        1943, p. 295.

1349.   "How Sgt. Joe Louis Sees the War," PM, April 8, 1945.

1350.   Hudson, Roy.   Post-War Jobs for Veterans, Negroes,
        Women.   New York: Workers Library, 1944.

1351.   Hurd, Charles.   "Democracy Challenged," Opportunity,
        Vol. 23, Spring, 1945, pp. 53-65.

1352.   Imbert, Dennis I.   The Negro After the War.   New
        Orleans, n.p., 1943.

1353.   "In Step! For America's Victory-To-Be," Pulse, Vol. 1,
        September, 1943, pp. 28-29.

1354.   Information and Education Division, Army Service
        Forces.   Opinions About Negro Infantry Platoons in
        White Companies of 7 Divisions Based on Survey Made
        in May-June, 1945.   Washington, DC: n.p., 1945.

1355.   "Items: Negro Soldiers," Monthly Summary of Events
        and Trends in Race Relations, February, 1945, p. 204.

1356.   Jackson, George F.   Black Women Makers of History: A
        Portrait.   Sacramento: Fong and Fong, 1977.   See
        "Military," pp. 279-283.

1357.   James, Parker.   "What Does War Prosperity Mean to the
        Negro?," Advertising and Selling, Vol. 36, February,
        1943, pp. 111-112.

1358.   "James Reese, Leader of World War II Jazz Band," Mich-
        igan Chronicle, February 21, 1981, p. C-6.

1359.   Janeway, Eliot.   "Fighting a White Man's War," Asia,
        January, 1943, p. 5.

1360.   Jefferson, Richard R.   "Negro Employment in St. Louis
        War Production," Opportunity, Vol. 22, Summer, 1944,
        pp. 116-119.

1361.   Jenkins, Martin D. et al.   The Black and White of
        Rejection for Military Service.   Montgomery, AL:
        American Teachers Association, 1944.

1362.   "Jim Crow Boomerang," Crisis, Vol. 49, October, 1943,
        p. 295.

1363.   "Jim Crow in the Army Camps, By A Negro Soldier,"
        Crisis, Vol. 49, December, 1940, p. 385.

1364.   "Joe Louis, Boxer, Honored by Army: 'Legion of Merit'
        Presented for His Exhibition in Camps Here and Over-
        seas," New York Times, September 24, 1945.

1365.   "Joe Louis: Example of How to Beat Hitler," New York
        Daily Worker, April 1, 1942, p. 4.

1366.   "Joe Louis Knocks Out (Abe) Simon for Second Time and
        Keeps His Championship: Negro Donates Entire Purse
        (ca.$45,000) to Army Emergency Relief," New York Herald-
        Tribune, March 28, 1942.

1367.   "Joe Louis Right: 'We're on God's Side'," Brown Amer-
        ican, Winter/Spring, 1944, p. 6.

1368.   "Joe Louis Visits Army Hospital in England," Pulse,
        Vol. 2, August, 1944, p. 31.

1369.   Johnson, Campbell Carrington. Fifty Years of Progress
        in the Armed Forces. Pittsburgh: Pittsburgh Courier,
        1950.

1370.   _____. "The Mobilization of
        Negro Manpower for the Armed Forces," Journal of Negro
        Education, Vol. 12, July, 1943, pp. 298-306.

1371.   _____. "The Unforgotten Man:
        The Negro Soldier," Opportunity, Vol. 23, Winter,1945,
        pp. 20-23, 54.

1372.   Johnson, Charles S. "The Negro," American Journal of
        Sociology, Vol. 47, May, 1942, pp. 854-864.

1373.   _____. "The Negro and the Present Crisis,"
        Journal of Negro Education, Vol. 10, July, 1941, pp.
        585-595.

1374.   _____. "The Negro in Post-War Reconstruc-
        tion: His Hopes, Fears and Possibilities," Journal of
        Negro Education, Vol. 11, October, 1942, pp. 465-470.

1375.   _____. "The Present Status of Race Re-
        lations in the South," Social Forces, Vol. 23, October,
        1944, pp. 27-32.

1376.   _____ and Associates. To Stem This Tide.
        Boston: Pilgrim Press, 1943, pp. 81-119.

1377.   Johnson, Ernest E. "Should Negroes Save Democracy?,"
        Scribner's Commentator, Vol. 11, November, 1941, pp.
        57-62.

1378.   Johnson, Guion Griff. "The Impact of War Upon the
        Negro," Journal of Negro Education, Vol. 10, July,
        1941, pp. 596-611.

1379.   Johnson, Haynes and George C. Wilson. Army in Anguish.
        New York: Pocket Books, 1972.

1380.   Johnson, Jesse J. Black Armed Forces Officers, 1936-
        1971. Hampton, VA: Hampton Institute, 1971.

1381.   _____. Black Women in the Armed Forces,
        1942-1974. Hampton, VA: Hampton Institute, 1974.

1382.   _____. Ebony Brass: An Autobiography of
        Negro Frustration Amid Aspiration. New York: Wil-
        liams-Frederick Press, 1967.

1383.   Johnson, J.R. Why Negroes Should Oppose the War.
        New York: Pioneer Publishers, 1939.

1384.   Johnson, Mordecai. "Negro Opportunity and National
        Morale," National Educational Association Journal, Vol.
        30, September, 1941, pp. 167-168.

1385.   Johnson, Reginald A. "In-Migration and the Negro
        Worker," Opportunity, Vol. 23, Spring, 1945, pp. 102-
        103.

1386.   Jollies, Naomi. "Four Negro Wacs Convicted-NAACP
        Leader Calls It Fair," New York Post, March 21, 1945.

1387.   Jones, Charles, Jr. "Black Soldiers in the National
        Guard, 1877-1949." Unpublished Doctoral Dissertation,
        Howard University, 1976.

1388.   Jones, Claudia. Jim Crow in Uniform. New York: New
        Age Publishers, 1940.

1389.   Jones, Lester M. "The Editorial Policy of Negro News-
        papers of 1917-1918 as Compared with That of 1941-1942,"
        Journal of Negro History, Vol. 29, January, 1944, pp.
        24-31.

1390.   Jones, Lucius. "Joe Louis' Tour of Army Camps of
        Nation Rekindles Interest Among Soldiers in His Illus-
        trious Career," Pittsburgh Courier, October 30, 1943,
        p. 17.

1391.   Jones, William. "Trade Boycotts," Opportunity, Vol.
        18, August, 1940, pp. 238-241.

1392.   Julian, Hubert Fauntleroy. Black Eagle. London:
        Jarrolds, 1964. Author discusses his military ex-
        periences in the U.S. Army during World War II.

1393.   Julian, Joseph. "Jim Crow Goes Abroad," Nation, Vol.
        155, December 5, 1942, pp. 610-612.

1394.   Karig, Walter and Kelley Wellbourn. Battle Report:
        Pearl Harbor to Coral Sea. New York: Farrar and
        Rinehart, 1944.

1395. Karolevitz, Robert F., Captain, Editor. The 25th Division and World War 2. Baton Rouge: Army and Navy Publishing Co., 1946.

1396. Kenworthy, E.W. "Taps for Jim Crow in the Services,"
New York Times Magazine, July 11, 1950, pp. 12, 24-27.

1397. _____ "The Case Against Army Segregation,"
Annals of the American Academy of Political and Social
Science, Vol. 275, May, 1951, pp. 27-33.

1398. King, Spencer Bidwell. Selective in North Carolina in
World War II. Chapel Hill: University of North Carolina Press, 1949.

1399. Klineberg, Otto. "Race Prejudice and the War," Annals,
Vol. 224, September, 1942, pp. 190-198.

1400. _____. Social Psychology. New York: Henry
Holt and Co., 1940.

1401. Klucholn, Frank L. "U.S. Negro Troops Crack Bougain-
ville Foe: Some from Harlem in Spirited Action," New
York Times, March 17, 1944, pp. 3-4.

1402. Koger, Azzie Briscoe. The Maryland Negro in Our Wars.
Baltimore: Clarke Press, 1942.

1403. _____. The Maryland Negro in Our Wars.
Baltimore: Clarke Press, 1944.

1404. LaFarge, Father John. "Our Jim Crow Army, America,
October, 1940.

1405. Lambert, Frank. "The Negro As A Military Airman,"
Flying and Popular Aviation, June, 1942, pp. 33, 34,
66, 68, 70.

1406. Lane, Layle. "The Negro and National Defense,"
American Teacher, Vol. 25, March, 1941, pp. 39-41.

1407. Lanier, R. O'Hara. "What the Negro Faces in A World
at War," Frontiers of Democracy, Vol. 8, March, 1940,
pp. 168-170.

1408. Lardner, John. "Jap Hunt on Saipan," Negro Digest,
Vol. 3, July, 1945, pp. 3-6.

1409. Lauiter, Louis. "Sidelights on the Negro and the Army,"
Opportunity, Vol. 22, Winter, 1944, pp. 5-8.

1410. Lawrence, Charles Radford. "Negro Organization in
Crisis: Depression, New Deal, World War II." Unpublished Doctoral Dissertation, Columbia University, 1953.

1411. Leach, Paul R. "Zero Hour for Black Doughboys,"
      Negro Digest, Vol. 2, December, 1943, pp. 83-84.

1412. Lee, Alfred M. "Subversive Individuals of Minority
      Status," Annals of the American Academy of Political
      and Social Science, Vol. 223, September, 1942, pp.
      167-168.

1413. Lee, Chauncey. "USO Camp Shows and the Soldier,"
      Crisis, Vol. 51, February, 1944, pp. 50, 61.

1414. Lee, Ulysses G., Jr. The United States Army in World
      War II, Special Studies: The Employment of Negro
      Troops. Washington, DC: United States Government
      Printing Office, 1966.

1415. Lee, Wallace. "Are Negroes Treated Better in This
      War Than in World War I," Negro Digest, Vol. 2, Janu-
      ary, 1944, p. 76.

1416. _____. "Are Negroes Good Soldiers?," Negro
      Digest, Vol. 3, December, 1945, pp. 28-33.

1417. Leigh, Randolph. 48 Million Tons to Eisenhower.
      Washington: The Infantry Journal, 1945.

1418. Leiser, Ernest. "For Negroes It's A New Army Now,"
      Saturday Evening Post, Vol. 225, December 13, 1952,
      pp. 26-27, 108, 110-112.

1419. "Let This People Fight Full Citizenship Rights for the
      Negro, A Crucial Issue in Winning the War," New Masses,
      Vol. 45, October, 1942, pp. 2-3.

1420. "Letters From the Jim Crow Army," Twice A Year, Fall/
      Winter, 1946-1947; New Republic, Vol. 110, March 13,
      1944, pp. 339-342.

1421. Lewis, Alfred Baker. "Reducing Racial Tension,"
      Opportunity, Vol. 21, October, 1943, pp. 156-157, 174.

1422. Lewis, Edward S. "Progress in Interracial Relation-
      ships," National Conference of Social Work, 1943, pp.
      277-289.

1423. Lewis, Robert. "Negroes Under Fire," The Progressive
      and La Follette's Magazine, Vol. 9, September 3, 1945,
      p. 4.

1424. Lewis, Roscoe L. "The Role of Pressure Grows in Main-
      taining Moral Among Negroes," Journal of Negro Educa-
      tion, Vol. 12, Summer, 1943, pp. 464-473.

1425. Lewis, Walter. "Brief History of 761st Tank Battalion
      in World War II," Negro History Bulletin, Vol. 29,
      November, 1965, pp. 46-47.

1426. Liebling, A.J. "Rolling Umpty-Seventh I," New Yorker,
       Vol. 107, December 5, 1942, pp. 52, 57-66.

1427. _____. "Rolling Umpty-Seventh II," New Yorker,
       Vol. 107, December 12, 1942, pp. 47-48, 53-54, 57-58.

1428. Lindenmeyer, Otto. Black and Brave: The Black Soldier
       in America. New York: McGraw Hill Co., 1970.

1429. Little, K.L. "Coloured Troops in Britain," New States-
       man and Nation, Vol. 21, August 29, 1942, p. 141.

1430. Lochard, Metz T.P. "Negroes and Defense," Nation,
       Vol. 152, January 4, 1941, pp. 14-16.

1431. _____. "Negro Soldiers," Scholastic, Vol.
       37, October 21, 1940, p. 2.

1432. Locke, Alain. "The Unfinished Business of Democracy,"
       Survey Graphic, Vol. 31, November, 1942, pp. 454-459.

1433. Logan, Rayford, Editor. What the Negro Wants. Chapel
       Hill: University of North Carolina Press, 1944.

1434. Logan, Spencer. A Negro's Faith in America. New York:
       Macmillan Co., 1946. Chapter 6, "The Negro Soldier,"
       pp. 61-80. About Negro soldiers in World War II.

1435. Long, Howard H. "The Negro Soldier in the Army of the
       United States," Journal of Negro Education, Vol. 12,
       July, 1943, pp. 307-315.

1436. Louis, Joe. My Life Story. New York: Duell, Sloan
       & Pearce, 1947. Author discusses his military exper-
       iences in the U.S. Army during World War II.

1437. "Louis Lands GI Boxer in Alaska," Pittsburgh Courier,
       September 8, 1945, p. 12.

1438. Low, Nat. "The War Department Is Sending Joe Lewis
       on an Exhibition Tour of the World," People Voice,
       July 14, 1943, p. 3.

1439. "Lynching and Liberty," Crisis, Vol. 47, July, 1940,
       p. 209.

1440. Macy, J. Noel. "Negro Women in the Wac," Opportunity,
       Vol. 23, Winter Issue, 1945, p. 14.

1441. MacDonald, Dwight. "The Novel Case of Winifred Lynn,"
       Nation, Vol. 156, February 20, 1943, pp. 268-270.

1442. _____. "The Supreme Court's New Moot Suit,"
       Nation, Vol. 159, July 1, 1944, pp. 13-14.

1443. MacDonald, Nancy and Dwight MacDonald. The War's
       Greatest Scandal! The Story of Jim Crow in Uniform.
       New York: The March on Washington Movement, 1943.

1444. MacGregor, Morris J. and Bernard C. Nalty, Editors.
       Blacks in the United States Armed Forces: Basic Docu-
       ments. Wilmington, DE: Scholarly Resources Inc., 1977,
       Vol. V, "Black Soldiers in World War II."

1445. _____.
       Blacks in the United States Armed Forces: Basic Docu-
       ments. Wilmington, DE: Scholarly Resources Inc., 1977,
       Vol. VI, "Blacks in the World War II and Naval Estab-
       lishment."

1446. Madden, Samuel H. A Brief Consideration of the Ameri-
       can Negro Soldiers. W.P.A. Public Archives Programs,
       Washington, DC: United States Government Printing
       Office, 1942.

1447. Maey, J. Noel. "Negro Women in the Wac," Opportunity,
       Vol. 23, Winter, 1945, p. 14.

1448. "Magazine Comment: Negro Soldiers," Monthly Summary
       of Events and Trends in Race Relations, January, 1945,
       p. 178.

1449. "Magazine Comment: Negro Soldiers," Monthly Summary
       of Events and Trends in Race Relations, September,
       1944, p. 48.

1450. Mandelbaum, David G. Soldier Groups and Negro Soldier,
       Berkeley, CA: University of California Press, 1952.

1451. "Maneuvers Show 93rd is Ready," Crisis, Vol. 50, June,
       1943, pp. 170-172.

1452. "Manpower Needs and Negro Soldiers," Christian Century,
       April 12, 1944, p. 451.

1453. "Many Women Replace Men," Black Dispatch, April 10,
       1943, p. 1.

1454. Marshall, S.L.A. Bastogne: The First Eight Days.
       Washington: The Infantry Journal Press, 1946.

1455. Martin, Harold H. "How Do Our Negro Troops Measure
       Up?," Saturday Evening Post, Vol. 193, June 16, 1951,
       pp. 30-31, 139, 141.

1456. Martin, Louis. "Fifth Column Among Negroes," Opportun-
       ity, Vol. 20, December, 1942, pp. 358-360.

1457. Martin, Ralph G. "Where Is Home?," New Republic, Vol.
       113, December 31, 1945, pp. 898-900.

1458. Matthews, Ernest L. Out of Bounds. New York: Univer-
       sal Publishing and Distributing Corp., 1954.

1459. Mays, Benjamin E. "Negroes and the Will to Justice,"
       Christian Century, Vol. 59, October 28, 1942, pp. 1316-
       1318.

1460. McCay, Donald R. and Richard S. Ruettan. Quest and
       Response. Lawrence, KS: University of Kansas Press,
       1973.

1461. McCulloch, Margaret. "What Should the American Negro
       Expect as the Outcome of a Real Peace?," Journal of
       Negro Education, Vol. 12, July, 1943, p. 557.

1462. McFadden, Iva M. "Women Answer America's Call," Pulse,
       Vol. 1, February, 1943, p. 4.

1463. McGuire, Philip. "Black Civilian Aides and the Problems
       of Racism and Segregation in the United States Armed
       Forces: 1940-1950." Unpublished Doctoral Dissertation,
       Howard University, 1975.

1464. _____. Taps for a Jim Crow Army. Santa
       Barbara, CA: ABC-CLIO, 1983.

1465. McGuire, Robert.   "Black Soldiers Under Fire,"
       Negro Digest, Vol. 4, November, 1945, pp. 3-5.

1466. McKay, Claude. "Once More the Germans Face Black
       Troops," Opportunity, Vol. 17, November,1939, pp.
       324-328.

1467. McMillan, Lewis K. "Light Which Two World Wars Throw
       Upon the Plight of the American Negro," Journal of
       Negro Education, Vol. 12, July, 1943, pp. 429-437.

1468. McNatt, Isaac. "I Was a Seabee," Politics, Vol. 1,
       June, 1944, pp. 137-140.

1469. McWilliams, Carney. "How the Negro Fared in the War,"
       Negro Digest, Vol. 4, May, 1946, pp. 67-74.

1470. _____. "Race Tensions: Second Phase,"
       Common Ground, Vol. 4, Autumn, 1943, pp. 7-12.

1471. "Mean Navy Action," Crisis, Vol. 50, December, 1943,
       p. 359.

1472. Meyer, Agnes C. "The Negro and the Army," Washington
       Post, March 19, 26, 1944, p. 29.

1473. "Military and Industrial Centers Plan for Recreational
       Activities of Negro Soldiers and Industrial Workers,"
       National Municipal Review, Vol. 31, December, 1942,
       pp. 620-621.

1474.   Miller, Arthur. Situation Normal. New York: Reynal
        and Hitchcock, 1944.

1475.   Miller, Donald M. An Album of Black Americans in the
        Armed Forces. New York: Watts, 1969.

1476.   Miller, Elliott M. "The Negro in the Army," Nation,
        Vol. 160, January 9, 1945, p. 72.

1477.   Miller, Kelly. "Race Prejudice in Germany and America,"
        Opportunity, Vol. 14, April, 1936, pp. 102-105.

1478.   Millis, Walter. The Martial Spirit. New York: Twen-
        tieth Century Fund, 1959.

1479.   Milner, Lucille B. "Jim Crow in the Army," New Repub-
        lic, Vol. 110, March 13, 1944, pp. 339-342.

1480.   Milton, H.S., Editor. The Utilization of Negro Man-
        power in the Army. Chevy Chase, MD: Operations
        Research Office, The John Hopkins University, 1955.

1481.   "Mixed Troops Not Mixed," Crisis, Vol. 52, August, 1945,
        p. 216.

1482.   Moody, Harold A. "Coloured Soldiers," New Statesman
        and Nation, Vol. 21, September 5, 1942, p. 158.

1483.   Moon, Bucklin. The High Cost of Prejudice. New York:
        J. Messner Inc., 1947.

1484.   Moore, H. Randolph. "Negro-White Relations During
        Demobilization," Sociology and Social Research, Vol.
        28, July, 1944, pp. 464-470.

1485.   Moran, Isaac. "What Negro Youth Expects from National
        Defense," Crisis, Vol. 48, August, 1941, pp. 253-255.

1486.   "More Houston 'Martyrs'?," Commonweal, Vol. 34, Septem-
        ber 19, 1941, p. 509.

1487.   "More Negro Women Needed in Cadet Nurse Corps Program,"
        Education for Victory, September 20, 1944, p. 31.

1488.   "More Varied Jobs Offered WAACS," Oklahoma Eagle, March
        20, 1943, p. 4.

1489.   Morrill, M.A. "A White Man's War?," Christian Century,
        Vol. 57, April 22, 1940, pp. 531-532.

1490.   Morton, Mary A. "The Federal Government and Negro
        Morale," Journal of Negro Education, Vol. 12, July,
        1943, pp. 452-463.

1491.   "Mrs. Clyde Ward Recalls Life for Black WAACS in World
        War II," Los Angeles Sentinel, February 26, 1980, p.
        A-13.

1492. Mueller, Nina J. "The Negro in World War II and After."
       Unpublished Master's Thesis, University of Texas at
       Austin, 1947.

1493. Mueller, Ralph and Jerry Turk. Report After Action:
       The Story of the 103rd Infantry Division. Hq. 103rd
       Infantry Division, Innsbruck, Austria, 1945.

1494. Mueller, William G. "The Negro in the Navy," Social
       Forces, Vol. 24, October, 1945, pp. 110-115.

1495. Mullen, Robert W. Blacks in America's War: The Shift
       in Attitudes from the Revolutionary War to Vietnam.
       New York: Monad Press, 1973.

1496. Mulzac, Hugh N. A Start To Steer By. New York: In-
       ternational Publishers, 1963. The author, who was the
       first Black to captain a ship in the U.S. Merchant
       Marine in 1942, discusses his combat experiences during
       World War II.

1497. Murray, Florence, Editor. The Negro Handbook, 1949.
       New York: MacMillan Co., 1949.

1498. Murray, Paul Thom. "Blacks and the Draft: An Analysis
       of Institutional Racism, 1917-1971." Unpublished Doc-
       toral Dissertation, Florida State University, 1972.

1499. Myrdal, Gunnar. An American Dilemma: The Negro Prob-
       lem and Modern Democracy. New York: Harper, 1963.

1500. _____. "The Negro and America's Uneasy Con-
       science," Free World, November, 1943, pp. 413-422.

1501. "Myth of Race Equality in the Army," Nation, Vol. 153,
       August 23, 1941, pp. 150-151.

1502. Nash, Roy. "Selected Negro Artillerymen," Nation,
       Vol. 151, October 19, 1940, pp. 375-376.

1503. National Negro Congress. Defense Training and Jobs
       For Negroes, Our War-Time Responsibility and Opportunity.
       Washington, DC: National Negro Congress, 1942.

1504. _____. Negro People Will Defend
       America. Washington, DC: National Negro Congress, 1941.

1505. National Urban League. Racial Aspects of Conversion.
       New York: National Urban League, 1945, pp. 18-22.

1506. "Navy Christens Ship for Dorie Miller, Black Hero,"
       Jet, Vol. 44, July 19, 1973, p. 18.

1507. "Navy First," Headlines, Vol. 1, January, 1945, p. 28.

1508. "Navy Salutes Black Navy Musicians of World War II,"
       New York Amsterdam News, March 28, 1981, p. 31; Nor-
       folk Journal and Guide, February 18, 1981, p. 1.

1509. "Negro Artillery in World War II," Field Artillery
       Journal, Vol. 36, April, 1946.

1510. "Negro Churches Protest Race Bars in War Efforts,"
       Christian Century, Vol. 59, March 18, 1942, p. 341.

1511. "Negro Division," Life, Vol. 15, August 9, 1943, p. 37.

1512. "Negro Leader Utters Solemn Warning," Christian Century,
       Vol. 61, March 8, 1944, p. 293.

1513. Negro Manpower in the Army. Army Talk, No. 170, April
       12, 1947. Washington, DC: United States Government
       Printing Office, 1947.

1514. "Negro Morale and World War II," Journal of Negro Edu-
       cation, Vol. 11, January, 1942, pp. 1-3.

1515. "Negro Officers in Two World Wars," Journal of Negro
       Education, Vol. 12, Summer, 1943, pp. 316-323.

1516. "Negro Pilots Got Wings," Life, Vol. 14, March 23,
       1942, pp. 30-31.

1517. "Negro Rights," Life, Vol. 16, April 24, 1944, p. 32.

1518. "Negro Soldier: Moving Picture," Saturday Review
       Literary Magazine, Vol. 27, March 18, 1944, p. 28.

1519. "Negro Soldiers," Scholastic, Vol. 37, October 21, 1940,
       pp. 2-3.

1520. "Negro Soldiers Blame War Department," Christian Cen-
       tury, Vol. 61, November 8, 1944, p. 1278.

1521. "Negro Tank Outfit Repeats Bastogne," New York Times,
       March 5, 1945, p. 21.

1522. "Negro Troops in Combat," Monthly Summary of Events
       and Trends in Race Relations, September, 1945, p. 47.

1523. "Negro Troops Remove Seattle Snow," Crisis, Vol. 50,
       March, 1943, p. 88.

1524. "Negroes at War," Life, Vol. 12, June 15, 1942, pp.
       83-93.

1525. "Negroes at War; All They Want Now Is a Fair Chance to
       Fight," Life, Vol. 14, June 15, 1941, pp. 83-87.

1526.   "Negroes in the Army," New Republic, Vol. 111, December
        25, 1944, pp. 871-872.

1527.   "Negroes Who Have Received Army Awards During the Cur-
        rent War," Opportunity, Vol. 23, Winter Issue, 1945,
        pp. 41-43, 50.

1528.   Nelson, Dennis D. The Integration of the Negro into
        the United States Navy, 1776-1947. Washington, DC:
        Department of the Navy Publication NAVEXOS-p-526, 1948.

1529.   _____. The Integration of Negro into the
        United States Navy. New York: Farrar, Straus, 1951.

1530.   Nesbitt, George B. "The Negro Soldier Speaks," Oppor-
        tunity, Vol. 22, Summer, 1944, pp. 120-121.

1531.   Newcomb, Harold. "The All-Black Air Force," Airman,
        Vol. 21, January, 1977, pp. 24-31.

1532.   Nicholas, Franklin. "The Negro's Status in the War,"
        Interracial Review, Vol. 14, November, 1942, pp. 168-
        169.

1533.   Nichols, Lee. Breakthrough on the Color Front. New
        York: Random House, 1954.

1534.   "Ninety-ninth Squadron," Time, Vol. 39, August 3,1942,
        p. 17.

1535.   "99th Pursuit Squadron, All Negro," Time, Vol. 38,
        September 15, 1941, pp. 32-33.

1536.   "No (Army) Commission For Joe Louis," Chicago Defender,
        March 31, 1945, p. 1.

1537.   "No Compulsory Training," Crisis, Vol. 51, December,
        1944, p. 376.

1538.   "No Jim Crow Army-Navy," Crisis, Vol. 52, November,
        1945, p. 315.

1539.   "No Negro Nurses Wanted," Crisis, Vol. 52, February,
        1945, p. 40.

1540.   "Now is the Time Not to be Silent," Crisis, Vol. 49,
        January, 1942, p. 7.

1541.   O'Gara, H.P. "The GI's Morale," Infantry Journal, Vol.
        56, 1945, pp. 49-50.

1542.   "Omissions from Newsreels," Crisis, Vol. 51, February,
        1944, p. 39.

1543.   "One of the First Blacks in Women's Army Corps,"
        Norfolk Journal and Guide, September 15, 1982, p. 1.

1544.   "One to Sixty-Four White Doctors," Crisis, Vol. 50,
        April, 1943, p. 102.

1545.   Osur, Alan M.   "Black-White Relations in the U.S. Mili-
        tary, 1940-1972," Air University Review, Vol. 33, No-
        vember/December, 1981, pp. 69-78.

1546.   _____. "Negroes in the Army Air Forces During
        World War II: The Problem of Race Relations." Unpub-
        lished Doctoral Dissertation, University of Denver,
        1974.

1547.   Ottley, Roi. "A White Folks' War?," Common Ground,
        Vol. II, Spring, 1972, pp. 29-31.

1548.   _____. "Negro Moral," New Republic, Vol. 105,
        November 10, 1941, pp. 613-615.

1549.   _____. New World A' Coming. Boston: Houghton
        Mifflin Co., 1943, pp. 306-347.

1550.   Ovington, Mary White. The Walls Came Tumbling Down.
        New York: Schocken Books, 1947. See Black soldiers
        in World War II, pp. 279-282.

1551.   Padmore, George. "Black Cloud Over Berlin," Negro
        Digest, Vol. 2, October, 1944, pp. 75-76.

1552.   Palmer, Robert R. et al. The Procurement and Training
        of Ground Combat Troops in the Official History of the
        U.S. Army in World War II. Washington, DC: United
        States Government Printing Office, 1948.

1553.   Parks, Robert J. "The Development of Segregation in
        U.S. Army Hospitals, 1940-1942," Military Affairs, Vol.
        37, 1973, pp. 145-150.

1554.   Parrish, Noel F. "Reflections on the Tuskegee Experi-
        ment," Aerospace Historian, Vol. 24, September, 1977,
        pp. 173-180.

1555.   _____. "The Segregation of Negroes in the
        Army Air Forces." Unpublished Air University Thesis,
        Maxwell Field Alabama, 1947.

1556.   Paszek, Lawrence J. "Negroes and the Air Force, 1939-
        1949," Military Affairs, Vol. 31, Spring, 1967, pp. 1-
        10.

1557.   _____. "Separate, But Equal: The Story
        of the 99th Fighter Squadron," Aerospace Historian,
        Vol. 24, September, 1977, pp. 135-135.

1558.   Paul, Felix L. "Yeoman First Class: Negro," Survey
        Graphic, Vol. 36, August,1947, pp. 444-446, 453.

1559. Peck, James L. H. "When Do We Fly?," Crisis, Vol. 47,
       December, 1940, pp. 376-378, 388.

1560. Peck, Phillips J. "The Negro in the AAF," Flying, Vol.
       26, June, 1945, pp. 24-25, 121-128.

1561. Perry, Pettis. The Negro's Stake in This War. San
       Francisco: Yates Collection, 1942.

1562. Pickens, William. "The American Negro Participates in
       War Finance," Opportunity, Vol. 13, Winter, 1945, pp.
       24-25, 55.

1563. "Pilots for 99th Pursuit Squadron Begin Training at
       Tuskegee," Opportunity, Vol. 19, August, 1941, pp. 247-
       248.

1564. Pitts, Lucia Mae. One Negro WAC'S Story. Los Angeles:
       Privately Printed, 1968.

1565. Ploski, Harry A. et al. Reference Library of Black
       America. New York: Bellewether Publishing Co., 1971.
       See Chapter I, "Black Servicemen and the Military
       Establishment."

1566. "Police Brutality Destroying the Morale of Negro Sold-
       iers," Service, Vol. 7, October, 1942, p. 12.

1567. Powell, Adam Clayton, Jr. "Is This a White Man's War?,"
       Common Sense, Vol. 11, April, 1942, pp. 111-115.

1568. _____. Marching Blacks. New York:
       Dial Press, 1945.

1569. Prattis, P.L. "The Morale of the Negro in the Armed
       Services of the United States," Journal of Negro Edu-
       cation, Vol. 12, Summer, 1943, pp. 355-363.

1570. "Press and Morale," Saturday Review and Literature,
       Vol. 25, July 4, 1942, pp. 5-6, 24-25.

1571. "Private Joe Louis Now in Uniform," New York Sun, Jan-
       uary 16, 1941, p. 1.

1572. Qualey, J.S. "Negro WAC'S Get Year For Defying Orders,"
       PM, March 21, 1945, p. 10.

1573. Quarles, Benjamin. "Will a Long War Aid the Negro?,"
       Crisis, Vol. 50, November, 1943, pp. 328-329.

1574. Queen, Stuart A. "Race Relations and the War," Oppor-
       tunity, Vol. 20, July, 1942, pp. 211-212.

1575. "Race Equality a War Issue," American City, September,
       1942, p. 69.

1576.   "Race Problem," Time, Vol. 41, February 8, 1943, p. 58.

1577.   "Racial Democracy-The Navy Way," Common Ground, Vol. 7, Winter, 1947, pp. 61-68.

1578.   "Racial Employment Trends in National Defense," Phylon, Vol. 2, 4th Quarter, 1941, pp. 337-358.

1579.   "Racial Front: U.S. Army's Policy of Segregating Negroes," Commonweal, Vol. 35, January 23, 1942, pp. 332-333.

1580.   "Racial Troubles Increasing," Intelligencer, (Stout Field, IN), September, 1944.

1581.   Ramsberger, Jack F., Editor. Battle History 473rd U.S. Infantry. n.p., 1945.

1582.   Randolph, Asa Phillip. Victory's Victims? The Negro's Future. New York: Socialist Party, 1943.

1583.   _____. "Why Should We March?," Survey Graphic, Vol. 31, November, 1942, pp. 488-489.

1584.   Raynor, William E. "Crow Car; Two Sailors and a Negro Officer," New Republic, Vol. 108, June 14, 1943, p. 792.

1585.   Reddick, Lawrence D. "The Negro in the United States Navy During World War II," Journal of Negro History, Vol. 22, April, 1947, pp. 201-219.

1586.   _____. "The Negro Policy of the United States Army, 1775-1945," Journal of Negro Education, Vol. 34, Winter, 1949, pp. 9-29.

1587.   _____. "The Relative Status of the Negro in the American Armed Forces," Journal of Negro Education, Vol. 22, Summer, 1953, pp. 380-387.

1588.   _____. "What Should the American Negro Reasonably Expect as the Outcome of a Real Peace?," Journal of Negro Education, Vol. 12, July, 1943, pp. 568-578.

1589.   Redding, J. Saunders. "Here's a New Thing Altogether," Survey Graphic, Vol. 33, August, 1944, pp. 358-359, 366-367.

1590.   _____. "A Negro Looks at This War," American Mercury, Vol. 55, November, 1942, pp. 585-592.

1591.   _____. "What the Negro Believes," Negro Digest, Vol. 2, January, 1944, pp. 3-4.

1592.   Reid, Ira de A., Editor. Racial Desegregation and Integration. Philadelphia: American Academy of Political and Social Science, 1956.

1593.   "Remember Pearl Harbor and Sikeston Too," Chicago Defender, March 14, 1942.

1594.   "Report on a Hero," Time, Vol. 45, March 26, 1945, p.22.

1595.   "Resentment Over Negro Policy Coming to a Head," Christian Century, Vol. 60, February 17, 1943, p. 189.

1596.   Reynolds, Grant. "What the Negro Soldier Thinks," Crisis, Vol. 51, November, 1944, pp. 352-353, 357.

1597.   _____. "What the Negro Soldier Thinks About the War Department," Crisis, Vol. 51, October, 1944, pp. 316-318, 328.

1598.   _____. "What the Negro Soldier Thinks About this War," Crisis, Vol. 51, September, 1944, pp. 289-291, 299.

1599.   Riddle, Estelle Massey. "The Negro Nurse and the War," Opportunity, Vol. 21, April, 1943, pp. 44-45.

1600.   Ripley, Herbert S. et al. "Mental Illness Among Negro Troops Overseas," The American Journal of Psychiatry, Vol. 103, January, 1947, pp. 499-512.

1601.   Roberts, Harry W. "Prior-Service Attitudes Toward Whites of 219 Negro Veterans," Journal of Negro Education, Vol. 22, Fall, 1953, pp. 455-465.

1602.   _____. "The Impact of Military Service Upon the Racial Attitudes of Negro Servicemen in World War II," Social Problems, Vol. 1, October, 1953, pp. 65-69.

1603.   Robinson, Jackie. Breakthrough to the Big League: The Story of Jackie Robinson. New York: Harper and Row, 1965. Author discusses his military service in the U.S. Army during World War II.

1604.   Robinson, James Herman, Editor. Love of This Land. Philadelphia: Christian Education Press, 1956.

1605.   Rose, Arnold M. "Army Policies Toward Negro Soldiers," Annals of the American Academy of Political and Social Science, Vol. 144, March, 1946, pp. 90-94.

1606.   _____. "Army Policies Toward Negro Soldiers: A Report on a Success and a Failure," Journal of Social Issues, Vol. 3, Fall, 1947, pp. 26-31.

1607.   _____. "Bases of American Military Morale in World War II," Public Opinion Quarterly, Vol. 9, Winter, 1945, pp. 411-417.

1608. Rose, Robert A. "Lonely Eagles (Black Airmen in WW II,"
American Aviation Historical Society, Vol. 20, Summer,
1975, pp. 118-127.

1609. Rosenberg, Anna M. "Womanpower and the War," Opportunity, Vol. 21, April, 1943, pp. 35-36.

1610. Ross, Irwin. "Negro Soldiers in Transportation,"
Crisis, Vol. 52, June, 1945, pp. 162-163.

1611. _____. "Negro Service Troops," New Republic,
Vol. 112, March 5, 1945, pp. 326-328.

1612. Russell, Charles E. National Unity, National Defense
and the Color Line: An Address Delivered ... on January 26, 1941 to Protest Discrimination in the Military
Service of the United States. Washington, DC: Interracial Committee of the District of Columbia, 1941.

1613. Rutherford, William de Jarnette. 165 Days: A Story
of the 25th Division on Luzon. Manila: n.p., 1945.

1614. Sancton, Thomas. "Something Happened to the Negro,"
New Republic, Vol. 108, February 8, 1943, pp. 175-179.

1615. Sandler, S.A. "Camptocormia: A Functional Condition
of the Back in Neurotic Soldiers," War Medicine, Vol.
7, 1945, pp. 36-45.

1616. Schiffman, Joseph. "The Education of Negro Soldiers
in World War II," Journal of Negro Education, Vol. 18,
Winter, 1949, pp. 22-28.

1617. Schoenfield, Seymour J. The Negro in the Armed Forces,
His Value and Status, Past, Present and Potential.
Washington: The Associated Publishers, 1945.

1618. Schuyler, George S. "A Long War Will Aid the Negro,"
Crisis, Vol. 50, November, 1943, pp. 328-329, 344.

1619. _____. Black and Conservative: The Autobiography of George S. Schuyler. New Rochelle, NY:
Arlington House, 1966.

1620. "Sees Threat to Negroes in Peacetime Conscription,"
Christian Century, Vol. 61, December 27, 1944, p. 1493.

1621. "Segregation," Commonweal, Vol. 34, September 26, 1941,
pp. 531-532.

1622. "Segregation for WAVES, Even in New York City," Afro-
American, November 4, 1944, p. 1.

1623. Selective Service in Peacetime: First Report of the
Director of Selective Service, 1940-1941. Washington,
DC: United States Government Printing Office, 1942.

1624.   Selvera, John Douglas. The Negro in World War II.
        Baton Rouge, LA: Military Press, Inc., 1964. Reprinted
        by Arno Press and New York Times, 1969.

1625.   "Seventy Per Cent Labor--Negro Soldiers," Crisis, Vol.
        51, December, 1944, pp. 377-392.

1626.   "Sgt. (Joe) Louis' Army Tour Helps Negro-White Goodwill,"
        New York Daily Worker, September 11, 1943, p. 6.

1627.   "Sgt. Joe Louis Wins Promotion," PM, April 10, 1945.

1628.   "Shall We Have Another Separate Officers' Training
        Camp?," Crisis, Vol. 48, December, 1941, p. 385.

1629.   Sherman, Lieutenant Colonel John H. "Are Negroes Good
        Soldiers," Negro Digest, Vol. 3, December, 1945, pp.
        28-33.

1630.   _____. "Command of Negro
        Troops," Vital Speeches, Vol. 12, January 15, 1946, pp.
        217-220.

1631.   _____. "Our Negro Sold-
        iers," New Republic, Vol. 113, November 19, 1945, pp.
        667-678.

1632.   Silvera, John D. The Negro in World War II. Baton
        Rouge: Military Press, Inc., 1946?

1633.   Sithoff, Howard. "Racial Militancy and Interracial
        Violence in the Second World War," Journal of American
        History, Vol. 58, December, 1971, pp. 661-681.

1634.   Smith, Ferdinand C. "National Maritime Union Fights
        Discrimination," Opportunity, Vol. 20, January, 1942,
        pp. 196-199.

1635.   Smith, Wendell. "The King of Sock, Sgt. Joe Louis Is
        Still the 'Big Guy'," Pittsburgh Courier, July 17, 1942.

1636.   Smythe, Mabel and H. Smythe. "The Negro College and
        the Negro Veteran," Negro College Quarterly, Vol. 2,
        September, 1944, pp. 116-128.

1637.   "Snow Cleaners, Cotton Pickers," Crisis, Vol. 50,
        March, 1943, p. 72.

1638.   Society for the Psychological Study of Social Issues.
        Opinions About Negro Infantry Platoons in White Com-
        panies of Seven Divisions. Washington, DC: U.S. War
        Department, 1947.

1639.   "Soldiers and the Rights of Negroes," Nation, Vol. 157,
        October 9, 1943, p. 418.

1640.   "Soldiers Cheated of Credit," _Crisis_, Vol. 51, November, 1944, p. 344.

1641.   Somerville, John Alexander.   _Man of Color, An Auto-biography: A Factual Report of the Status of the American Negro Today_. Los Angeles: Lorrin L. Morrison Publishing Co., 1949.

1642.   Spore, John B.   "Our Negro Soldiers," _The Reporter_, Vol. 6, January 22, 1952, pp. 6-9.

1643.   "Staff Sergeant Joe Louis Morale Builder For Our Soldiers at Front," _Los Angeles Weekly_, June 24, 1944.

1644.   Stauffer, Samuel, et al.   _The American Soldier: Adjustment to Army Life_. Princeton: Princeton University Press, 1949. See Chapter on "Negro Soldiers."

1645.   Steele, A.T.   "Unsung Jungle Heroes," _Negro Digest_, Vol. 2, June, 1944, pp. 51-52.

1646.   Sterling, Dorothy.   _I Have Seen War_. New York: Hill and Wang, 1960. See Chapter entitled "In a Strange (England) Country."

1647.   Stevens, Rutherford B.   "Racial Aspects of Emotional Problems of Negro Soldiers," _Journal of Clinical Psychopathology_, Vol. 103, January, 1947, pp. 493-498.

1648.   Steward, Maxwell S.   _The Negro in America_. New York: Public Affairs Committee, Inc., 1944 (?), pp. 28-29.

1649.   Stewart, Ollie.   "The Negro-American Nationalist," _Scribner's Commentator_, Vol. 9, March, 1941, p. 68.

1650.   Stillman, Richard Joseph.   _Integration of the Negro in the United States Armed Forces_. New York: Frederick A. Prager Publishing Co., 1968.

1651.   Stokes, Anson Phelps.   "American Race Relations in War Time," _Journal of Negro Education_, Vol. 14, Fall, 1945, pp. 535-551.

1652.   Stouffer, Samuel A. et al.   _The American Soldier: Adjustment During Army Life_. Vol. I. Princeton, NJ: Princeton University Press, 1949. See Black soldiers in World War II, pp. 486-599.

1653.   "Tan Yanks," _Time_, Vol. 43, May 29, 1944, pp. 66-68, 70.

1654.   "Tan Yanks Come Through," (All Negro 93rd Division 1), _Negro Digest_, Vol. 2, January, 1944, pp. 31-37.

1655.   "10,000 Soldiers Turn Out, Hail Sergt. Joe Louis, Ray Robinson," _New York Amsterdam News_, September 25, 1943.

1656.   "The Air Force Goes Interracial," Ebony, Vol. 4, September, 1949, pp. 15-18.

1657.   "The Champ in Camp: A Day With Joe Louis at Fort Riley," The Ring, Vol. 21, October, 1942, pp. 5, 7.

1658.   The Colored Soldier in the U.S. Army. Prepared in the Historical Section, Army War College, May, 1942. Manuscript in the Office of the Chief of Military History.

1659.   "The Fate of Democracy," Opportunity, Vol. 20, January, 1942, p. 2.

1660.   "The Fort Dix Straw," New York Amsterdam Star-News, March 28, 1942.

1661.   "The Front Page: Negro Soldiers," Monthly Summary of Events and Trends in Race Relations, March, 1945, p.23.

1662.   "The Front Page: Negro Soldiers," Monthly Summary of Events and Trends in Race Relations, November, 1945, p. 124.

1663.   "The Front Page: Negro Soldiers," Monthly Summary of Events and Trends in Race Relations, December, 1945, p. 158.

1664.   "The Front Page: Negro Soldiers," Monthly Summary of Events and Trends in Race Relations, September, 1944, p. 239.

1665.   "The Front Page: Negro Soldiers," Monthly Summary of Events and Trends in Race Relations, May, 1945, p. 303.

1666.   "The Luckless 92nd," Newsweek, Vol. 25, February 26, 1945, p. 34.

1667.   "The Navy: Where Do We Stand," Crisis, Vol. 49, May, 1942, p. 161.

1668.   "The Negro and Nazism," Opportunity, Vol. 18, July, 1940, pp. 194-195.

1669.   "The Negro in the Army Today," The Annals of the American Academy of Political and Social Science, Vol. 223, September, 1942, pp. 55-59.

1670.   "The Negro in the United States Army," Crisis, Vol. 49, February, 1942, p. 47.

1671.   "The Negro in the United States Navy," Crisis, Vol. 47, July, 1940, p. 200.

1672.   "The Negro Policy of the U.S. Army 1775-1945," Journal of Negro History, Vol. 34, January, 1949, pp. 9-20.

1673.   "The Negro Soldier Betrayed," Crisis, Vol. 52, April, 1945, p. 97.

1674.   "The Negro's War," Fortune, Vol. 25, June, 1942, pp. 77-80, 157-158.

1675.   "The Pattern of Race Riots Involving Negro Soldiers," Monthly Summary of Events and Trends in Race Relations, August, 1944, p. 15.

1676.   The President's Committee on Civil Rights. To Secure These Rights. Washington, DC: United States Government Printing Office, 1945.

1677.   The President's Committee on Equality of Treatment and Opportunity in the Armed Services. Freedom to Serve. Washington, DC: United States Government Printing Office, 1950.

1678.   "The Role of the Negro in National Defense," School and Society, Vol. 52, December 7, 1940, p. 580.

1679.   "The Social Front: Negro Soldiers," Monthly Summary of Events and Trends in Race Relations, August, 1944, p. 8.

1680.   "The Social Front: Negro Soldiers," Monthly Summary of Events and Trends in Race Relations, October, 1944, p. 64.

1681.   "The Social Front: Negro Soldiers," Monthly Summary of Events and Trends in Race Relations, November, 1944, p. 94.

1682.   "The Social Front: Negro Soldiers," Monthly Summary of Events and Trends in Race Relations, March, 1945, p. 219.

1683.   "The Social Front: Negro Soldiers," Monthly Summary of Events and Trends in Race Relations, April, 1945, p. 219.

1684.   "The Social Front: Negro Soldiers," Monthly Summary of Events and Trends in Race Relations, May, 1945, p. 286.

1685.   "The Social Front: Negro Soldiers," Monthly Summary of Events and Trends in Race Relations, June, 1945, p. 318.

1686.   "The Social Front: Negro Soldiers," Monthly Summary of Events and Trends in Race Relations, July, 1945, p. 353.

1687.   "The Social Front: Negro Soldiers," Monthly Summary of Events and Trends in Race Relations, November, 1945, p. 103.

1688.   "The Story of the 477th Bombardment Group," Politics, Vol. 1, June, 1944, pp. 141-142.

1689.   "The WAAC-The Girl Who Wouldn't Be Left Behind,"
        Aframerican Woman's Journal, Vol. 3, 1942, p. 7.

1690.   "The Winifred Lynn Case Again: Segregation," Social
        Service Review, Vol. 18, September, 1944, pp. 369-371.

1691.   "They Also Serve," Brown American, Vol. 5, Summer,
        1943, p. 12.

1692.   Thomas, Jesse O. "Your American Red Cross Is At His
        (Negro Soldier) Side," Opportunity, Vol. 23, Winter,
        1945, pp. 15-19.

1693.   Thompson, Charles H. "American Negro and the National
        Defense," Journal of Negro Education, Vol. 9, October,
        1940, pp. 547-552.

1694.   _____. "American Negro and the National
        Defense, II," Journal of Negro Education, Vol. 10,
        October, 1941, pp. 623-630.

1695.   _____. "American Negro in World War I
        and World War II," Journal of Negro Education, Vol. 12,
        July, 1943, pp. 263-267.

1696.   _____. "Negro Morale and World War II,"
        Journal of Negro Education, Vol. 11, January, 1942, pp.
        1-3.

1697.   _____. "Peacetime Compulsory Military
        Training and the Negro's Status in the Armed Forces,"
        Journal of Negro Education, Vol. 14, April, 1945, pp.
        127-131.

1698.   _____. "Role of Race Relations in World
        War II," Journal of Negro Education, Vol. 11, April,
        1942, pp. 105-112.

1699.   Tobias, Channing H. "The U.S.O. Service to Negroes,"
        Opportunity, Vol. 20, April, 1942, pp. 132-134.

1700.   "Together 'Not Against'," Richmond News Leader, April
        3, 1942.

1701.   "Too Dark for Army Air Corps," Crisis, Vol. 47, Sep-
        tember, 1940, p. 279.

1702.   Townsend, Willard S. "Full Employment and the Negro
        Worker," Journal of Negro Education, Vol. 14, June,
        1945, p. 6.

1703.   Tucker, Roger. The Negro in World War II. Trenton,
        NJ: Commission on the Urban Population, 1945.

1704.   Tunnell, Emlen. Footsteps of a Giant. Garden City,
        NY: Doubleday, 1966. Author discusses his military
        service in the U.S. Coast Guard during World War II.

1705.   "2 Former Members of Women's Auxiliary Army Corps (WAC)," Michigan Chronicle, August 28, 1982, p. A-4.

1706.   "Two Negro Fighters With Mixed Units in Germany Receive DSC's for Heroism," Opportunity, Vol. 24, Winter, 1946, p. 33.

1707.   "Unhappy Soldier," Time, Vol. 44, July 10, 1944, pp. 65-68.

1708.   "U.S.A. Needs a Sharp Break with the Past," Crisis, Vol. 49, May, 1942, p. 151.

1709.   United States, American Battle Monuments Commission. American Armies and Battlefields in Europe. Washington, 1938.

1710.   _____, 92nd Division. Summary of Operations in the World War. Washington, 1944.

1711.   _____, 93rd Division. Summary of Operations in the World War. Washington, 1944.

1712.   United States Army. Negro Troops. Commission of Inquiry into the Effects of Segregation and Discrimination on the Morale and Development of Negro Servicemen, Public Hearing, City Hall, St. Louis, Missouri, 1949. Washington, DC: United States Government Printing Office, 1950.

1713.   United States Army. With the 92nd Infantry Division, October, 1942-June, 1945. Washington, DC: United States Government Printing Office, 1945.

1714.   United States Army. Negro Manpower in the Army. Washington, DC: Department of Army, 1949.

1715.   United States Army Service Forces. Leadership and the Negro Soldier. Washington, DC: United States Government Printing Office, 1944.

1716.   United States Congressional Record 76th Congress, 3rd Session, 1940.

1717.   United States Congressional Record 78th Congress, 2nd Session, 1944.

1718.   United States Congressional Record 80th Congress, 2nd Session, 1948.

1719.   United States Department of the Army. Office Civilian Aide. The Negro in the Army, Policy and Practice. Washington, DC: United States Government Printing Office,1948.

1720.   United States Government, Navy Department, Press Release.   "The Negro Soldier," January 15, 1944.

1721.   United States Government, Navy Department, Press Release, "The Negro Soldier," March 16, 1944.

1722.   United States Government, Navy Department, Press Release, "The Negro Soldier," April 25, 1944.

1723.   United States Government, Navy Department, Press Release, "The Negro Soldier," July 20, 1944.

1724.   United States Government, Navy Department, Press Release, "The Negro Soldier," July 21, 1944.

1725.   United States Government, Navy Department, Press Release, "The Negro Soldier," July 29, 1944.

1726.   United States Government, Navy Department, Press Release, "The Negro Soldier," October 19, 1944.

1727.   United States Government, Navy Department, Press Release, "The Negro Soldier," March 8, 1945.

1728.   United States Government, Navy Department, Press Release, "The Negro Soldier," July 13, 1945.

1729.   United States Government, Navy Department, Press Release, "The Negro Soldier," July 29, 1945.

1730.   United States Government, Navy Department, Press Release, "The Negro Soldier," November 1, 1945.

1731.   United States Government, Navy Department, Press Release, "The Negro Soldier," January 15, 1946.

1732.   United States Government, Navy Department, Press Release, on "Negro Enlisted Strength of the Navy," 1943-1945.

1733.   United States Government, Navy Department, Press Release, on "Ship's History of the U.S.S.P.C. 1268." n.d.

1734.   United States Government, War Department, Press Release, "The Negro Soldier," January/December, 1944.

1735.   United States Government, War Department, Press Release, "The Negro Soldier," January/December, 1945.

1736.   United States Government, War Department, Press Release, "The Negro Soldier," August 13, 1945.

1737.   United States Government, War Department, Press Release, "The Negro Soldier," November 15, 1945.

1738.   United States Government, War Department, Press Release, "The Negro Soldier," November 16, 1945.

1739.   United States Government, War Department, Press Release,
        "The Negro Soldier," November 30, 1945.

1740.   United States Government, War Department, Press Release,
        "The Negro Soldier," October 1, 1945.

1741.   United States Government, War Department, Press Release,
        "The Negro Soldier," October 22, 1945.

1742.   United States Government, War Department, Press Release,
        "The Negro Soldier," February 7, 1946.

1743.   United States Government, War Department, Press Release,
        "The Negro Soldier," February 11, 1946.

1744.   United States Housing and Home Finance Agency. The
        Housing of Negro Veterans. Washington, DC: United
        States Government Printing Office, 1948.

1745.   United States Office of War Information. Negroes and
        the War. Washington, DC: United States Government
        Printing Office, 1942.

1746.   United States Senate Committee on Armed Services, Hear-
        ing ... on Universal Military Training. Washington,
        DC: United States Government Printing Office, 1948.

1747.   United States War Department. Command of Negro Troops.
        Washington, DC: United States Government Printing
        Office, 1944.

1748.   "U.S. Negro Troops Are Based in Liberia," Life, Vol. 13,
        December 21, 1942, pp. 36-37.

1749.   "U.S. Negro Troops Begin Front-Line Action in Pacific,"
        Washington Post, March 17, 1944.

1750.   Villard, Oswald Garrison. "Justice for the Negro,"
        Christian Century, Vol. 57, December 18, 1940, pp.
        1582-1584.

1751.   _____. "The Negro Great Gains,"
        Christian Century, Vol. 59, November 4, 1942, pp.
        1351-1352.

1752.   _____. "Shall It Be A War of Color,"
        Christian Century, Vol. 59, February 4, 1942, pp. 145-
        146.

1753.   _____. "The War Between the Races,"
        Christian Century, Vol. 60, July 7, 1943, pp. 795-796.

1754.   "WAAC's Cure For Narrow Nationalsim," Norfolk Journal
        and Guide, November 21, 1942.

1755. "WAAC's Open Ranks to Colored Applicants," Philadelphia Tribune, October 3, 1942.

1756. "WAC Promoted," Headlines, Vol. 1, November, 1944, p. 24.

1757. "WAC Swears Menial Duties Go To Negroes," PM, March 20, 1945.

1758. "WAC Technicians," Service, Vol. 8, March, 1944, p. 8.

1759. "WACs Left Intact," Headlines, Vol. 2, August, 1945, p. 31.

1760. "WACs Meet Jim Crow," Headlines, Vol. 1, February, 1945, p. 11.

1761. "WACs Released, Back to Work," Headlines, Vol. 1, February, 1945, p. 11.

1762. "War and Race Relations: Student Opinion," Crisis, Vol. 50, September, 1943, p. 269.

1763. "War Departments Enlisted Negro Recruits for Air Corps," Opportunity, Vol. 19, April, 1941, p. 119.

1764. "War Department Wasted Talents," Atlanta Daily World, January 29, 1943.

1765. "War Industry Training for Atlanta Negroes," Opportunity, Vol. 20, December, 1942, pp. 377-390.

1766. "Wave Head, Race Women Hold Confab," Chicago Defender, July 31, 1944, p. 1.

1767. "Wave Officers," Headlines, Vol. 1, January, 1945, p. 29.

1768. "We Are Accused of Inciting to Riot and Being Traitors," Crisis, Vol. 49, June, 1942, p. 183.

1769. Weaver, Robert G. "Defense Industries and the Negro," Annals, Vol. 223, September, 1942, pp. 60-66.

1770. _____. "The Negro Veterans," Annals, Vol. 225, March, 1945, pp. 127-132.

1771. _____. "When the GIs Come Home," Negro Digest, Vol. 3, July, 1945, pp. 21-23.

1772. Weil, Frank C. "The Negro in the Armed Forces," Social Forces, Vol. 26, October, 1947, pp. 95-98.

1773. Weiss, Isidor. "Psychoses in Military Prisoners," Journal of Clinical Psychopathology, Vol. 8, April, 1947, pp. 689-705.

1774. Wellver, Warman. "Report on the Negro Soldier," Harper's Magazine, Vol. 192, April, 1946, pp. 333-339.

1775. Werrell, Kenneth P. "Mutiny at Army Air Force Station 569: Bamber Bridge, England, June, 1943," Aerospace Historian, Vol. 22, 1975, pp. 202-209.

1776. West, Levon. Flight to Everywhere. New York: Whittlesey House, McGraw-Hill Book Company, 1944.

1777. Wheeler-Nicholson, Major Malcolm. "Are Negroes Good Soldiers?," Negro Digest, Vol. 2, December, 1943, pp. 21-23.

1778. "White House Blesses Jim Crow," Crisis, Vol. 48, September, 1940, pp. 350-351.

1779. "White Man's War," Time, Vol. 41, March 2, 1942, pp. 13-14.

1780. White, Walter F. A Rising Wind. Garden City, NY: Doubleday Doran and Co., Inc., 1945.

1781. _____. "Brown Americans," Coronet, Vol. 17, November, 1944.

1782. _____. How Far the Promised Land? New York: Viking Press, 1955.

1783. _____. "It's Our Country Too: The Negro Demands the Right To Be Allowed To Fight For It," Saturday Evening Post, Vol. 212, December 14, 1940, pp. 26, 61-68.

1784. _____. "Race Relations in the Armed Services of the United States," Journal of Negro Education, Vol. 12, July, 1943, pp. 350-354.

1785. _____. "The Right to Fight for Democracy," Survey Graphic, Vol. 31, November, 1942, pp. 472-474.

1786. _____. "What the Negro Thinks of the Army," Annals, Vol. 223, September, 1942, pp. 67-71.

1787. White, William L. "Negro Officers, 1917 and Now," Survey Graphic, Vol. 31, April, 1942, pp. 192-194.

1788. _____. "The Negro in the Army," Reader's Digest, Vol. 40, April, 1942, pp. 51-54.

1789. Wieck, Fred D. "Soldier in the South," Common Ground, Vol. 4, 1942, pp. 30-36.

1790. Wiley, Major Bell. The Training of Negro Troops. Washington, DC: Historical Section Army Ground Forces, 1946.

1791.   Wilkins, Roy. "Maneuvers Show 93rd Is Ready," _Crisis_,
        Vol. 50, June, 1943, pp. 170-172.

1792.   _____. "Nurses Go To War," _Crisis_, Vol. 50,
        February, 1943, pp. 42-44.

1793.   _____. "Still a Jim-Crow Army," _Crisis_, Vol.
        53, April, 1946, pp. 106-109, 125.

1794.   _____. "The Old Army Game?," _Crisis_, Vol. 52,
        May, 1945, pp. 130-131, 140, 145.

1795.   _____. "The West in War Time," _Crisis_, Vol. 50,
        May, 1943, pp. 142, 153.

1796.   Williams, John Alfred. _Flashbacks: A Twenty-Year
        Diary of Article Writing_. Garden City, NY: Doubleday,
        1973. Author discusses his military service in the
        U.S. Navy during World War II.

1797.   Williams, John Henry. _A Negro Looks At The War_. New
        York: Workers Library Publishers, 1940.

1798.   Williams, Mary H., Compiler. _Chronology: 1941-1945,
        A Volume in the Official Series UNITED STATES ARMY IN
        WORLD WAR II_. Washington: United States Government
        Printing Office, 1959.

1799.   Wilson, Ruth Danehower. _Jim Crow Joins Up: A Study
        of Negroes in the Armed Forces of the United States_.
        New York: Clark Press, 1944.

1800.   Wilson, William. "Negroes Find the British Draw Line
        Too, But Subtly," _Newsweek_, Vol. 26, November 5, 1945,
        pp. 58, 63.

1801.   _____. "Old Jim Crow in Uniform," _Crisis_,
        Vol. 46, February, 1939, pp. 42-44; March, 1939, pp.
        71-73, 82, 93.

1802.   Winston, Henry. _Old Jim Crow Has Got To Go!_ New York:
        New Age Publishers, 1941.

1803.   Wirth, Louis. "Morale and Minority Groups," _American
        Journal of Sociology_, Vol. 47, November, 1941, pp.
        415-433.

1804.   Wolf, Stewart. "Mental Illness Among Negro Troops
        Overseas," _American Journal of Psychiatry_, Vol. 103,
        January, 1947, pp. 508-512.

1805.   "Women In The Army," _Service_, Vol. 7, October, 1942,
        p. 14.

1806.   Wormser, Robert. "Race and Draft," _Nation_, Vol. 156,
        May 29, 1943, pp. 789-792.

1807. Wright, Richard R. What the Negro Needs: A Post-War Plan to Integrate the Negro's Activities and Build Toward Full Social and Economical Security. New York: 194-?

1808. Wynn, Neil A. "The Afro-American and the Second World War." Unpublished Doctoral Dissertation, The Open University, England, 1973.

1809. Yancey, Francis. This Is Our War. Chicago: Afro-American Co., 1945.

1810. Yearwood, Ruby Bryant. "Women Volunteers Unite To Serve," Opportunity, Vol. 21, April, 1943, pp. 60-62, 88-89.

1811. Yerby, Frank. "Health Cards," Harper's Magazine, Vol. 178, May, 1944, pp. 548-553.

VIII.

Blacks in the Korean War

1812.   "Ahead of the Country," Time, Vol. 55, June 5, 1950, p. 18.

1813.   Albert, Alain. The Crossing. New York: G. Braziller, 1964.

1814.   Appleman, Roy E. United States Army in the Korean War: South to the Naktong, North to the Yalu. Washington, DC: United States Government Printing Office, 1961.

1815.   Banks, Samuel L. "The Korean Conflict," Negro History Bulletin, Vol. 38, October, 1973, pp. 122-125.

1816.   Barth, George B. Tropic Lightning and Taro Leaf in Korea. n.p., 1953.

1817.   _____. Tropic Lightning and Taro Leaf in Korea, July, 1950-May, 1951. Athens, n.p., 1955.

1818.   Billington, Monroe. "Freedom to Service: The President's Committee on Equality of Treatment and Opportunity in the Armed Forces, 1949-1950," Journal of Negro History, Vol. 51, October, 1966, pp. 262-274.

1819.   Bogart, Leo. "The Army and Its Negro Soldiers," The Reporter, Vol. II, December 30, 1954, pp. 8-11.

1820.   _____, Editor. Social Research and the Desegregation of the U.S. Army: Two Original 1951 Field Reports. Chicago: Markham, 1969.

1821.   Clark, Mark. "Does Integration Work in the Armed Forces," U.S. News and World Report, May 11, 1956, pp. 54-56.

1822. Clay, Revella L. "Recent Advances Towards the Elimin-
       ation of Segregation in the United States Army," Negro
       History Bulletin, Vol. 15, October, 1951, pp. 20, 24.

1823. Clytus, John. Black Man in Red Cuba. Coral Gables,
       FL: University of Miami Press, 1970. Author was in
       the U.S. Air Force during the Korean War.

1824. David, Allan A., Editor. Battleground Korea. The
       Story of the 25th Infantry Division. Tokyo: Kyoya
       Co., 1952.

1825. Dwyer, Robert J. "The Negro in the United States Army,"
       Sociology and Social Research, Vol. 38, November/Decem-
       ber, 1943, pp. 103-112.

1826. Feldman, J. Arnold. "The 1960 Audit of Negro Veterans
       and Servicemen," Journal of Intergroup Relations, Vol.
       2, Winter, 1960-1961, pp. 79-81.

1827. Foreman, Paul B. "The Implication of Project Clark,"
       Phylon, Vol. 16, September, 1955, pp. 263-274.

1828. Forman, James. The Making of Black Revolutionaries:
       A Personal Account. New York: Macmillan, 1972.
       Author discusses his duties in the U.S. Air Force, es-
       pecially on Okinawa during the Korean War.

1829. Gropman, Alan L. "Integration Transition in the U.S.
       Armed Services, 1948-1954." Unpublished Doctoral Dis-
       sertation, Tufts University, 1969.

1830. Harrison, Robert E. When God Was Black. Grand Rapids,
       MI: Zondervan Publishing House, 1971. Author dis-
       cusses his military experiences in the U.S. Army during
       the Korean War.

1831. Hermes, Walter G. Truce Tent and Fighting Front.
       Washington, DC: United States Government Printing
       Office, 1966.

1832. "How Do Our Negro Troops Measure Up?," Saturday Evening
       Post, Vol. 223, June 16, 1951, pp. 30-31, 139, 141.

1833. Howell, Jinxy R.L. All Hairs on My Head Hurt. New
       York: Exposition Press, 1964. Author discusses his
       life as a dental surgeon in the U.S. Air Force during
       the Korean War.

1834. Jacobs, Bruce. "Tropic Lightning (25th Infantry Divi-
       sion)," Chapter 13 in Soldiers: The Fighting Divisions
       of the Regular Army. New York: W.W. Norton and Com-
       pany, 1958.

1835.   Jamal, Hakin Abdullah (formerly Allen Donaldson).
        From the Dead Level: Malcolm X and Me. New York:
        Random House, 1972. Author discusses his military ex-
        periences with the U.S. Army in New Jersey and Japan
        during the Korean War.

1836.   Lee, Ulysses Grant. The Employment of Negro Troops.
        Washington, DC: United States Government Printing
        Office, 1966.

1837.   Leiser, Ernest. "For Negroes It's A New Army Now,"
        Saturday Evening Post, Vol. 225, December 13, 1952,
        pp. 26-27, 108, 110-112.

1838.   MacGregor, Morris J. and Bernard C. Nalty, Editors.
        Blacks in the United States Armed Forces: Basic Docu-
        ments. Wilmington, DE: Scholarly Resources, Inc.,
        1977. Vol. XII, "Integration (1948-1963)."

1839.   _____. Integration of the Armed Forces,
        1940-1965. Washington, DC: Center of Military His-
        tory, 1981.

1840.   Mack, Raymond W. "The Prestige System of an Air Base:
        Squadron Rankings and Morale," American Sociological
        Review, Vol. 19, June, 1954, pp. 281-287.

1841.   Martin, Harold H. "How Do Our Negro Troops Measure
        Up?," Saturday Evening Post, Vol. 223, June 16, 1951,
        pp. 30-31, 139, 141.

1842.   Marshall, Thurgood. Report on Korea; the Shameful
        Story of the Court Martial of Negro GI's. New York:
        N.A.A.C.P., 1951.

1843.   _____. "Summary Justice: The Negro GI
        in Korea," Crisis, Vol. 58, May, 1951, pp. 297-305,
        350-355.

1844.   Meredith, James Howard. Three Years in Mississippi.
        Bloomington, IN: University Press, 1966. Author dis-
        cusses his service duty in the U.S. Air Force during
        the Korean War.

1845.   Middleton, Harry J. The Compact History of the Korean
        War. New York: Hawthorn Books, 1966.

1846.   Millis, Walter. The Martial Spirit. New York: Twen-
        tieth Century Fund, 1959.

1847.   Morgan, Gordon Daniel. Poverty Without Bitterness.
        Jefferson City, MO: New Scholar Press, 1969. Author
        discusses his military service with the U.S. Army in
        Korea.

1848. Moskos, Charles C. "Has the Army Killed Jim Crow?,"
       Negro History Bulletin, Vol. 21, November, 1952, pp.
       27-29.

1849. _____. "Racial Integration in the Armed
       Forces," American Journal of Sociology, Vol. 72, Sep-
       tember, 1966, pp. 132-148.

1850. "Negro General Possible," Army Navy Air Force Registar,
       Vol. 91, September 26, 1953, p. 117.

1851. Nelson, Dennis D. "A Report on Military Civil Rights,"
       Negro History Bulletin, Vol. 16, January, 1953, pp. 75-
       78.

1852. Nichols, Lee. Breakthrough on the Color Front. New
       York: Random House, 1954.

1853. Operations Research Office. Project Clear: The Util-
       ization of Negro Manpower in the Army. Chevy Chase,
       MD: Operations Research Office, Johns Hopkins Univer-
       sity, April, 1955.

1854. Parnell, C.F. "Taps For Jim Crow in the Services;
       Reply," New York Times Magazine, June 25, 1950, p. 4.

1855. Pictorial Album of Henry Kaserne, 370th Armored Infan-
       try Battalion, and 29th Transportation Truck Battalion.
       London: Montgomery Publishing Company, 1952.

1856. Pullen, Richard T., et al., Editors. 25th Infantry
       Division, Tropic Lightning in Korea. Atlanta: Albert
       Love Enterprises, 1954.

1857. Puner, Morton. "What the Armed Forces Taught Us About
       Integration," Coronet, Vol. 48, June, 1960, pp. 105-110.

1858. Rackleff, Robert B. "The Black Soldier in Popular
       American Magazines, 1900-1971," Negro History Bulletin,
       Vol. 34, December, 1971, pp. 185-189.

1859. Reddick, Lawrence D. "The Negro Policy of the American
       Army Since World War II," Journal of Negro History, Vol.
       58, April, 1953, pp. 194-215.

1860. Reid, Ira de A., Editor. Racial Desegregation and
       Integration. Philadelphia: American Academy of Poli-
       tical and Social Science, 1956.

1861. Rose, Arnold M. "Psychoneurotic Breakdown Among Negro
       Soldiers," Phylon, Vol. 17, First Quarter, 1956, pp.
       61-69.

1862. Rutherford, William A. "Jim Crow: A Problem of Diplo-
       macy," Nation, Vol. 175, November 8, 1952, pp. 428-429.

1863. Seale, Bobby G. Seige the Time: The Story of the
       Panther Party and Huey P. Newton. New York: Random
       House,1970. Author discusses his military service in
       the U.S. Air Force during the Korean War.

1864. Selective Service System. Special Groups: Special
       Monograph No. 10. Washington, DC: United States Gov-
       ernment Printing Office, 1953.

1865. Sher, Ronald. Integration of Negro and White Personnel
       in the U.S. Army, Europe, 1952-1954. Historical Divi-
       sions, Headquarters, United States Army, Europe, 1956.

1866. "Ship Shape: Josephine Delores Rosa Is the First Negro
       WAVE to Get Sea-Going Duty," Our World, Vol. 9, Febru-
       ary, 1954, pp. 58, 60-61.

1867. Stillman, Richard Joseph. Integration of the Negro in
       the U.S. Armed Forces. New York: Frederick A. Praeger
       Publishing Company, 1968.

1868. "Taps For Jim Crow in the Services," New York Times
       Magazine, June 11, 1950, pp. 12, 24-27.

1869. Teague, Robert L. Letters To A Black Boy. New York:
       Walker, 1968. Author discusses his military service
       in the U.S. Navy during the Korean War.

1870. The 25th Infantry Division (Tropic Lightning), 1941-
       1955. Honolulu: n.p., 1955.

1871. 370th Armored Infantry Battalion, Munich, Germany,
       1953. Munich: L. Stopr, 1953.

1872. Treadwell, Mattie E. The Women's Army Corps. Wash-
       ington, DC: U.S. Department of the Army, Office of
       Military History, 1954.

1873. Troman, Mary E. and Nelle K. Perry. "Demonstrated
       Ability (of Chappie James)," Ladies Home Journal, Vol.
       74, February, 1957, pp. 149-157.

1874. Westover, John G. Combat Support in Korea. Washing-
       ton: Combat Forces Press, 1955.

1875. Wiant, John. "Integration A Fact in Services, But-,"
       Army-Navy-Air Force Register & Defense Times, Vol. 28,
       November, 1959, pp. 9-11.

1876. Williams, Robin M., Jr. "Social Change and Social
       Conflict: Race Relations in the United States, 1944-
       1964," Sociological Inquire, Vol. 35, Winter, 1966,
       pp. 8-25.

1877. Wright, Charles Stevenson. Absolutely Nothing to Get
       Alarmed About. New York: Farrar, Straus and Giroux,
       1973. Author discusses his military service in the
       U.S. Army during the Korean War.

1878.   "U.S. Negroes Make Reds See Red," Reader's Digest,
        January, 1954, pp. 38-40.

1879.   U.S. President's Committee on Equality of Treatment
        and Opportunity in the Armed Service. Freedom to Serve,
        Equality of Treatment and Opportunity in the Armed Ser-
        vices. Washington, DC: United States Government Print-
        ing Office, 1950.

1880.   "Yesterday in Negro History," Jet, Vol. 4, July 23,
        1953, p. 10.

IX.

Blacks in the Vietnam War

1881. "Abolish the Draft! Enact the 'Freedom Budget'!," _Freedomways_, Vol. 6, Fall, 1966, pp. 293-295.

1882. "Admiral Says Navy Is Open to Black Input," _Jet_, Vol. 43, May 11, 1972, p. 44.

1883. "AFROTC To Graduate First Black Woman," _Air Force Times_, Vol. 33, May 16, 1973, p. 10.

1884. "Air Force Accused," _Amsterdam News_, September 4, 1971, p. A-10.

1885. "Air Force Jim Crow," _Crisis_, Vol. 77, June/July, 1970, pp. 227-229.

1886. "Air Force Questioning Some Proposals Listed in Integration Report," _Air Force Times_, Vol. 23, July 17, 1963, p. 3.

1887. "Air Force Racism Charged in Study," _New York Times_, August 31, 1971.

1888. "Air Force's 'Ugly Racism' Blamed on Supervisors," _Baltimore Afro-American_, September 11, 1971, p. 1.

1889. "Airman Keeps Up Fight for Afro Hairstyle," _Pittsburgh Courier_, March 14, 1970, p. 2.

1890. Allen, Mark. "The Case of Billy Dean Smith," _Black Scholar_, Vol. 4, October, 1972, pp. 15-17.

1891. "Anti-War G.I. Sentenced," _Pittsburgh Courier_, January 10, 1970, p. 1.

1892. "Are Our G.I.'s On Dope," _Sepia_, Vol. 17, July, 1968, pp. 10-12.

1893. "Armed Forces Recruiting Centers Target of New Black Coalition Unit," Washington Post, July 14, 1971, p. C-2.

1894. "Army Confirms It Denied Bias Plea," Baltimore Afro-American, April 10, 1971, p. 1.

1895. "Army Promotes Three in Historic Move," Baltimore Afro-American, May 22, 1971, p. 1.

1896. "Army Tries to Oust Six WACS in Protest," Washington Post, June 1, 1971, p. A-1.

1897. "As Negro Veterans Come Home, Stabilizing Force?," U.S. News and World Report, February 5, 1968, pp. 52-53.

1898. "As Race Issue Hits Armed Forces," U.S. News and World Report, September 1, 1969, pp. 26-27.

1899. Bailey, P. "Getting Together at 'The Point'," Ebony, Vol. 26, December, 1971, pp. 136-137.

1900. Banks, L.J. "Black Admiral Signals 'New Look' for U.S. Navy," Ebony, Vol. 26, September, 1971, pp. 72-74†.

1901. Bates, Robert G. "Problems in Recruiting Blacks For the Service Academies: A Perspective," Naval War College Review, Vol. 26, July/August, 1973, pp. 54-63.

1902. Bennett, L. Howard. "Command Leadership and the Black Serviceman," U.S. Naval Institute Proceedings, Vol. 197, April, 1971, pp. 42-47.

1903. Bernstein, Carl. "Viet War Racism Assailed," Washington Post, April 3, 1971, p. B-5.

1904. Bevel, Diane Nash. "Journey to North Vietnam," Freedomways, Vol. 7, Spring, 1967, pp. 118-128.

1905. "Bias Still Exists in Armed Forces: Lt. Gen. Davis," Jet, Vol. 41, January 29, 1970, p. 10.

1906. "Bill Increasing Vet Loan Limit Signed by Nixon," Jet, Vol. 39, November 12, 1970, p. 19.

1907. Billington, Monroe. "Freedom To Serve: The President's Committee on Equality of Treatment and Opportunity in the Armed Forces, 1949-1950," Journal of Negro History, Vol. 51, October, 1966, pp. 262-274.

1908. "Billy Smith Is on Trial for Refusing to Kill," Black Panther, August 2, 1971, p. 7.

1909. "Black America 1970," Time, April 6, 1970, pp. 13-35, 45-100.

1910. "Black Army Captain Freed in 'Racism' Trial," Jet, Vol. 43, March 2, 1972, p. 20.

1911. "Black Army Officers," Chicago Daily Defender, February 22, 1971, p. 13.

1912. "Black General Named To Command Ft. Carson," Jet, Vol. 44, September 21, 1972, p. 26.

1913. "Black General Takes Over a New Command Post in Washington," Jet, Vol. 45, December 6, 1973, p. 66.

1914. "Black General Tells of Army Gains Against Bias," Jet, Vol. 44, June 8, 1972, p. 2.

1915. "Black GI Death Rate in Vietnam Cut in Half," Jet, Vol. 44, September 7, 1972, p. 46.

1916. "Black GI Escapee Turns Self In; Awaits United States Action," Jet, Vol. 43, July 22, 1971, p. 8.

1917. "Black GI with Sickle Cell Victimized by Failure of Army to Screen Inductees," Jet, Vol. 44, February 24, 1972, pp. 46-47.

1918. "Black Named Top Enlisted Man in U.S. Air Force," Jet, Vol. 45, October 4, 1973, p. 28.

1919. "Black Naval Officer Named Commander of Navy Air Squadron," Jet, Vol. 44, January 13, 1972, p. 29.

1920. "Black Officer Total Decline," Air Force Times, Vol. 31, August 19, 1970, p. 5.

1921. "'Black Power' Activity Described in Vietnam," Norfolk Journal and Guide, January 23, 1971, p. 1.

1922. "Black Red Cross Volunteer Brings Lots of Soul to Vietnam," Black Times, February 15, 1971, p. 12.

1923. "Black Sailors Refuse to Testify at Riot Hearings," Jet, Vol. 44, December 28, 1972, p. 27.

1924. Black Scholar. November, 1970. Special issue dealing with the Black Soldier.

1925. "Black Servicemen's Group Eases Racial Tensions," Jet, Vol. 44, January 2, 1972, p. 2.

1926. "Black Soldier; Symposium," Ebony, August, 1968, pp. 31-34†.

1927. "Black Soldiers Fight Two Wars in Vietnam," Sepia, Vol. 18, February, 1969, pp. 61-62.

1928. "Black, White Airmen in Racial Battle; 70 Arrested, Many Hurt on California Base," Jet, Vol. 43, June 10, 1971, p. 12.

1929. "Blacks Warn Nixon on Effect of Dishonorable Discharges," Washington Post, July 13, 1971, p. A-2.

1930. Bohn, R.D. "A Marine General Speaks His Mind," Sepia, Vol. 20, August, 1971, p. 35.

1931. Bonsal, Stephen. "The Negro Soldier in War and Peace," North American Review, Vol. 185, No. 616, June, 1970, pp. 312-327.

1932. Booker, Simon. "Negroes in Vietnam: We, Too, Are Americans," Ebony, Vol. 21, November, 1965, pp. 89-90.

1933. Borders, Lt. Thomas. "Coast Guard Equality Programs Limited by Societal Attitudes," Black Times, February 15, 1971, p. 2.

1934. Borus, Jonathan F. et al. "Adjustment Issues Facing the Vietnam Returnee," Archives of General Psychiatry, Vol. 28, 1973, pp. 501-506.

1935. _____. "The Racial Perceptions Inventory," Archives of General Psychiatry, Vol. 29, 1973, pp. 270-275.

1936. _____. "Racial Perceptions in the Army: An Approach," American Journal of Psychiatry, Vol. 28, 1972, pp. 1369-1374.

1937. Boyd, George M. "A Look at Racial Polarity in the Armed Forces," Air University Review, Vol. 21, September/October, 1970, pp. 42-50.

1938. Brecher, Ruth and Edward Brecher. "The Military's Limited War Against Segregation," Harper's Magazine, Vol. 217, September, 1963, pp. 79-92.

1939. Brittain, Victoria. "GI's Fight For Peace," New States-man, Vol. 77, May 9, 1969, pp. 643-644.

1940. Browne, Robert S. "The Freedom Movement and the War in Vietnam," Freedomways, Vol. 5, Fourth Quarter, 1965, pp. 467-480.

1941. Burchard, Hank. "Draft Director Doesn't Like Draft, But-," Washington Post, September 23, 1971, p. G-1.

1942. Butterfield, Roger. "The Mobilization of Black Strength," Life, Vol. 65, December 6, 1968, pp. 93-106.

1943. "Captain Gravely Goes for Admiral Position," <u>Amsterdam News</u>, May 8, 1971, p. 2.

1944. Casey, Leon A. "Black Moses (Chaplain I.V. Tolbert)," <u>Airman</u>, Vol. 16, October, 1972, p. 41.

1945. "'Chappie' James Next General," <u>Amsterdam News</u>, January 31, 1970, p. 2.

1946. "Cherry Point, North Carolina Air Station Is Accused of Racial Bias," <u>Norfolk Journal and Guide</u>, June 12, 1971, p. 11.

1947. "Chicagoan Gets Top AF Badge," <u>Chicago Daily Defender</u>, September 18-24, 1971, p. 5.

1948. Chiricos, Theodore, et al. "Status Inconsistency, Militancy and Black Identification Among Black Veterans," <u>Social Science Quarterly</u>, Vol. 51, December, 1970, pp. 572-586.

1949. "City and State: Fort Meade Sets Up Office to Hear Bias Complaints," <u>Washington Post</u>, June 23, 1971, p. B-4.

1950. Clarke, John. <u>Black Soldier</u>. Garden City, NY: Doubleday, 1968.

1951. Cleaver, Eldridge. <u>Soul On Ice</u>. New York: McGraw Hill Book Co., 1968. See Chapter entitled, "The Black Man's Stake in Vietnam."

1952. "Cleveland Woman Becomes Marines' First Woman Judge," <u>Jet</u>, Vol. 44, May 24, 1973, p. 32.

1953. "CM Sgt. Thomas N. Barnes Named New CMSAF;First Black Airman To Hold Post," <u>Air Force Magazine</u>, Vol. 56, November, 1973, pp. 26-27.

1954. Coates, Charles H. <u>Military Sociology: A Study of American Military Institutions and Military Life</u>. University Park, MD: The Social Science Press, 1965, pp. 350-355.

1955. "Col. Ruth A. Lucas, First Negro Woman in Air Force Promoted to Colonel," <u>Armed Forces Journal</u>, Vol. 106, January 4, 1969, p. 14.

1956. "Collins Appeals to Supreme Court," <u>Southern Patriot</u>, September, 1970, p. 1.

1957. "Commission (On Civil Rights) Report: Negro Does Better in Service Than Out But Ills Found," <u>Air Force Times</u>, Vol. 24, October 9, 1963, p. 13.

1958.   "Course In Black Studies Introduced at Phan Rang, AB, Vietnam," _Air Force Times_, Vol. 31, December 30, 1970, p. 18.

1959.   Crist, George B. "Black is Beautiful and the Military Establishment." Unpublished Master's Thesis, Air War College, 1970.

1960.   Crouch, Julius T. "The Black Junior Officer in Today's Army," _Military Review_, Vol. 52, May, 1972, pp. 61-67.

1961.   Dalfiume, Richard M. "The Fahy Committee and Desegregation of the Armed Forces," _The Historian_, Vol. 31, November, 1968, pp. 1-28.

1962.   "Daniel 'Chappie' James: Big Man, Big Message," _Sepia_, Vol. 17, April, 1968, pp. 64-66.

1963.   David, Jay and Elaine Crane. _The Black Soldier-From the American Revolution to Vietnam_. New York: William Morrow and Co., 1971.

1964.   "Death of Black G.I. Sets Off Clash in Germany," _New York Times_, January 5, 1971, p. 2.

1965.   "Death Rate of Black GIs Lower in Vietnam," _Norfolk Journal and Guide_, May 29, 1971, p. 9.

1966.   Dell, Nat. "The Black Soldier--A Situation Report," _Soldier_, February, 1973, pp. 6-15.

1967.   "Dispute Over Army Civil Rights Role," _Senior Scholastic_, October 25, 1963, p. 16.

1968.   Dobkin, Robert A. "Richmond Man Selected As First Black Admiral," _Washington Post_, April 28, 1971, p. 1.

1969.   "Dr. Fleming Named Bias Officer in Westmoreland's Office," _Jet_, Vol. 43, March 11, 1971, p. 19.

1970.   "8 Black GIs Held in Attack on White," _Washington Post_, August 1, 1970, p. A-4.

1971.   "80 Negroes At Academies; Total Doubles 1963 Figure," _Air Force Times_, Vol. 26, August 10, 1966, p. 10.

1972.   Endicott, William and Stanley Williford. "Uptight in the Armed Forces," _Nation_, Vol. 209, November 3, 1969, pp. 464-466.

1973.   "Enforcement Is Needed," (Editorial) _Baltimore Afro-American_, April 3, 1971, p. 4.

1974.   Everett, Robert P. "Brotherhood is the Name of the Game," _Airman_, Vol. 15, August, 1971, pp. 18-22.

1975. "Ex-Norfolk Football Star Slated To Be Admiral," Norfolk Journal and Guide, May 8, 1971, p. 8.

1976. "Failure to Report for Induction," Race Relations Law Reporter, Vol. 12, Winter, 1967, pp. 19, 231.

1977. "Fair Deal Ordered for Black Soldiers," Norfolk Journal and Guide, March 27, 1971, p. 1.

1978. Fendrich, James and Michael Pearson. "Black Veterans Return," Trans-Action, Vol. 7, March, 1970, pp. 32-37.

1979. _____ et al. "Marital Status and Political Alienation Among Black Veterans," American Journal of Sociology, Vol. 77, 1971, pp. 245-261.

1980. _____. "The Returning Black Vietnam Veteran," The Vietnam Veteran in Contemporary Society, L. Sherman and E. Caffey, Editors. Washington, DC: United States Government Printing Office, 1972.

1981. Field, R.L. "The Black Midshipmen at the U.S. Naval Academy," Naval Institute Proceeding, April, 1973, pp. 28-36.

1982. Friederich, Rudolf J. "54 Black Heroes: Medal Honor Winners," Crisis, Vol. 76, June/July, 1969, pp. 243-245.

1983. "Four at the Helm: Blacks Win Class Election at U.S. Naval Academy," Ebony, Vol. 28, January, 1973, pp. 100-102+.

1984. "Fourteen Black GIs Reported Jailed on Mutiny Charge in Vietnam," Washington Post, October 16, 1971, p. A-11.

1985. "Fugitive Black GIs Ask Pentagon Aid in German Court," Washington Post, June 9, 1971, p. A-3.

1986. "Gen. James in Highest Post Held by Black at Pentagon," Jet, Vol. 44, May 10, 1973, p. 31.

1987. "General Davison Named First Black Division Commander," Jet, Vol. 43, May 4, 1972, p. 5.

1988. "General GIs Wanted Tried on Bias Rap Cited by Army," Baltimore Afro-American, April 17, 1971, p. 1.

1989. "General Hunton Confirmed by Senate," Norfolk Journal and Guide, June 12, 1971, pp. 1-2.

1990. George, Vinson. "Battling the Pentagon," U.S. News and World Report, Vol. 55, September 30, 1963, p. 16.

1991. "Georgia's Vinson: Battling the Pentagon," U.S. News and World Report, Vol. 55, September 30, 1963, p. 16.

1992.   "GI Afro," <u>First Tuesday</u>, March, 1971, p. 6.

1993.   "GIs Blame 'No Dance' Girls in Panama," <u>Baltimore Afro-American</u>, May 22, 1971, p. 1.

1994.   "GI Race War in Germany," <u>Sepia</u>, Vol. 20, June, 1971, pp. 56–57.

1995.   "GIs Death Sparks Riot," <u>Chicago Daily Defender</u>, January 5, 1971, p. 19.

1996.   "GI Movement," <u>Southern Patriot</u>, September, 1970, p. 6.

1997.   "GIs Marched in Augusta," <u>Southern Patriot</u>, September, 1970, p. 1.

1998.   Goshko, John M. "Army Drops Charges Against Twenty-nine Black GI's," <u>Washington Post</u>, October 23, 1971, p. A-1.

1999.   _____. "Black Troops Distrust United States Military Justice," <u>Washington Post</u>, October 31, 1971, p. A-1.

2000.   _____. "Race Rifts Follow the Flag," <u>Washington Post</u>, September 27, 1970, p. B-1.

2001.   Gould, William Stuart. "Racial Conflict in the U.S. Army," <u>Race</u>, Vol. 15, July, 1973, pp. 1–27.

2002.   Grady, John. "The 'Less Than Honorable' Solution," <u>Nation</u>, Vol. 216, February 19, 1973, pp. 233–236.

2003.   Grant, Zali B. "Whites Against Blacks in Vietnam," <u>New Republic</u>, Vol. 160, January 18, 1969, pp. 15–16.

2004.   "Groups Rally to Support GI Charged with Murder," <u>Jet</u>, Vol. 48, September 28, 1972, p. 18.

2005.   Grove, Greene. "The Army and the Negro," <u>New York Times Magazine</u>, July 24, 1966, pp. 4–5, 49–51.

2006.   "Guard Nominates First Negro General," <u>Washington Post</u>, May 7, 1971, p. C-1.

2007.   "Guerrilla Trainer; Southeast Asian Jungles," <u>Ebony</u>, Vol. 20, April, 1964, pp. 47–48†.

2008.   Guild, H. "GI Race War in Germany, <u>Sepia</u>, Vol. 20, June, 1971, pp. 56–61.

2009.   Guimond, Gary. "Equal For All," <u>Airman</u>, Vol. 15, February, 1971, pp. 28–31.

2010.   Hall, N.J. "The Tragedy of Black Deserters," <u>Sepia</u>, Vol. 21, May, 1972, pp. 54–62.

2011.   Halloran, Richard. "General Combats Racial Irritants,"
        New York Times, September 2, 1971, p. 13.

2012.   Halstead, Fred. GI's Speak Out Against the War: The
        Case of the Fort Jackson Eight. New York: Pathfinder
        Press, 1970.

2013.   Hawkins, Augustus F. "Racism in the Military," Journal
        and Guide, January 1, 1972, p. 1.

2014.   Henderson, Lenneal J., Jr. "Impact of Military Base
        Shut-downs," Black Scholar, Vol. 5, October, 1973, pp.
        9-15.

2015.   "How Negro Americans Perform in Vietnam," U.S. News
        and World Report, August 15, 1966, p. 62.

2016.   "Ignoring Feelings of Blacks Leads to Riot on U.S. Air
        Force Base, General Says," Jet, Vol. 20, July 1, 1971,
        p. 46.

2017.   "Increase in Negroes Planned," Air Force Times, Vol.
        28, November 8, 1967, p. 4.

2018.   "Institutional Racism in the Military," Congressional
        Record 118, 92nd Congress, 2d Session, March 2, 1972.

2019.   "Investigation Planned on Racism in Military," Norfolk
        Journal and Guide, June 12, 1971, p. 9.

2020.   Jackson, Donald. "Black People and Vietnam," Liberator
        Magazine, December, 1965, pp. 9-10.

2021.   _____. "Unite or Perish," Liberator Maga-
        zine, February, 1967, pp. 16-18.

2022.   Jackson, George L. "Constraints of the Negro Civil
        Rights Movement on American Military Effectiveness:
        A Survey," Naval War College Review, Vol. 22, January,
        1970, pp. 100-107.

2023.   Jefferson, R.S. "The Results of Group Therapy with a
        Population of Black Enlisted Personnel in the United
        States Air Force," National Medical Association, Sep-
        tember, 1972, pp. 414-442.

2024.   Jefferson, William. "We Must Have the Most Talented,"
        Air Reservist, Vol. 22, July, 1970, pp. 8-9.

2025.   "Jesse Brown Largest Ship Named for Black American,"
        Jet, Vol. 43, February 22, 1973, p. 9.

2026.   Johnson, Haynes and George C. Wilson. Army in Anguish.
        New York: Pocket Books, 1972.

2027.   Johnson, Jesse J. A Pictorial History of Black Ser-
        vicemen: Missing Pages in United States History.
        Hampton, VA: Hampton Institute, 1970.

2028.   _____. Black Armed Forces Officers, 1736-
        1971. Hampton, VA: Hampton Institute, 1971.

2029.   _____. Black Women In the Armed Forces,
        1942-1974. Hampton, VA: Hampton Institute, 1974.

2030.   Johnson, Thomas T. "Negroes in the Nam," Ebony, August,
        1968, pp. 31-40.

2031.   _____. "Negro in Vietnam Uneasy About
        U.S.," New York Times, May 1, 1968.

2032.   _____. "Negro Veteran is Confused and
        Bitter," New York Times, July 29, 1968.

2033.   _____. "The U.S. Negro in Vietnam," New
        York Times, April 29, 1968, p. 1-F.

2034.   Jones, J. "The U.S. Army Reserve: It Pays to Go to
        Meetings," Essence, Vol. 30, November, 1972, p. 34.

2035.   Jones, Nathaniel R. et al. The Search For Military
        Justice: Report of an NAACP Inquiry Into the Problems
        of Negro Servicemen in West Germany. New York: NAACP
        Special Contribution Fund, 1971.

2036.   Karsten, Peter. The Naval Aristocracy. New York:
        Free Press, 1972.

2037.   King, Edward L. The Death of the Army. New York:
        Saturday Review Press, 1972.

2038.   King, Martin Luther, Jr. "A Time to Break Silence,"
        Freedomways, Vol. 7, Spring, 1967, pp. 103-117.

2039.   Lane, David A. "An Army Project in Duty-Time General
        Education of Negro Troops in Europe, 1947-1951,"
        Journal of Negro Education, Vol. 33, Spring, 1964, pp.
        117-124.

2040.   Lathan, Aaron. "Gen. Davis Buried in Arlington,"
        Washington Post, December 1, 1970, p. C-8.

2041.   Lee, U. "Draft and the Negro," Current History, July,
        1968, pp. 28-33.

2042.   Lewis, David L. and Judy Mia. "America's Greatest
        Negroes: A Survey," Crisis, Vol. 77, January, 1970,
        pp. 17-21.

2043.   Lewis, Flora. "The Rumble at Camp Lejeune," Atlantic
        Monthly, Vol. 225, January, 1970, pp. 35-41.

2044.   Lewis, Jesse W.   "A Star For 'Chappie' James--and a
        New, Top Job in the Pentagon," Air Force and Space
        Digest, Vol. 53, March, 1970, pp. 32-34.

2045.   Little, Roger W., Editor.   Selective Service and Amer-
        ican Society.   New York: n.p., 1969.

2046.   Llorens, David.   "Why Negroes Re-enlist," Ebony, Vol.
        23, August, 1968, pp. 87-92.

2047.   Lucas, R.   "The Navy's First Black Admiral," Sepia,
        Vol. 20, July, 1971, pp. 12-13.

2048.   Mabra, Fred J.   "Manpower Utilization," Military Review,
        Vol. 46, December, 1966, pp. 92-97.

2049.   MacGregor, Morris J. and Bernard C. Nalty, Editors.
        Blacks in the United States Armed Forces: Basic
        Documents.   Wilmington, DE: Scholarly Resources, Inc.,
        1977.   Vol. XII, "Equal Treatment and Opportunity:
        The McNamara Doctrine (1962-1973)."

2050.   "Mac's Other War; Negro Servicemen in Off-base Housing,"
        Time, September 29, 1967, p. 24.

2051.   "Major C.W. Sears Promoted in Vietnam," Norfolk Journal
        and Guide, January 9, 1971, p. 1.

2052.   "Malcolm X Association Charges Air Force Racial Bias,"
        Los Angeles Times, December 3, 1970, p. II-1.

2053.   Mallette, Rev. Daniel J.   "Vietnam: Only the Privileged
        are Exempt," Liberator Magazine, May, 1967, pp. 16-17.

2054.   "Man Refuses Draft: No Blacks on Board," Los Angeles
        Sentinel, December 3, 1970, p. D-1.

2055.   Marchbanks, V.H.J.   "The Black Physician and the USAF,"
        National Medical Association, January, 1972, pp. 73-74.

2056.   "Marine Gets Ten Year Term in Death in Racial Brawl,"
        New York Times, April 12, 1971, p. 5.

2057.   McHale, Tony.   "Black Airmen Feel Racism--Communica-
        tions Need Cited," Air Force Times, Vol. 31, March 10,
        1971, p. 19.

2058.   _____.   "Blacks at Ramey (AFB,PR) Tell of Pre-
        judice," Air Force Times, Vol. 31, July 28, 1971, p. 20.

2059.   McKissick, Floyd B. and Whitney M. Young, Jr.   "The
        Negro and the Army: Two Views," New Generation, Vol.
        48, Fall, 1966, pp. 10-15.

2060.   McLean, L. Deckle.   "The Black Man and the Draft,"
        Ebony, August, 1968, pp. 61-66.

2061.   McPhee, Mary. "The Colonel Is a Lady," _Sepia_, Vol. 21,
        June, 1972, pp. 30-32, 34, 36.

2062.   "Military Racial Education," _Tuesday Magazine_, April,
        1971, p. 26.

2063.   "Military Racism," _Civil Liberties_, February, 1973.

2064.   "Military's Black Generals Get Pentagon Duty," _Jet_,
        Vol. 39, April 16, 1970, p. 3.

2065.   "More Black Reservists Sought by National Guard," _Jet_,
        Vol. 42, November 25, 1971, p. 16.

2066.   Morris, Joe Alex, Jr. "Black GI's Crime Up in Europe,"
        Washington Post, November 12, 1971, p. A-24.

2067.   Morris, Steven. "How Blacks Upset the Marine Corps:
        'New Breed' Leathernecks are Tackling Racist Vestiges,"
        Ebony, Vol. 22, December, 1969, pp. 55-62.

2068.   Moskos, Charles C., Jr. "Racial Integration in the
        Armed Forces," _American Journal of Sociology_, Vol. 72,
        September, 1966, pp. 132-148.

2069.   _____. "The American Dilemma in
        Uniform: Racism in the Armed Forces," _Annals_, Vol.
        406, March, 1973, pp. 94-106.

2070.   _____. _The American Enlisted Man._
        New York: Russell Sage Foundation, 1970.

2071.   "Muhammad Ali-The Measure of a Man," _Freedomways_, Vol.
        7, Spring, 1967, pp. 101-102.

2072.   "NAACP Probers Cite Reasons for GI Unrest," _Norfolk
        Journal and Guide_, February 27, 1971, p. 1.

2073.   "NAACP Says Black Officer Beaten by Whites on Ship,"
        Jet, Vol. 43, December 14, 1972, p. 6.

2074.   "Navy Chief Raps Bias Against Blacks," _Jet_, Vol. 43,
        November 3, 1972, pp. 16-17.

2075.   "Navy Fires Mrs. Helen Bowers," _Black Panther_, August
        2, 1971, p. 5.

2076.   "Navy Lawyer Returns from Vietnam with More Experience,"
        Pittsburgh Courier, March 21, 1970, p. 6.

2077.   "Navy Names First Ship for Black Naval Officer," _Negro
        History Bulletin_, Vol. 34, March, 1971, p. 62.

2078.   "Navy Secretary Names Destroyer After First Black Naval
        Aviator," _Black Times_, February 25/March 3, 1971, p. 6.

2079.   "Navy Selects Fourth Black Captain, Second Line Offi-
        cer," Jet, Vol. 42, March 25, 1971, p. 18.

2080.   "Navy Steps Up Negro Commissioning Drive," Journal of
        Armed Forces, Vol. 105, December 23, 1967, p. 21.

2081.   "Navy Stops Exclusive Steward Recruiting," Black Times,
        February 25/March 3, 1971, p. 6.

2082.   "Navy to Grade on Ability to Deal with Blacks, Others,"
        Jet, Vol. 41, June 17, 1971, p. 1.

2083.   Navy USMC Seek More Negro Officers," Journal of Armed
        Forces, Vol. 105, November 4, 1967, p. 1.

2084.   "Negro Field Graders Rise 134% in 3 years," Air Force
        Times, Vol. 29, January 15, 1969, p. 4.

2085.   "Negro Progress in Armed Forces," Armed Forces Journal,
        Vol. 105, August 10, 1968, p. 2.

2086.   "Negro Re-Up Rates Double That of White," Air Force
        Times, Vol. 26, March 23, 1966, p. 3.

2087.   "Negro Service Rate Rises," Air Force Times, Vol. 27,
        March 1, 1967, p. 15.

2088.   "Negro Total Rises Slightly to 77,495," Air Force Times,
        Vol. 27, August 31, 1966, p. 6.

2089.   "Negroes in the Service," Army, Vol. 16, October, 1966,
        p. 26.

2090.   "New Jersey's Fort Dix Hit by High Crime and Race Ten-
        sion," Washington Post, April 6, 1971, p. A-3.

2091.   "New Opportunities for Blacks in Navy National News-
        paper Publishers Association Topic," Norfolk Journal
        and Guide, June 5, 1971, p. 8.

2092.   Newlry, John Henry, Jr. "An Assessment of the Rela-
        tionship Between Racial Perceptions and Patterns of
        Leadership Behavior Among Black and White Army Company
        Commanders." Unpublished Doctoral Dissertation, Cath-
        olic University of America, 1973.

2093.   Newson, Moses J. "Pentagon Not Enforcing Rights Laws,"
        Baltimore Afro-American, September 4, 1971, pp. 1†.

2094.   Newton, Isham G. "The Negro in the National Guard,"
        Phylon, Vol. 23, First Quarter, 1962, pp. 18-28.

2095.   "Nixon OK's 5 Black Army Officers for Generals," Jet,
        Vol. 43, June 22, 1972, p. 1.

2096.   Nommo (Black Students Union Newspaper at UCLA), March
        9, 1971. Special Issue on the Black Soldier and the
        War in Vietnam.

2097.   "Norfolk Is Next Stop for Navy's BLK Aviator," Norfolk
        Journal and Guide, February 27, 1971, p. 8.

2098.   "Norfolkian Supervisor of Vietnam Honor Unit," Norfolk
        Journal and Guide, March 27, 1971, p. 8.

2099.   Odom, Herbert G. "The Real Dorie Miller Story," Chi-
        cago Daily Defender, March 2, 1971, p. 9.

2100.   "Off to Germany," Chicago Daily Defender, February 9,
        1971, p. 3.

2101.   "Off-base Housing; Policy of the Defense Department,"
        New Republic, August 5, 1967, p. 9.

2102.   Olsen, P. "The Negro and the Sea," Negro History
        Bulletin, Vol. 35, February, 1972, pp. 4-43.

2103.   "100 Black Soldiers Battle Police on German Streets,"
        Jet, Vol. 43, August 31, 1972, p. 45.

2104.   "Only One Color: Negroes in Vietnam," Newsweek, Vol.
        66, December 6, 1965, pp. 42-43.

2105.   "Opportunities for Negroes in Military Called Best
        Ever," Air Force Times, Vol. 22, April 21, 1962, p. 25.

2106.   "Our First Admiral," Atlanta Daily World, May 6, 1971,
        p. 4.

2107.   "Oxford Occupation: Here's Chapter II," U.S. News and
        World Report, October 22, 1962, pp. 38†.

2108.   "Paradox of the Black Soldier," Ebony, Vol. 23, August,
        1968, p. 142.

2109.   Parks, David. GI Diary. New York: Harper and Row,
        1968.

2110.   Patton, Gwendolyn. "Black People and War," Liberator
        Magazine, February, 1967, pp. 10-11.

2111.   Payne, Ethel L. "Wilkins Optimistic on Bias Change
        in Services," Pittsburgh Courier, May 8, 1971, p. 29.

2112.   Pfautz, Harold W. "The New Negro: Emerging American,"
        Phylon, Vol. 24, Fourth Quarter, 1963, pp. 360-368.

2113.   Phillips, Larry. "Military Racism Cited By (Congres-
        sional Black) Caucus," Air Force Times, Vol. 32, De-
        cember 8, 1971, p. 63.

2114.   "Philly Coed Nominated for Air Force Academy," _Jet_,
        Vol. 43, March 16, 1972, p. 8.

2115.   Pierce, Ponchitta, and Peter Bailey. "The Returning
        Veteran," _Ebony_, Vol. 23, August, 1968, pp. 145-151.

2116.   "Pondexteur Williams Honored at Last," _Washington Post_,
        August 30, 1970, p. D-4.

2117.   "Poor Communication Seen as Cause of Marine Trouble,"
        Baltimore Afro-American, January 10, 1970, p. 14.

2118.   Pound, Michael C. "Details in Black: A Case Study
        Investigation and Analysis of the Content of the United
        States War Department Non-Fiction Motion Picture of the
        Negro Soldier." Unpublished Doctoral Dissertation, New
        York University, 1982.

2119.   "President Forms Advisory Group on Equal Opportunity
        in Forces," _Air Force Times_, Vol. 22, June 30, 1962,
        p. 24.

2120.   "Prejudice Fight Shifts Overseas," _Air Force Times_,
        Vol. 24, September 4, 1963, pp. 1, 6.

2121.   "Probe Bigotry on U.S. Bases in Europe," _Norfolk Jour-
        nal and Guide_, October 3, 1970, p. 9.

2122.   Puner, M. "What the Armed Forces Taught Us About In-
        tegration," _Coronet_, June, 1960, pp. 105-110.

2123.   "Race Relations Program in Army Gets Wilkins Approval,"
        Jet, Vol. 43, August 17, 1972, p. 54.

2124.   "Racism in the Military," _Congressional Record_, 118,
        92d Congress, 2d Session, October 14, 1972.

2125.   "Racism Led to New Group for Viet Vets," _Jet_, Vol. 41,
        November 5, 1970, p. 25.

2126.   "Rapping With Chappie (James)," _Air University Review_,
        Vol. 23, July, 1972.

2127.   "Render Resigns DOD Post," _Chicago Daily Defender_,
        August 28/September 3, 1971, p. 2.

2128.   "Report From Black America--A Newsweek Poll," _Newsweek_,
        Vol. 73, June 30, 1969, pp. 16-35.

2129.   "Reserves Get Black General; Only Marines Left Now,"
        Jet, Vol. 42, July 1, 1971, p. 46.

2130.   Resor, Stanley R. "Meeting the Challenge of a Changing
        World," _Army_, Vol. 18, November, 1968, pp. 19-21.

2131. "Samaritans On Wings: Black Nurses in Vietnam,"
       Ebony, Vol. 25, May, 1970, pp. 60-62, 64, 66-67.

2132. "SCEF Discredits Conspiracy Witness," _Baltimore Afro-_
       American, January 10, 1970, p. 14.

2133. Schanche, Don A. "Burn the Mother Down," _Saturday_
       Evening Post, Vol. 241, November 16, 1968, pp. 31-32,
       65-71.

2134. Schexnider, Alvin James. "The Development of National-
       ism: Political Socialization Among Blacks in the U.S.
       Armed Forces." Unpublished Doctoral Dissertation,
       Northwestern University, 1973.

2135. Schweitz, Bob. "Defense Council Set Up To End Dis-
       crimination," _Air Force Times_, Vol. 26, May 18, 1966,
       p. 2.

2136. _____. "Services Act Fast To Draft No Bias
       Plan," _Air Force Times_, Vol. 23, July 10, 1963, p. 10.

2137. Schweitz, R.E. "Our Integrated Army: Education and
       Housing for Servicemen's Families," _The Reporter_, No-
       vember 22, 1962, pp. 35-37.

2138. "Sergeant Found Innocent," _Norfolk Journal and Guide_,
       November 28, 1970, p. 2.

2139. "Service Careers for Negroes," _Journal of Armed Forces_,
       Vol. 104, April 29, 1967, p. 5.

2140. "Settlement Sought in Black GI Burial," _Miami Herald_,
       December 1, 1970, p. D-16.

2141. "Shuttle Fight Another Milestone in Black Aviation:
       Lt. Col. Guion S. Bluford, Jr., A Veteran of 144 Com-
       bat Missions in Vietnam," _Winston-Salem (NC) Journal_,
       August 28, 1983, p. 1.

2142. "Skepticism on Volunteer Army," _Black Times_, February
       15, 1971, p. 9.

2143. "Small Wave Washes Away Naval Tradition," _Ebony_, Vol.
       27, October, 1972, pp. 124+.

2144. Smith, Mary. "Black Women in Uniform," _Sacremento_
       Observer, June 1, 1972, p. D-18.

2145. Snellings, Rolland. "Vietnam; Whitey: I Will Not
       Severe," _Liberator Magazine_, March, 1966, pp. 8-9.

2146. Southall, Rita. _The Black Letters: Love Letters From_
       A Black Soldier in Vietnam. Washington, DC: Nuclas-
       sics and Science Publishing Co., 1972.

2147.   Stern, Sol.   "When The Black G.I. Comes Back From Viet-
        nam," New York Times Magazine, March 24, 1968, pp. 26-
        27.

2148.   Stewart, T.   "The Marines Vs. Prejudice," Sepia, Vol.
        20, August, 1971, pp. 32-39.

2149.   Stillman, Richard J.   "Negroes in the U.S. Armed For-
        ces," Phylon, Vol. 30, Summer, 1969, pp. 139-159.

2150.   Stokes, R.   "Race Riot at Long Binh; Army Stockade
        North of Saigon," Newsweek, Vol. 84, September 30,
        1968, p. 35.

2151.   Swift, Pamela.   "Black Midshipmen," Washington Post-
        Parade, January 16, 1972, p. 17.

2152.   Taylor, Clyde, Editor.   Vietnam and Black America: An
        Anthology of Protest and Resistance. Garden City, NY:
        Anchor Books, 1973. Many of the Articles were written
        by former soldiers.

2153.   "The Air Force Academy Blows Its Mind," Ebony, Vol. 27,
        March, 1972, pp. 33-42+.

2154.   "The Army Clears the Record," Newsweek, Vol. 80, Oc-
        tober 16, 1972.

2155.   "The Black Experience in Air Force Blue," Air Force
        Magazine, Vol. 55, June, 1972, pp. 30-34.

2156.   "The Black Junior Officer in Today's Army," Military
        Review, Vol. 52, May, 1972, pp. 61-67.

2157.   "The Black Soldier," Ebony, Vol. 24, August, 1968.
        Entire issue.

2158.   "The Drill Sergeant Is a Lady," Ebony, Vol. 27, Decem-
        ber, 1972, pp. 84-89.

2159.   "The Great Society in Uniform," Newsweek, Vol. 67,
        August 22, 1966, pp. 46-48.

2160.   "The Integrated Society," Time, Vol. 88, December 23,
        1966, p. 22.

2161.   "The Pentagon Jumps into The Race Fight," U.S. News and
        World Report, August 19, 1963, pp. 49-50.

2162.   The President's Committee on Equal Opportunity in the
        Armed Forces, Initial Report. Mimeographed. June 13,
        1963. - -, Final Report. Mimeographed, November, 1964.

2163.   The Search for Military Justice: Report of an NAACP
        Inquiry into the Problems of the Negro Serviceman in
        West Germany. New York: NAACP, 1971.

2164. "The Terms Defined," Ebony, Vol. 25, August, 1970, p. 35.

2165. "The Volunteer Army: Black Misgivings," Christian Century, Vol. 90, February 28, 1973, p. 252.

2166. "The War in Vietnam," Freedomways, Spring, 1965, pp. 229-230.

2167. "These Truly are the Brave: History of U.S. Black Soldier," Ebony, Vol. 23, August, 1968, pp. 164-170, 177.

2168. "Three Black Colonels Picked for Brigadier Generals," Washington Post, May 14, 1971, p. A-2.

2169. "'There Is Racism and It Is Ugly'," New York Times, September 5, 1971, p. E-5.

2170. "Travis Air Force Base Erupts," Black Panther, May 29, 1971, p. 17.

2171. "Two Black Generals," Negro History Bulletin, Vol. 34, April, 1971, p. 93.

2172. United States Commission on Civil Rights. Family Housing and the Negro Serviceman. Washington, DC: United States Government Printing Office, 1963.

2173. United States Commission on Civil Rights. "The Negro in the Armed Forces," in Civil Rights '63. Washington, DC: United States Government Printing Office, 1963, pp. 169-224.

2174. "United States General Rebuked," Pittsburgh Courier, August 14, 1971, p. 12.

2175. U.S. Selective Service System. The Classification Process. Washington, DC: United States Government Printing Office, 1950.

2176. United States Commission on Civil Rights. Employment: 1961 Report. Washington, DC: United States Government Printing Office, 1961.

2177. U.S. Commission on Civil Rights, South Dakota Advisory Committee. Negro Airmen in a Northern Community, Discrimination in Rapid City, South Dakota. Washington, DC: United States Government Printing Office, 1963.

2178. U.S. President's Committee on Equal Opportunity in the Armed Forces. Equality of Treatment and Opportunity for Negro Military Personnel Stationed within the U.S. Washington, DC: United States Government Printing Office, 1963.

2179.   "U.S. Air Force Cites Four Black Men as 'Outstanding'," Jet, Vol. 43, October 26, 1972, p. 2.

2180.   "U.S. Army Appoints Three New Black Generals," Norfolk Journal and Guide, May 22, 1971, p. 9.

2181.   "U.S. Backs Black GI Burial in White Plot," Washington Post, August 26, 1970, p. A-23.

2182.   "U.S. Navy's First Black Admiral," Newsweek, Vol. 79, May 10, 1971, p. 63.

2183.   "Vietnam Hero Goes on Trial in Germany," Washington Post, October 27, 1970, p. A-8.

2184.   "Voluntary Segregation to End in U.S. Marines," Jet, Vol. 43, September 14, 1972, p. 24.

2185.   Watson, D.L. "Search for Justice Continues," Crisis, Vol. 43, October, 1971, pp. 258-259.

2186.   Watts, Daniel H. "Reverend King and Vietnam," Liberator Magazine, May, 1967, p. 3.

2187.   Webb, Percy R. Memoranda of a Soldier. New York: Vantage Press, 1961.

2188.   Weigert, Kathleen Maas. "Stratification and Minority Group Ideology: Black Soldiers' Beliefs About Military and Civilian Opportunities." Unpublished Doctoral Dissertation, University of Notre Dame, 1972.

2189.   White, Jack. "The Angry Black Soldier," The Progressive, Vol. 34, March, 1970, pp. 22-26.

2190.   White, James S. "Race Relations in the Army," Military Review, Vol. 50, July, 1970, pp. 3-12.

2191.   White, Milton. "Malcolm X in the Military," Black Scholar, Vol. 1, May, 1970, pp. 31-35.

2192.   Whitmore, Terry. Memphis-Nam-Sweeden: The Autobiography of a Black American Exile. Garden City, NY: Doubleday and Co., 1971.

2193.   Williams, Fenton A. Just Before the Dawn: A Doctor's Experiences in Vietnam. New York: Exposition Press, 1971. Author discusses his military experience in the U.S. Army during the Vietnam War.

2194.   Williams, John A. Captain Blackman. Garden City, NY: Doubleday and Co., 1972.

2195.   Willis, William S. "Divide and Rule: Red, White and Black in the Southeast," Journal of Negro History, Vol. 48, July, 1963, pp. 157-176.

2196.   Wilson, C.E.   "A Negro at the War in Vietnam," Liber-
        ator Magazine, March, 1966, pp. 31-32.

2197.   "Witnesses Testify Against Black GI in My Lai Trial,"
        Jet, Vol. 41, November 5, 1970, p. 57.

2198.   "Women In Uniform," Ebony, Vol. 18, December, 1962,
        pp. 62-67.

2199.   Young, Whitney M.,Jr.   "When Negroes in Vietnam Come
        Home," Harper's Magazine, Vol. 234, June, 1967, pp.
        63-69.

2200.   Zelik, Melvin.   "The Census and Selective Service,"
        Eugenics Quarterly, Vol. 15, September, 1968, pp. 173-
        176.

X.

Blacks in the Post-Vietnam Era

2201. "A Salute to Navy Professionals During Black History Month," Arizona Informant, February 18, 1981, p. 1.

2202. "Admiral Gravely to Lead U.S. Navy's Third Fleet," Jet, Vol. 50, August 19, 1976, p. 6.

2203. "Admiral L.C. Chambers," Michigan Chronicle, June 18, 1977, p. D-1

2204. "Afro-American Military Physicians Currently on Active Duty (as of June, 1974)," National Medical Association, July, 1974, pp. 350-352.

2205. "Air Force Academy Names First Black Cadet Commander," Jet, Vol. 53, September 8, 1977, p. 5.

2206. "Air Force Gets First Black Woman Chaplain," Baltimore Afro-American, August 9, 1980, p. 12.

2207. "Alexander Is Confirmed as Army Secretary," Baltimore Afro-American, February 19, 1977, p. 1.

2208. "Army Changing Discharge of Status of D. Willis," Chicago Defender, May 15, 1982, p. 15.

2209. "Army General A.P. Chambers," New York Amsterdam News, May 30, 1981, p. 55.

2210. "Army Major General Fred Sheffey Plans to Retire," Baltimore Afro-American, August 9, 1980, p. 10.

2211. "Army May Be 42-50% Black in a Decade," Cleveland Call and Post, February 5, 1977, p. A-13.

2212.   "Army Position on Military Unions Viewed," Atlanta
         Daily World, January 19, 1977, p. 2.

2213.   "Army Secretary Clifford Alexander," Atlanta Daily
         World, March 27, 1977, p. 4.

2214.   "Army Secretary Supports Aid for Viet Vets," Baltimore
         Afro-American, July 2, 1977, p. 1.

2215.   "Army Seeks To Recruit Black Chaplains," Chicago De-
         fender, February 18, 1978, p. 6.

2216.   "Army Studies Black Discharges," Baltimore Afro-Ameri-
         can, January 8, 1977, p. 8.

2217.   "Army's First Female Dental Intern Completes Studies,"
         Jet, Vol. 47, October 3, 1974, p. 18.

2218.   "Army Trainee Accuses Drill Instructor of Abuse,"
         Atlanta World, December 10, 1978, p. 2.

2219.   "AUSA Report on Military Compensation," Atlanta Daily
         World, July 19, 1977, p. 5.

2220.   "AUSA Report on Minimum Army Requirements," Atlanta
         Daily World, July 15, 1977, p. 6.

2221.   "AUSA Report on Strategic Mobility," Atlanta Daily
         World, July 18, 1977, p. 4.

2222.   Avillo, Phillip. "Beyond Integration: The Air Force
         and Racial Justice," Air University Review, Vol. 32,
         January/February, 1981, pp. 116-120.

2223.   Bailey, Peter. "Black Veterans: The Forgotten Victims
         of Vietnam," Ebony, Vol. 28, September, 1974, pp. 33-
         34†.

2224.   Berg, Gene. "Uncovering a Cover-up: The Marines and
         the KKK," Encore, Vol. 6, January 17, 1977, pp. 17-18.

2225.   "Black Admiral To Command Largest U.S. Naval District,"
         Jet, Vol. 48, June 5, 1975, p. 18.

2226.   "Black Army Colonel Named First District Engineer,"
         Jet, Vol. 47, February 14, 1974, p. 16.

2227.   "Black Lawyer Named to U.S. Army's Top Post," Jet, Vol.
         50, February 10, 1977, pp. 22-23.

2228.   "Black Marines and the Ku Klux Klan," Black Scholar,
         Vol. 9, April, 1977, p. 1.

2229.   "Black Marines Battle Ku Klux Klan at Camp Pendleton
         Base," Black Scholar, Vol. 9, April, 1977, pp. 46-49.

2230. "Black Percentage of Air Forces Rises--Total Decrease,"
       Air Force Times, Vol. 36, October, 1975, p. 19.

2231. "Black Women In Court Martial Over Corn Row," Jet, Vol.
       47, February 20, 1975, p. 19.

2232. "Blacks' OERs Slightly Below Whites': Difference Held
       Insignificant," Air Force Times, Vol. 36, October 29,
       1975, p. 8.

2233. Booker, Simeon. "General 'Chappie' James Laid to Rest
       with Honors," Jet, Vol. 51, March 16, 1978, pp. 12-15.

2234. _____. "Navy Trains First Black Woman Pilot,"
       Jet, Vol. 47, November 28, 1974, pp. 20-24.

2235. _____. "Throng Honors Gen. James at End of
       35-Year Stint," Jet, Vol. 51, February 16, 1978, pp.
       6-7.

2236. _____. "What the Vietnam War Did to Blacks,"
       Jet, Vol. 48, May 22, 1975, pp. 14-17.

2237. "Boss Man of the Army," Ebony, Vol. 32, June, 1977,
       pp. 33-36†.

2238. "Boss of the Vaunted VII Army Corps," Ebony, Vol. 34,
       July, 1979, pp. 44-46†.

2239. Brown, Tony. "Nation's Security Depends on Black
       Soldier," New York Voice, June 26, 1982, p. 6.

2240. Bullock, James A. "The Great Air Force Experiment,"
       Negro Heritage, Vol. 14, 1975, pp. 50-62.

2241. Butler, John S. and Malcolm D. Holmes. "Perceived
       Discrimination and the Military Experience," Journal
       of Political and Military Sociology, Vol. 9, Spring,
       1981, pp. 17-30.

2242. "Camp Pendleton Marines Case Discussed," Atlanta Daily
       World, January 16, 1977, p. 1.

2243. "Carl Brashear, Navy's First Black Diver," Atlanta World,
       April 5, 1979, p. 5.

2244. "Carl Brashear Retires as Diver for U.S. Navy," Norfolk
       Journal and Guide, March 30, 1979, p. B-11.

2245. "Chappie James Confirmed as Four-star General," Jet,
       Vol. 48, August 14, 1975, p. 40.

2246. "C. Hayes First Black To Command Navy Hospital Corps
       School," Michigan Chronicle, August 22, 1981, p. A-7.

2247. "Christine Knightson Becomes Army's 2nd Black Woman Aviator," Cleveland Call and Post, September 20, 1980, p. A-10.

2248. "Clifford Alexander Is Sworn in as Army Secretary," Atlanta Daily World, February 22, 1977, p. 1; Norfolk Journal and Guide, February 26, 1977, p. A-1.

2249. "Closest Black to Carter Is Naval Commander Who Carries U.S. Secret Code," Jet, Vol. 50, March 31, 1977, p. 6.

2250. Cobb, W. Montague. "New Spirit in the Navy," Crisis, Vol. 86, November, 1979, pp. 393-394.

2251. "Col. Thomas Hughley Gets Army Meritorious Service Medal," Cleveland Call and Post, March 1, 1980, p. A-11.

2252. Couch, William Jr. "The Image of the Black Soldier in Selected American Novels," CLA Journal, Vol. 20, December, 1976, pp. 176-184.

2253. "Dean Mann Appointed Army Hospital Commander," National Medical Association, July, 1974, p. 343.

2254. Dell, Nat. "Black Soldier Update," Soldiers, Vol. 31, January, 1976, pp. 6-10.

2255. Dellums, Ron. "Don't Slam Door to Military," Joint Center for Political Studies Focus, June, 1975, p. 6.

2256. Department of Defense. Black Americans in Defense of Our Nation. Washington, DC: United States Government Printing Office, 1982.

2257. DeSilva, Antoinette. "Top Ranking Blacks in the Air Force," Dawn Supplement, July, 1981, pp. 6, 12.

2258. "Detroit G.I. Selected Mayor of Army Area," Michigan Chronicle, October 14, 1978, p. 1.

2259. "Donna Davis, Army Paratrooper," Michigan Chronicle, January 27, 1979, p. D-2.

2260. Drew, Robin. "Army's (2d Lt. Marcella A.) Hayes, 1st Black Woman Military Aviator in U.S. Forces," United States Army Aviation Digest, Vol. 26, January, 1980, p. 1.

2261. Editorial. "Bias in Army Discipline," Chicago Defender," October 28, 1978, p. 6.

2262. Editorial. "General Rogers Views on Racism and Sexism in Army," Baltimore Afro-American, November 28, 1981, p. 4.

2263.   Editorial. "Number of Blacks in U.S. Armed Forces,"
        Chicago Defender, July 12, 1982, p. 9.

2264.   "Editorial Questions Possibility of All-Black U.S.
        Army," Michigan Chronicle, November 12, 1977, p. A-8.

2265.   Esaw, R.H. "Racial Pendulum Has Swung Too Far,"
        Marine Corps Gazette, Vol. 61, April, 1977, pp. 12-13.

2266.   "European View of Black American Soldiers," Cleveland
        Call and Post, July 24, 1982, p. A-9.

2267.   Fiman, Bryon G. "Black-White and American-Vietnamese
        Relations Among Soldiers in Vietnam," Journal of Social
        Issues, Vol. 3, 1975, pp. 39-48.

2268.   "1st Black Woman Selected for Shuttle Missions," Air
        Force Times, Vol. 42, May 3, 1982, p. 4.

2269.   "First Female Army G.I. D. Aldrich Promoted to High-
        est Rank," New York Amsterdam News, October 14, 1978,
        p. B-1.

2270.   "Five Receive Commissions at Norfolk State College,"
        Norfolk Journal and Guide, January 29, 1977, p. B-18.

2271.   Fleming, Robert. "Col. Frank Petersen 'The Godfather'
        - In Line for Star Rank," Encore, Vol. 8, April 2,
        1979, p. 22.

2272.   Foster, George. "For Blacks: Statistics Tell Story,"
        Air Force Times, Vol. 34, July 10, 1974, pp. 1, 4.

2273.   Friederich, Rudolf J. "Medal of Honor for 21 Black
        Vietnam Heroes," Crisis, Vol. 81, August/September,
        1974, pp. 227-228.

2274.   "Ft. Stewart, Georgia, Soldier Sees No Future for
        Blacks in Army," Baltimore Afro-American, November 18,
        1978, p. 7.

2275.   Futernick, Allah J. "Racial References and Degree of
        Prejudice Among White Southern ROTC Cadets," Journal
        of Political and Military Sociology, Vol. 15, Spring,
        1977, pp. 53-62.

2276.   Gatling, Wade S. "Equal Opportunity in the Air Force,"
        Crisis, Vol. 83, August/September, 1976, pp. 250-252.

2277.   "General James Gets 4th Star at Air Force Ceremonies,"
        Jet, Vol. 97, September 18, 1975, pp. 24-26.

2278.   "General John Q.T. King: Portrait of a Citizen-Sol-
        dier," Crisis, Vol. 85, December, 1978, pp. 347-349.

2279.   "Gen. William Brown Named Commander USAF in Europe,"
        New York Amsterdam News, August 9, 1980, p. 25.

2280.   Goode, M.A.   "The Long and Shorthand of It," Airman,
        Vol. 23, October, 1979, pp. 17-19.

2281.   Harrod, Frederick S.   "Integration of the Navy," U.S.
        Navy Institute Proceedings, Vol. 105, October, 1979,
        pp. 40-47.

2282.   "Hazel Johnson Becomes First Black Woman General," Jet,
        Vol. 51, June 21, 1979, p. 18.

2283.   "He Flies the Largest Airplane in the World," Ebony,
        Vol. 34, April, 1979, pp. 98-100†.

2284.   "High Dropout Rate Plagues Volunteer Army," Atlanta
        World, December 17, 1978, p. 2.

2285.   Holt, Bryan D.   "Miss Mines Is First Black Woman Mid-
        shipman," Key News, July 29, 1976, p. 1.

2286.   "Howard Grad Becomes First Black Female Navy Lawyer,"
        Jet, Vol. 47, April 10, 1975, p. 29.

2287.   Hunt, James W.   "The Effects of Two Teaching Methods
        on Perceived Discrimination Against Blacks and Feelings
        of Reverse Racism in a United States Combat Service
        Support Organization."   Unpublished Doctoral Disserta-
        tion, North Carolina State University at Raleigh, 1976.

2288.   "Illinois Names First Black Woman to Merchant Marines,"
        Jet, Vol. 50, April 1, 1976, p. 42.

2289.   "It's Official: First Black Marine General Is In-
        stalled," Jet, Vol. 56, May 17, 1979, p. 13.

2290.   James, Felix.   "The Attitude Toward the Recruitment of
        Black Troops in Ohio, 1862-1863," Journal of Afro-
        American Issues, Vol. 2, 1974, pp. 49-58.

2291.   Janowitz, Morris.   "Focus on Blacks in the Military,"
        Joint Center for Political Studies Focus, June, 1975,
        pp. 3-5.

2292.   _____ and Charles Moskos.   "Racial Composi-
        tion in the All-Volunteer Forces," Armes Forces Society,
        Vol. 1, November, 1974, pp. 109-123.

2293.   "Joan Bynum Is Navy's First Black Female Captain," Jet,
        Vol. 55, November 23, 1978, p. 5.

2294.   Johnson, Herschel.   "Stand-in for the Enemy," Ebony,
        Vol. 33, February, 1978, pp. 87-90†.

2295. Johnson, Patrice. "Cadet Benjamin Tries Her Wings,"
      Encore, Vol. 6, January 8, 1977, pp. 17-18.

2296. _____. "Changing Face of the Military,"
      Encore, Vol. 6, August 1, 1977, pp. 9-10†.

2297. Johnson, Ralph. "America's First Black Four-star
      General vs. His Militant Critics," Sepia, Vol. 25,
      February, 1976, pp. 34-41.

2298. Jones, Caroline R. "Black Women in the Army: Where
      the Jobs Are," Crisis, Vol. 82, May, 1975, pp. 175-177.

2299. _____. "Making a Career out of the Mili-
      tary," Encore, Vol. 4, June 23, 1975, p. 76.

2300. Jones, Lafayette. "Marketing and Merchandising to the
      Black Military Patron," Interservice, Vol. 2, Winter,
      1982, pp. 27-30†.

2301. Jordan, Vernon E., Jr. "Blacks in the Army: Numbers
      Aren't the Point," Washington Star, July 13, 1975.

2302. "Joy Harris Describes Racism in the Navy," Norfolk
      Journal and Guide, December 10, 1980, p. A-1.

2303. Keller, Ella Tates. "Black Families in the Military
      System." Unpublished Doctoral Dissertation, Missis-
      sippi State University, 1980.

2304. "L. Branch Becomes 1st Black Catholic Chaplain for
      U.S. Navy," Atlanta World, September 12, 1982, p. 2.

2305. "Life for African-Americans in U.S. Army," World Muslim
      News, March 24, 1982, p. 1.

2306. "Lt. Col. Melvin Bowdan Retires from U.S. Army," Los
      Angeles Sentinel, December 6, 1979, p. A-10.

2307. "Lt. Comdr. Kelley Promotes Careers in the Navy," Los
      Angeles Sentinel, June 2, 1977, p. A-2.

2308. "Marine Base Named after Late Black Drill Sgt. Major,"
      Jet, Vol. 47, May 16, 1974, p. 50.

2309. "Marine Jailed in KKK Case," Baltimore Afro-American,
      January 8, 1977, p. 3.

2310. Massquoi, Hans J. "Battle the Army Can't Afford to
      Lose," Ebony, Vol. 29, February, 1974, pp. 116-118†.

2311. "Moments in Black Military History," Air Force Times,
      Vol. 41, March 16, 1981, pp. 43-44.

2312. Moore, Nathaniel. "Procurement of Black Army Officers
      Is In Trouble," Parameters, Vol. 8, December, 1978,
      pp. 55-61.

2313.   "Mother Is a Sergeant: Single WAC Noncom Becomes A-
        doptive Parent after Rule Change," Ebony, Vol. 29,
        October, 1974, pp. 156-158†.

2314.   "NATO Leaders Reportedly Object to Number of Black
        GI's in Europe," Cleveland Call and Post, June 12,
        1982, p. A-1.

2315.   "Navy Chaplain Carolyn Higgins," Norfolk Journal and
        Guide, February 12, 1980, p. 1.

2316.   "Navy Gets Its First Black Woman in Medical Corps,"
        Jet, Vol. 48, May 29, 1975, p. 24.

2317.   "Navy Names First Black Air Patrol Squadron Chief,"
        Jet, Vol. 47, December 12, 1974, p. 50.

2318.   "Navy Tabs First Black as Air Wing Commander," Jet,
        Vol. 54, August 24, 1978, p. 26.

2319.   "Navy's Efforts to Combat Racism," Atlanta World, Sep-
        tember 4, 1979, p. 1.

2320.   Nikolayev, G. "Racist Army," Soviet Military Review,
        Vol. 11, November, 1978, pp. 49-50†.

2321.   "Norfolk NAACP to Probe Military Personnel's Bias Com-
        plaints," Norfolk Journal and Guide, July 21, 1982,
        p. 1.

2322.   "Number of American Blacks Who Would Die in War,"
        Michigan Chronicle, July 17, 1982, p. A-6.

2323.   "Number of Blacks in the Army," Norfolk Journal and
        Guide, March 23, 1979, p. A-10.

2324.   Ochipinti, Laura. "I Am an American," Sergeants, Vol.
        19, October, 1918, pp. 18-20.

2325.   "Old Soldier Who Wouldn't Surrender," Ebony, Vol. 29,
        November, 1974, pp. 86-88†.

2326.   "Outstanding Airmen Honored at Air Force Association
        Convention," Norfolk Journal and Guide, January 1,
        1977, p. A-6.

2327.   Pecorella, Patricia Anne. "Racial Inequalities in
        Army Reward Systems: A Definition and Empirical Eval-
        uation." Unpublished Doctoral Dissertation, Universiy
        of Michigan, 1976.

2328.   Philpott, Tom. "Racial Balance Called Vital to AVF
        Effectiveness," Air Force Times, Vol. 41, November 24,
        1980, p. 10.

2329.   Philpott, Tom.   "Racial Imbalance Cause for Dilemma,"
        Air Force Times, Vol. 42, July 12, 1982, p. 7.

2330.   _____.   "Should AVF's Racial Mix Concern Us?,"
        Air Force Times, Vol. 41, November 17, 1980, pt. 1, p.7.

2331.   Pilisuk, Marc.   "The Legacy of the Vietnam Veteran,"
        Journal of Social Issues, Vol. 31, Fall, 1975, pp. 3-12.

2332.   Poinsett, Alex.   "Gen. Daniel (Chappie) James, Jr.:
        New Boss of the Nation's Air Defense," Ebony, Vol. 30,
        December, 1975, pp. 48-51†.

2333.   Poole, Isaiah J.   "New Pilot at Army," Black Enter-
        prise, Vol. 70, November, 1979, p. 17.

2334.   "(Pres.) Carter Nominates 2 Army Brigadier Generals for
        Promotions," Norfolk Journal and Guide, April 27, 1979,
        p. B-13.

2335.   "Pretty Petty Officer Is Navy Electronics Expert,"
        Jet, Vol. 49, December 18, 1975, p. 3.

2336.   "Problems Facing New Secretary Alexander," Pittsburgh
        Courier, March 5, 1977, p. 6.

2337.   "Recruiting: Blacks Up," Air Force Times, Vol. 35,
        November 13, 1974, p. 22.

2338.   Reed, Fred.   "Fear Expressed for Jailed Blacks (In
        November Racial Assaults at Camp Pendleton, Calif.),"
        Air Force Times, Vol. 37, June 3, 1977, p. 4.

2339.   "Robert Goodrum Named 'Midshipman of the Year'," At-
        lanta Daily World, February 22, 1977, p. 1.

2340.   "ROTC Grads May Be Assigned to the Reserves," Norfolk
        Journal and Guide, March 12, 1977, p. B-18.

2341.   Rowan, Carl T.   "Racial Issues In Debate on Draft Reg-
        istration," St. Louis Argus, June 19, 1980, pp. 1, 10.

2342.   Ryan, Paul B.   "USS Constellation Flare-up: Was It
        Mutiny?," U.S. Naval Institute Proceedings, Vol. 102,
        January, 1976, pp. 45-53.

2343.   "Salute to Blacks in the Navy," Baltimore Afro-American,
        March 6, 1982, p. 16.

2344.   Schexnider, Alvin J.   "Expectations from the Ranks:
        Representativeness and Value Systems," American Be-
        havioral Scientist, Vol. 19, May/June, 1976, pp. 523-
        542.

2345.   _____.   "Race and the All-Volunteer Army,"
        Armed Forces and Society, Vol. 2, 1976, pp. 421-434.

2346.   Schilling, Jane. "Charge! 54th! Charge!," The Afro-American Journal, Vol. 2, April, 1974, pp. 1, 3, 6.

2347.   Schweitz, Bob. "A Look at the Rate of Blacks in the Armed Forces and Its Effect on Recruitment of Whites," Air Force Times, Vol. 35, December 25, 1974, p. 13.

2348.   _____. "Blacks in the Service: A Rebuttal," Air Force Times, Vol. 35, June 11, 1975, p. 11.

2349.   "Second Black Officer Named as Navy Admiral," Jet, Vol. 50, February 14, 1974, p. 5.

2350.   "Second Marine Stands Trial in KKK Case at Camp Pendleton," Atlanta Daily World, January 14, 1977, p. 1.

2351.   "Secretary Alexander Names Five New Black Army Generals," Jet, Vol. 55, February 8, 1979, p. 16.

2352.   "Sergeant Sentenced for Death of Recruit," Baltimore Afro-American, December 23, 1978, p. 7.

2353.   "7 S.L. Army Recruiters Honored for Outstanding Performance," St. Louis Argus, January 31, 1980, pp. 1, 3.

2354.   Shapiro, Richard Laurence. "American Military and Race Relations: A Case Study of Racial Attitudes and Behavior at American Air Force Bases Overseas." Unpublished Doctoral Dissertation, University of Denver, 1974.

2355.   Shields, Patricia M. "The Burden of the Draft: The Vietnam Years," Journal of Political and Military Sociology, Vol. 9, Fall, 1981, pp. 215-228.

2356.   "Shuttle Flight Another Milestone in Black Aviation: Lt. Col. Guion S. Bluford, Jr. Becomes the First Black to Fly in Space," Winston-Salem (NC) Journal, August 28, 1983, p. 1.

2357.   Strayer, Richard et al. "Vietnam Veterans: A Study Exploring Adjustment Patterns and Attitudes," Journal of Social Issues, Vol. 3, Fall, 1975, pp. 81-93.

2358.   "The Drill Sergeant Is a Lady," Ebony, Vol. 27, December, 1973, pp. 84-89.

2359.   "The Military and the KKK," Los Angeles Sentinel, January 6, 1977, p. A-6.

2360.   "3 Sailors Face Courts-Martial After Racial Incident," Atlanta Daily World, September 7, 1979, p. 1.

2361.   "Top Brass-24 Make Grade: Military Ranks Open to Dozen Black Flag Rank Officers," Ebony, Vol. 32, May, 1978, pp. 40+.

2362. "Top Black Women Officers of U.S. Armed Forces," New York Amsterdam News, April 11, 1981, p. 36.

2363. "Top Ranking Black in Navy," Dawn Supplement, September, 1981, pp. 6. 23.

2364. "2 Naval Advisors Discuss Racial Progress in the U.S. Navy," Chicago Defender, February 10, 1979, p. 5.

2365. "Two More Black Marines on Trial at Camp Pendleton," Los Angeles Sentinel, February 17, 1977, p. A-12.

2366. "USAF Sgt. Hughes Interviewed About Being Held Hostage in Iran," Norfolk Journal and Guide, November 30, 1979, p. A-1.

2367. "U.S. Air Force's Top Kick," Ebony, Vol. 28, May, 1974, pp. 45-48+.

2368. "U.S. Army: Discharge Reviews," Encore, Vol. 4, October 4, 1976, pp. 13-14.

2369. "U.S. Naval Academy Gets First Black Female Student," Jet, Vol. 50, July 29, 1976, p. 6.

2370. "U.S. Navy's First Black Woman Pilot, B. Robinson," Baltimore Afro-American, June 14, 1980, p. 1.

2371. "Vice Admiral Samuel Gravely Retires," Baltimore Afro-American, July 12, 1980, p. 3.

2372. "Views Problems with Young Blacks in the Army," Michigan Chronicle, November 18, 1978, p. A-8.

2373. "Volunteer Army and Blacks," Atlanta Daily World, May 5, 1979, p. 4.

2374. "Volunteer Army Viewed," Norfolk Journal and Guide, March 12, 1977, p. B-12.

2375. Walker, Elvoid, Jr. "Race Relations in the United States Army." Unpublished Doctoral Dissertation, United States International University, 1978.

2376. Weigert, Kathleen M. "Stratification, Ideology, and Opportunity Beliefs Among Black Soldiers," Public Opinion Quarterly, Vol. 38, Spring, 1974, pp. 57-68.

2377. West, Malcolm R. "Blacks Take Strain of Army Life Better: Chaplain," Jet, Vol. 51, March 10, 1977, pp. 20-21.

2378. "West Point Names First Black Brigade Leader," Jet, Vol. 56, September 6, 1979, p. 16.

2379. Willis, John. "Variations in State Casualty Rates in
       World War II and the Vietnam War," Social Problems,
       Vol. 22, 1975, pp. 558-558.

2380. Wilson, Dale E. "The Army's Black Tank Battalions,"
       Armor, Vol. 91, March/April, 1982, pp. 30-31.

2381. Wilson, Walter Peete, Jr. "A Survey of Cultural Values
       and Perceptions of Black and White Managers at a Mili-
       tary Installation."   Unpublished Doctoral Dissertation,
       United States International University, 1980.

2382. "Woman General," Sacramento Observer Magazine, Vol. 16,
       June 14-20, 1979, p. F-3.

2383. "Women in the Service Academies," Ebony, Vol. 32, No-
       vember, 1976, pp. 31-34, 36, 38.

2384. Wright, Thomas E. "Big Man in the New Army," Sepia,
       Vol. 26, October, 1977, pp. 51-54.

2385. "Woman Navigator Spans the Globe for U.S. Air Force,"
       Ebony, Vol. 33, December, 1978, pp. 85-86+.

2386. "Young Black Couple Has On-the-job Marriage," Jet, Vol.
       48, June 6, 1974, pp. 28-29.

Appendixes

I.

Black American Generals and Flag Officers

A. THE FIRST BLACK GENERALS

Major General Robert B. Elliott, Commanding General, National Guard of the State of South Carolina (1870).

Brigadier General Samuel J. Lee, Chief of Staff, National Guard of the State of South Carolina (1872).

Brevet Brigadier General William Beverly Nash, National Guard of the State of South Carolina (1873).

Brigadier General H.W. Purvis, Adjutant and Inspector General, National Guard of the State of South Carolina (1873).

Brigadier General Joseph Hayne Rainey, Judge Advocate General, National Guard of the State of South Carolina (1873).

Major General Prince R. Rivers, Commanding General, Third Division, National Guard of the State of South Carolina (1873).

Major General Robert Smalls, National Guard of the State of South Carolina (1873).

Major General First Division, National Guard of the State of South Carolina (1873).

Brigadier General William J. Whipper, Second Brigade, Second Division, National Guard of the State of South Carolina (1873).

Brigadier General T. Morris Chester, Fourth Brigade, National Guard of the State of Louisiana (1873-1874).

B. THE FIRST BLACK GENERAL IN THE REGULAR ARMED FORCES

Benjamin Oliver Davis Sr. was promoted to Brigadier General on August 1, 1941. He retired in 1948.

C.   THE SECOND BLACK GENERAL IN THE REGULAR ARMED FORCES

Benjamin Oliver Davis, Jr. was promoted to Brigadier General
in 1954. In February 1965 he was appointed Assistant Deputy
Chief of Staff, Programs and Requirements. He retired in
February 1970.

D.   BLACK AMERICAN GENERAL OFFICERS IN THE ARMY

Lieutenant General Julius Wesley Becton, Jr.

Lieutenant General Arthur James Gregg (Retired).

Lieutenant General Roscoe Robinson, Jr.

Major General Harry William Brooks, Jr. (Retired).

Major General Adnrew Phillip Chambers

Major General Jerry Ralph Curry

Major General Frederic Ellis Davison (Retired)

Major General Oliver Williams Dillard (Retired)

Major General Henry Doctor, Jr.

Major General Robert Clarence Gaskill (Retired)

Major General Edward Greer (Retired)

Major General James Frank Hamlet (Retired)

Major General Emmett Paige, Jr.

Major General Hugh Granville Robinson

Major General Charles Calvin Rogers

Major General Fred Clifton SSheff (Retired)

Major General Harvey Dean Williams

Brigadier General Robert Bradshaw Adams

Brigadier General Leo Austin Brooks

Brigadier General Dallas Coverdale Brown, Jr.

Brigadier General John Mitchell Brown

Brigadier General Alfred Jackal Cade (Retired)

Brigadier General Roscoe Conklin Cartwright (Deceased)

Brigadier General Eugene R. Cromartie

Brigadier General B.O. Davis, Sr. (Deceased)

Brigadier General Donald J. Delandro

Brigadier General Johnie Forte, Jr.

Brigadier General James Reginald Hall, Jr.

Brigadier General Arthur Holmes, Jr.

Brigadier General Edward Honor

Brigadier General Hazel Winifred Johnson

Brigadier General Marion C. Mann (Retired)

Brigadier General James Franklin McCall

Brigadier General Julius Parker, Jr.

Brigadier General Colin Luther Powell

Brigadier General George Baker Price (Retired)

Brigadier General Jackson E. Rozier

Brigadier General George Macon Shul (Retired)

Brigadier General Isaac D. Smith

Brigadier General Guthrie Lewis Turner, Jr.

E.   BLACK AMERICAN FLAG AND GENERAL OFFICERS
     IN THE NAVY AND MARINE CORPS

Vice Admiral Samuel L. Gravely, Jr. (Retired)

Rear Admiral Gerald E. Thomas

Rear Admiral Lawrence C. Chambers (Retired)

Rear Admiral L.A. Williams

Rear Admiral Benjamin Thurman Hacker

Brigadier General Frank E. Petersen, Jr., U.S. Marine Corps.

F.   BLACK AMERICAN GENERAL OFFICERS IN THE AIR FORCE

General Daniel James (Deceased)

Lieutenant General B.O. Davis, Jr. (Retired

Major General Rufus L. Billips (Retired)

Major General Titus C. Hall

Major General Winston D. Powers

Major General Lucius Theus (Retired)

Major General William E. Brown, Jr.

Major General Thomas E. Clifford (Retired)

Brigadier General Archer L. Durham

Brigadier General Alonzo L. Ferguson

Brigadier General David M. Hall

Brigadier General Charles B. Jiggetts

Brigadier General James Timothy Boddie

Brigadier General Elmer T. Brooks

Brigadier General Avon C. James

Brigadier General Norris W. Overton (Retired)

Brigadier General Bernard P. Randolph

G.   BLACK AMERICAN GENERAL OFFICERS IN THE ARMY
         AND AIR FORCE RESERVES

Major General Benjamin Lacy Hunton USAR (Retired)

Major General John Q.T. King USAR

Brigadier General William C. Banton USAFR (Retired)

Brigadier General Albert Bryant USAR

Colonel (Brigadier General upon mobilization) Vance Coleman
USAR

H. BLACK AMERICAN GENERAL OFFICERS IN THE ARMY AND AIR NATIONAL GUARD

Major General Cunningham C. Bryant, District of Columbia, National Guard

Brigadier General Cornelius O. Baker, Pennsylvania Army National Guard (Retired)

Brigadier General Carl E. Briscoe, New Jersey Army National Guard

Brigadier General Louis Duckett, New York Army National Guard

Brigadier General Calvin G. Franklin, California Army National Guard

Brigadier General William S. Frye, New Jersey Army National Guard (Retired)

Brigadier General Edward O. Goardin, Massachusetts Army National Guard (Retired)

Brigadier General Chauncey M. Hooper, New York Army National Guard (Retired)

Brigadier General Richard Lee Jones, Illinois Army National Guard (Retired)

Brigadier General Raymond Watkins, Illinois Army National Guard (Retired)

II.

Ships Named After Black Americans and Black Institutions

Leonard R. Harmon

Booker T. Washington

George Washington Carver

Frederick Douglass

John Merrick

Robert L. Vann

Paul Laurence Dunbar

James Weldon Johnson

John Hope

John H. Murphy

Toussant L'Ouverture

Robert S. Abbott

Harriet Tubman

Edward A. Savoy

Bert Williams

James Kyron Walker

Robert J. Banks

William Cox

George A. Lawson

Dorie Miller

Jesse L. Brown

Fisk Victory

Tuskegee Victory

Howard Victory

Lane Victory

III.

Black Soldiers in Films

1. DOCUMENTARIES AND SEMI-DOCUMENTARIES

    A. ALL OF THE WARS

       1. "The Black Soldier" (1978)

    B. WORLD WAR ONE

       1. "Doing Their Bit" (1918)

       2. "Our Colored Fighters" (1918)

    3. "The Heroic Black Soldiers of the War" (1919)

       4. "The Unknown Soldier Speaks" (1919)

    C. WORLD WAR TWO

       1. "At Their Side" (1944)

       2. "Fighting Americans" (1943)

    3. "Fighting Liberators Hailed" (1944)

    4. "From Whence Cometh My Help" (1949)

      5. "Men of Color to Arms" (1943(?))

    6. "Negro Troops in Clark's Army Rout
        Nazis in Italian Front" (1944)

      7. "One Tenth of Our Nation" (1940)

8.   "Team Work" (1944)

9.   "The Call of Duty" (1946)

10.   "The Negro Soldier" (1944)

11.   "This Is The Army" (1943(?))

12.   "Sergeant Joe Louis on Tour" (1943)

13.   "Wings For This Man" (1944)

D.   KOREAN WAR

1.   "Army Ends Segregation: Korea" (1957)

2.   "The Navy Steward" (1953)

E.   VIETNAM WAR

1.   "No Vietnamese Ever Called Me Nigger" (1968)

2.   "The Black G.I." (1970)

3.   "The Twentieth Century: Integration in
     The Military" (1966)

4.   "The Vietnam War: Black and White" (1967)

2.   FEATURE FILMS

A.   CIVIL WAR

1.   "Sergeant Rutledge" (1960)
     Starring Woody Strodes

2.   "Soul Soldier" (1970)
     Starring Rafer Johnson

B.   SPANISH-AMERICAN WAR

1.   "The Trooper of Troop K" (1916)
     Starring Noble Johnson

C.   WORLD WAR TWO

1. "Spying the Spy" (1917)
Starring Sam Robinson

2. "Battaan" (1943)
Starring Kenneth Spencer

3. "Crash Dive" (1942)
Starring Ben Carter

4. "Home of the Brave" (1949)
Starring James Edwards

5. "Paisan" (1946)
Starring Dots M. Johnson

6. "Red Ball Express" (1952)
Starring Sidney Poitier

7. "The Story of a Three-Day Pan" (1968)
Starring Harry Baird

8. "To Live In Peace" (1946)
Starring John Kitzmiller

9. "Without Pity" (1948)
Starring John Kitzmiller

D.   VIETNAM WAR

1. "The Anderson Platoon" (1967)
Starring Joseph Anderson

IV.

"Documents of World War I"

Collected by W.E. Burghardt DuBois*

FRENCH MILITARY MISSION
  Stationed with the American Army
                  August 7, 1918

SECRET INFORMATION CONCERNING BLACK AMERICAN TROOPS

1. It is important for French officers who have been called upon to exercise command over Black American troops, or to have an exact idea of the position occupied by Negroes in the United States. The information set forth in the following communication ought to be given to these officers and it is to their interest to have these matters known and widely disseminated. It will devolve likewise on the French Military Authorities, through the medium of the Civil Authorities, to give information on this subject to the French population residing in the cantonments occupied by American colored troops.

2. The American attitude upon the Negro question may seem a matter for discussion to many French minds. But we French are not in our province if we undertake to discuss what some call "prejudice". American opinion is unanimous on the "color question" and does not admit of any discussion.

The increasing number of Negroes in the United States (about 15,000,000) would create for the white race in the Republic a menace of degeneracy were it not that an impassable gulf has been made between them.

As this danger does not exist for the French race, the French public has become accustomed to treating the Negro with familiarity and indulgence.

*Reprinted with the permission of the Crisis Publishing Co.

This indulgence and this familiarity are matters of grievous concern to the Americans. They consider them an affront to their national policy. They are afraid that contact with the French will inspire in black Americans aspirations which to them (the whites) appear intolerable. It is of the utmost importance that every effort be made to avoid profoundly estranging American opinion.

Although a citizen of the United States, the black man is regarded by the white American as an inferior being with whom relations of business or service only are possible. The black is constantly being censured for his want of intelligence and discretion, his lack of civic and professional conscience and for his tendency toward undue familiarity.

The vices of the Negro are a constant menace to the American who has to repress them sternly. For instance, the black American troops in France have, by themselves, given rise to as many complaints for attempted rape as all the rest of the army. And yet (black American) soldiers sent us have been the choicest with respect to physique and morals, for the number disqualified at the time of mobilization was enormous.

CONCLUSION

1. We must prevent the rise of any pronounced degree of intimacy between French officers and black officers. We may be courteous and amiable with these last, but we cannot deal with them on the same plane as with the white American officers without deeply wounding the latter. We must not eat with them, must not shake hands or seek to talk with them outside of the requirements of military service.

2. We must not commend too highly the black American troops, particularly in the presence of (white) Americans. It is all right to recognize their good qualities and their services, but only in moderate terms, strictly in keeping with the truth.

3. Make a point of keeping the native cantonment population from "spoiling" the Negroes. (White) Americans become greatly incensed at any public expression of intimacy between white women with black men. They have recently uttered violent protests against a picture in the "Vie Parisienne" entitled "The Child of the Desert" which shows a (white) woman in a "cabinet particulier" with a Negro. Familiarity on the part of white women with black men is furthermore a source of profound regret to our experienced colonials who see in it an over-weening menace to the prestige of the white race.

Military authority cannot intervene directly in this question, but it can through the civil authorities exercise some influence on the population.

(Signed)   LINARD.

THE FOLLOWING DOCUMENT IS A SPECIMEN
OF THE NUMEROUS AND CONTINUOUS REQUESTS
MADE BY WHITE COMMANDERS OF COLORED
REGIMENTS TO GET RID OF COLORED OFFICERS.
IT WILL BE NOTED THAT AT THE DATE THIS
DOCUMENT WAS SENT COLORED OFFICERS HAD
HAD VERY LITTLE CHANCE TO PROVE THEIR
EFFICIENCY.

G.H.G., A.E.F.
8/25/1918

11440-A124

.Headquarters 372nd Infantry
S.P. 179, France

August 24, 1918

From: The Commanding Officer, 372nd Infantry.

To: The Commanding General, American E.F.

Subject: Replacement of Colored Officers by White Officers

1.   Request that colored officers of this regiment be replaced by white officers for the following reasons:

First: The racial distinctions which are recognized in civilian life naturally continue to be recognized in the military life and present a formidable barrier to the existence of that feeling of comradeship which is essential to mutual confidence and esprit de corp.

Second: With a few exceptions there is a characteristic tendency among the colored officers to neglect the welfare of their men and to perform their duties in a perfunctory manner. They are lacking in initiative.   These defects entail a constant supervision and attention to petty details by battalion commanders and other senior officers which distract their attention from their wider duties; with harmful results.

2.   To facilitate the desired readjustment of officer personnel it is recommended,

A.   That no colored officers be forwarded to this regiment as replacements, or otherwise.

B.   That officers removed upon recommendation of efficiency boards be promptly replaced by white officers of like grade. But, if white officers are not available as replacements; white officers of lower grades be forwarded instead.

C. That the opportunity be afforded to transfer the re-
maining colored combat officer personnel to labor organizations
or to replacement units for other colored combat organizatios
according to their suitability.

3. Reference letter No. 616-3s written by Commanding
General, 157th D.I. on the subject August 21, 1918, and forwarded to your office through military channels.

(Signed) Herschel Tupes
Colonel, 372nd Infantry

Received A. G. O.
    26th Aug., 1918,
        G.H.Q., A.E.F.
            2st Ind. (Endorsement)

G.H.Q., A.E.F., France, August 28, 1918

--To Commanding Officer, 372nd Infantry,

A.E.F.

1. Returned.

2. Paragraph two is approved.

3. You will submit by special courier requisition for white
officers to replace officers relieved upon the recommendation
of efficiency board.

4. You will submit list of names of officers that you recom-
mend to be transferred to labor organization or to replacement
units for other colored combat organizations; stating in each
case the qualifications of the officers recommended.
    By command of General Pershing:
            (Signed) W.P. Bennett
                    Adjutant General.

        2nd Ind. (Endorsement)
    Hg. 372nd Infantry, S. P., 179, France.
    September 4, 1918--To Commanding General, A.E.F., France.

1. Requisition in compliance with par. 3, 1st. Ind. is
enclosed herewith. Special attention is invited to the filling
of two original vacancies by app.

THE FOLLOWING LETTER WAS SENT CONTRARY TO
MILITARY REGULATIONS TO A U.S. SENATOR BY
THE MAN WHO WAS CHIEF OF STAFF OF THE
COLORED NINETY-SECOND DIVISION: IN OTHER
WORDS, BY THE MAN WHO MORE THAN ANY OTHER
SINGLE PERSON WAS RESPONSIBLE FOR THE MORALE
AND EFFICIENCY OF THIS DIVISION. WE SHALL
PROVE LATER THAT EVERY ESSENTIAL STATEMENT
MADE IN THIS LETTER AGAINST NEGRO TROOPS IS
EITHER FALSE OR MISLEADING.

Headquarters VI Army Corps
American Expeditionary Forces

Dec. 6, 1918

My Dear Senator:

Now that a reorganization of the army is in prospect, and
as all officers of the temporary forces have been asked if
they desire to remain in the regular army, I think I ought to
bring a matter to your attention that is of vital importance
not only from a military point of view but from that which all
Southerners have. I refer to the question of Negro officers
and Negro troops.

I have been Chief of Staff of the 92nd (Colored) Division
since its organization, and shall remain on such duty until it
starts its movement in a few days back to the United States,
when I go to the 6th Corps as the Chief of the Operation Section of that unit. My position has been such that I can speak
from intimate knowledge and what I have to say is based on
facts which I know fully and not from secondhand information.

To start with: all company officers of infantry, machine
guns and engineers were Negroes; as were also most of the artillery lieutenants and many of the doctors. Gradually as
their incompetence became perfectly evident to all, the engineers and artillery-men, were replaced by white officers.
They remained with the infantry until the end, and also with
a few exceptions with the machine guns.

The record of the division is one which will probably
never be given full publicity, but the bare facts are about
as follows. We came to France in June, were given seven weeks
in training area instead of the four weeks in training area
usually allotted, then went to a quiet sector of the front.
From there we went to the Argonne and in the offensive start-
ing there on September 26 had one regiment in the line, at-
tached to the 38th French Corps. They failed there in all
their missions, laid down and sneaked to the rear, until they
were withdrawn. Thirty of the officers of this regiment alone
were reported either for cowardice or failure to prevent their
men from retreating--and this against very little opposition.
The French and our white field officers did all that could
possibly have been done; but the troops were impossible. One

of our majors commanding a battalion said "The men are rank cowards there is no other word for it."

Next we were withdrawn to another defensive sector where we remained until the armistice; having some minor engagements against any enemy who had no offensive intentions.

During our career, counting the time in America, we have had about thirty cases of rape, among which was one where twenty-two men at Camp Grant raped one woman, and we have had eight (I believe) reported in France with about fifteen attempts besides. There have been any number of self-inflicted wounds, among one captain.

There have been numerous accidental shootings, several murders, and also several cases of patrols or sentinels shooting at each other. And at the same time, so strict had been the supervision and training that many officers passing through our areas would remark that our men actually had the outer marks of better discipline than the other divisions. They were punctillious about saluting, their appearance was excellent. They kept their animals and equipment in good condition. General Bullard, commanding our Second Army, asked me my estimate and I said they could do anything but fight. They have in fact been dangerous to no one except themselves and women.

In these organizations where we have white company officers, namely the artillery and engineers, we have had only one case of rape. The undoubted truth is that the Colored officers neither control nor care to control the men. They themselves have been engaged very largely in the pursuit of French women, it being their first opportunity to meet white women who did not treat them as servants.

During the entire time we have been operating there has never been a single operation conducted by a colored officer, where his report did not have to be investigated by some field officer to find out what the real facts were. Accuracy and ability to describe facts is lacking in all and most of them are just plain liars in addition.

The foregoing is just to give you an insight into the facts. Should any effort be made to have Negro officers, or for that matter Negro troops, the career of the division should be asked for and every officer who has been a field officer of the 92nd Division should be summoned before the Committee to give his experience and opinions. Their statements, based on a year's experience should certainly carry a great deal of weight, and all of them state the same thing, only varying in extremes.

With best wishes, I am

      Sincerely yours,
      (Signed) Allen J. Greer,
      Colonel, General Staff, U.S.A.

Hon. Kenneth D. McKellar,
  United States Senate
    Washington, D.C.

THE FOLLOWING LETTER WRITTEN BY A
NEGRO OFFICER TO AN AMERICAN
FRIEND ILLUSTRATES THE TEMPER AND
DIFFICULTIES OF THE SITUATION IN
FRANCE.

19 Feb., 1919

I have been hoping that you would be able to drop in on us here before our departure. We are slated to leave here at 4 A.M. on the 21st supposedly aboard the _Aquitania_. It was my desire to talk with you about the offer to officers and men in the A.E.F. to attend a school in France or England. I made application and was shown the endorsement by Regt. Commander, that the offer did not apply to transient officers. The knowledge was obtained from a telegram received from Hdq. One of our officers went to the Commanding General of this Camp to obtain a copy of the telegram which could not be or was not produced. Capt. _____ _____ went in person to the General and requested permission to attend stating that he volunteered for service, left his practise and family at a sacrifice and that he thought the Govt. owed it to him to give him a chance and attend school here. The General took his name and the Organization to which he belongs promising to let him hear from him, but as yet nothing has been done. This Camp is practically a penal institution and prejudice against us is very strong. Some day there is likely to be some grave disturbance here. The conditions are simply awful: mud everywhere, leaky tents and barracks and lack of sufficient and proper toilets. The men are worked quite hard, some at night and others in the day, rain or shine. As a consequence there are quite a number of sick men in our organization. Since our arrival here, the roads have been improved quite a bit (due to the work of the 92nd div.) and you do not have to wade in ankle deep mud. Board walks here to nearly all the tents and barracks. There is so much talk about the rotten conditions that the Camp officials are making feverish efforts to be ready for the proposed inquiry.

The work of each organization is graded by the Camp Officer in Charge of details and if not satisfactory, the organization may be placed at the bottom of the sailing list or removed temporarily. Commanding Officers of separate units or regiments are practically helpless and if they complain too much against the treatment accorded them are kept here until the Commanding General sees fit to let them go.

I am beginning to wonder whether it will ever be possible for me to see an American (white) without wishing that he were in his Satanic Majesty's private domain. I must pray long and earnestly that hatred of my fellow man be removed from my heart and that I can truthfully lay claim to being a Christian.

THE FOLLOWING INSTANCES OF COLOR
DISCRIMINATION ARE TAKEN AT
RANDOM FROM AMONG NUMBERS OF
SIMILAR CASES.

This memorandum was sent to the Commanding Officer, 367th Infantry:

1. Company "D" of your organization has been designated by the Central Embarkation Office as a coaling detail for U.S.S. Virginia.

2. This detail with all officers and men will report at Naval Surgeon's Office, foot of Rue de Siam, Brest, at 8:30 a.m., February 9, 1919. Detail with march from camp not later than 7 a.m.

3. All equipment and officers' hand baggage will be taken. You will arrange for truck with Camp Transportation Officer Building No. 2, Camp Headquarters. Truck will be furnished at 5 a.m.

4. All embarkation regulation will be followed. The detail will be checked aboard the vessel by an officer from the Central Embarkation Office. The detail will not return to camp.

By Command of Brig. General Butler,
          L.S. Schmidt,
          Major A.G., Adjutant.

There was an order issued from the Central Embarkation Office to the effect that when troops were designated as a coaling detail, they would go on board with all regulations for embarkation completed and would not return to camp, but would proceed to the United States on board the ship that they had coaled. When the Executive Officer of the Virginia discovered that these troops were Colored, he requested Admiral Halstead to have these Colored troops taken off board, after having coaled the vessel, as it was a precedent in the navy that no Colored troops had ever traveled on board of a United States battleship. This request was then sent by Admiral Halstead to the Central Embarkation Office, and the Colored Troops were placed on board a tug and sent back to Brest. When they arrived in Brest, it was late at night, they had no orders as to where to proceed, were without a place to stay and anything to eat.

Before leaving the ship the Colored commanding officer of the troops received the following letter from the officer under whom the men worked:

U.S.S. <u>Virginia</u>
Brest, France,
11 February, 1919.

1. I take pleasure in commending you and the officers
and men under your command in connection with the coaling of
this ship and at the same time wish to express my apprecia-
tion of the good conduct and the high state of discipline of
your command.

H.J. Ziegmine,
<u>Captain</u>, U.<u>S</u>. <u>Navy</u>
<u>Commanding</u>

*   *   *

During November, 1918, Colored Artillery officers were in
school at Vannes; a number of dances was given by the French
ladies which were called the Franco-American dances. These
dances were given for charity and a fee was charged for ad-
mission. The Colored Officers, who composed what was known
as the 167th Brigade Detachment, attended several of these
dances, and were entertained by and danced with the French
ladies of the town. The matter was then brought to the attention of General Horn, who was in command of the school,
whereupon he issued an order that no officer of the 167th
Brigade Detachment would be permitted to attend a dance where
a fee was charged. The 167th Brigade Detachment was composed
entirely of Colored officers, so that the order referred only
to them, but had no effect upon the white officers who were
in attendance at the school.

*   *   *

Headquarters, Area "D"
January 25, 1919.

MEMORANDUM

To C.O. 367th Infantry:

<u>White</u> <u>officers</u> desiring meals in their quarters will have
orderlies <u>report</u> to Lieutenant Williams at the Tent adjoining
Area Headquarters for cards to present at Officers' Mess.

All colored officers will mess at Officers' Mess in D-17.

F.M. Crawford,
First Lieutenant Infantry
Area "D"

Headquarters Forwarding Camp
American Embarkation Center

A.P.O. 766, A.E.F.
January 21, 1919.
Memorandum: No. 229, E.O.

To All Organizations:

1. For your information and guidance.
Program Reference Visit of General Pershing, 9:30 A.M.
Arrive Forwarding Camp. All troops possible, except Colored,
to be under arms.

Formation to be as designated by General Longan. Only
necessary supply work and police work to be performed up to
time troops are dismissed in order that they may prepare for
reception of General Pershing. As soon as dismissed men to
get into working clothes and to go to their respective tasks
in order that Commander-in-Chief may see construction going
on. (Work of altering dry delousing plant not to be inter-
rupted). Colored troops who are not at work to be in their
quarters or at their tents .....

By command of

Brigadier-General Longan.
Richard I. Levy,
Major, C.A.C., U.S.A. Camp,
Adjutant

Index

Including authors, joint authors, and editors.
Numbers refer to individual entry numbers.

About the Compilers

LENWOOD G. DAVIS is Associate Professor of History at Winston-Salem State University. Dr. Davis has compiled more than seventy-eight bibliographies. He is the author of numerous books, including *I Have a Dream: The Life and Times of Martin Luther King, Jr.* (1973), *The Black Woman in American Society: A Selected Annotated Bibliography* (1975), *The Black Family in the United States: A Selected Bibliography of Annotated Books, Articles, and Dissertations on Black Families in America* (1978), *Black Artists in the United States: An Annotated Bibliography*, coauthored with Janet L. Sims (1980), *Marcus Garvey: An Annotated Bibliography*, coauthored with Janet L. Sims (1980), *Black Aged in the United States* (1980), *Black Athletes in the United States: A Bibliography*, coauthored with Belinda S. Daniels (1981), *A Paul Robeson Research Guide* (1982), *Joe Louis: A Selected Bibliography* (1983), *Malcolm X: A Selected Bibliography* (1984), *The Ku Klux Klan: A Bibliography* (1984), and *Black-Jewish Relations in the United States, 1752-1984: A Selected Bibliography* (1984).

GEORGE H. HILL, APR, journalist, television and radio producer, and lecturer is director of the Institute of Research, vice president of Nightingale Communications & Media, and is instructor of media classes at Los Angeles Southwest College. He holds seven college degrees including a Ph.D. in communications and is accredited by the Public Relations Society of America. Dr. Hill's other books include: *Black Media in America: A Resource Guide and Bibliography, Airwaves to the Soul, Religious Broadcasting, 1920-1983: A Selectively Annotated Bibliography* (with Lenwood G. Davis), *Black Business and Economic Conditions: A Bibliography, Jessie Louis Jackson—From Country Preacher to Presidential Candidate: A Bibliography* (with Janet Sims-Wood), *Ebony Images: Black Americans & Television, Michael Joe Jackson: A Bio-Bibliography* (forthcoming), and *Civil Rights Leaders and Organizations: A Bibliography* (forthcoming).

3 5282 00103 5768